Content Syndication
with RSS

Content Syndication
with RSS

Ben Hammersley

O'REILLY®

Beijing · Cambridge · Farnham · Köln · Paris · Sebastopol · Taipei · Tokyo

Content Syndication with RSS
by Ben Hammersley

Published by O'Reilly & Associates, Inc., 1005 Gravenstein Highway North, Sebastopol, CA 95472.

O'Reilly & Associates books may be purchased for educational, business, or sales promotional use. Online editions are also available for most titles (*safari.oreilly.com*). For more information, contact our corporate/institutional sales department: (800) 998-9938 or *corporate@oreilly.com*.

Editor:	Simon St. Laurent
Production Editor:	Brian Sawyer
Cover Designer:	Ellie Volckhausen
Interior Designer:	David Futato

Printing History:

March 2003:	First Edition.

ISBN: 0-596-00383-8
[C]

Table of Contents

Preface

This book is about RSS, the massively popular content-syndication technology. From distributing headlines across web sites and delivering complete content to specialist applications, to providing the building blocks of the Semantic Web, RSS is one of the Internet's fastest growing technologies.

There are over one million RSS feeds available across the Web; this book shows you how to read them and how to create your own. This book covers:

- RSS 0.91, 0.92, 1.0, and 2.0 in detail
- How to create and parse feeds
- Extending RSS through modules
- RDF and the Semantic Web
- Web-based aggregators
- Desktop readers
- Publish and Subscribe

Audience

This book was written with two somewhat interrelated groups in mind:

Web developers and web site authors
> This book should be read by all web developers who want to share their site with others by offering RSS-based feeds of their content. This group includes everyone from bloggers and amateur journalists, to those running large-budget, multiuser sites. From multinational news organizations to neighborhood sports groups, the use of RSS can extend the reach, power, and utility of your product—this book shows you how.

Developers
> This book is also for developers who want to use the content that other people are syndicating. This group includes everyone from fan-site developerss wanting

the latest gaming news, or intranet builders needing up-to-date financial information on the corporate Web, to developers looking to incorporate news feeds into artificially intelligent systems or build data-sharing applications across platforms. For you, this book delves into the interpretation of metadata, different forms of content syndication, and the increasing use of web services technology in this field.

Assumptions This Book Makes

The skill level needed for the book varies. In general, the book gets harder as you go. For the web author, Chapters 1 through 4, covering the history and implications of the subject and the basic details of writing and using RSS feeds, might be as far as you need to go. These chapters assume familiarity with HTML and XML, although you will be reminded of important technical points. Don't worry if this seems daunting now: it's all very straightforward. (Appendix A provides a brief introduction to XML if you need one.)

Delve further, however, and you'll find that with a little confidence you can do all sorts of great things. Most developers will be unfazed by most of the book, although some of the XSLT and web services sections are quite new. Knowledge of Perl is useful but not required. The code should be commented sufficiently to make all things clear.

Conventions Used in This Book

I use the following font conventions in this book.

Italic is used for:

- Unix pathnames, filenames, and program names
- Internet addresses, such as domain names and URLs
- New terms where they are defined

Boldface is used for:

- Names of GUI items: window names, buttons, menu choices, etc.

`Constant width` is used for:

- Command lines and options that should be typed verbatim
- Names and keywords in Java programs, including method names, variable names, and class names
- XML element tags

Comments and Questions

Please address comments and questions concerning this book to the publisher:

O'Reilly & Associates, Inc.
1005 Gravenstein Highway North
Sebastopol, CA 95472
(800) 998-9938 (in the United States or Canada)
(707) 829-0515 (international or local)
(707) 829-0104 (FAX)

There is a web page for this book, which lists errata, examples, or any additional information. You can access this page at:

http://www.oreilly.com/catalog/consynrss/

To comment or ask technical questions about this book send email to:

bookquestions@oreilly.com

For more information about books, conferences, Resource Centers and the O'Reilly Network, see the O'Reilly web site at:

http://www.oreilly.com

Acknowledgments

This book owes a great deal to many people. RSS is blessed with an extremely passionate development community. To the citizens of the rss-dev, syndication, and Syndic8 lists and the lurkers of the rss-dev chatroom, I pay homage. I must make special notice, however, of a few key people. My deep thanks go to Bill Kearney, Kevin Hemenway, and Micah Dubinko for their technical reviewing genius. Not to forget Dave Winer, Jeff Barr, James Linden, DJ Adams, Rael Dornfest, Brent Simmons, Chris Croome, Kevin Burton, and Dan Brickley, and, closer to home, Andy Losowsky.

My editor, Simon St. Laurent, deserves as much thanks as he has shown patience: infinite.

But most of all, I thank my wife, Anna, who now knows more about angle brackets than she really quite expected when she married me.

## CHAPTER 1

Introduction

Whatever we possess becomes of double value when
we have the opportunity of sharing it with others.
—Jean Nicolas Bouilly

In this chapter, we discuss the definition of content syndication within the scope of the Internet and give a little of its history. We then move on to the business cases for syndicating your own content and a discussion of the philosophy behind content syndication. The chapter finishes with a brief discussion of the legal issues surrounding the provision and use of syndication feeds.

What Is Content Syndication?

Content syndication makes part or all of a site's content available for use by other services. The syndicated content, or *feed*, can consist of both the direct content itself and *metadata*—information about the content.

The feed can be anything from just headlines and links to stories, to the entire content of the site, stripped of its layout and with metadata liberally applied. The technology to do this ranges from the simple beginnings of RSS 0.91, through to the RDF-based RSS 1.0, all the way to the industrial strength NewsML, ICE, and Prism. Content syndication can allow users to experience a site on multiple devices and be notified of updates over a variety of services. It can range from a simple list of links sent from site to site, to the beginnings of the Semantic Web.

Content syndication can also start as easy as you like and quickly give inspiration for new, innovative services, as its development has already shown.

A Short History

In the main, this book deals with the most common XML content-syndication standard: RSS. As with other Internet standards, it helps to know some of its history before diving into the technicalities.

While it is only three years old, RSS is a somewhat troubled set of standards. Its upbringing has seen standards switch, regroup, and finally split apart entirely under the pressures of parental guidance. To fully understand this wayward child, and to get the most out of it, it is necessary to understand the motivations behind it and how it evolved into what it is today.

HotSauce: MCF and RDF

The deepest, darkest origins of the current versions of RSS began in 1995 with the work of Ramanathan V. Guha. Known to most simply by his surname, Guha developed a system called the *Meta Content Framework* (MCF). Rooted in the work of knowledge-representation systems such as CycL, KRL, and KIF, MCF's aim was to describe objects, their attributes, and the relationships between them.

MCF was an experimental research project funded by Apple, so it was pleasing for management that a great application came out of it: ProjectX, later renamed HotSauce. By late 1996, a few-hundred sites were creating MCF files that described themselves, and HotSauce allowed users to browse around these MCF representations in 3D.

It was popular, but experimental, and when Steve Jobs' return to Apple's management in 1997 heralded the end of much of Apple's research activity, Guha left for Netscape.

There, he met with Tim Bray, one of the original XML pioneers, and started moving MCF over to an XML-based format. (XML itself was new at that time.) This project later became the *Resource Description Framework* (RDF). RDF is, as the World Wide Web Consortium (W3C) RDF Primer says, "a general-purpose language for representing information in the World Wide Web." It is specifically designed for the representation of metadata (see Chapter 5) and the relationships between things. In its fullest form, it is the basis for the concept known as the *Semantic Web*, the W3C's vision of a web of information that computers can understand.

Channel Definition Format

This was in 1997, remember. XML, as a standard way to create data formats, was still in its infancy, and much of the Internet's attention was taken up by the increasingly frantic war between Microsoft and Netscape.

Microsoft had not ignored the HotSauce experience. With others, principally a company called Pointcast, they further developed MCF for the description of web sites and created the *Channel Definition Format* (CDF).

CDF is XML-based and can describe content ratings, scheduling, logos, and metadata about a site. It was introduced in Microsoft's Internet Explorer 4.0 and later into the Windows desktop itself, where it provided the backbone for what was then called Active Desktop.

By 1999, MCF was well and truly steeped in XML and becoming RDF, and the Microsoft/Netscape bickering was about to start again. Both companies were due to launch new versions of their browsers, and Netscape was being circled for a possible takeover by AOL.

RSS First Appears

So, Netscape's move was to launch a portal service, called the "My Netscape Network," and with it RSS.

Short for *RDF Site Summary*, RSS allowed the portal to display headlines and URLs from other sites, all within the same page. A user could then personalize their My Netscape page to contain the headlines from any site that interested them and had an RSS file available. It was, basically, a web page–based version of everything Hot-Sauce and CDF had become. It was a great success.

My Netscape benefited from this in many ways: they suddenly had a massive amount of content given to them for free. Of course, they had no control over it or any real way of making money from it directly, but the additional usefulness of their site to the user made people stick around longer. In the heat of the dot-com boom, allowing people to put their own content on a Netscape page, alongside advertising sold by Netscape, was a very good idea: the portal could both save money on content and make more on ad sales. The user also benefited. She had her favorite sites summarized on one page—a one-stop shop for a day's browsing, which many users found extremely useful. The RSS provider didn't lose out either, gaining from both additional traffic and wider exposure.

These abilities, aided by the relative simplicity of the RSS 0.9 standard itself, proved so useful that RSS didn't stay unique to Netscape for long. Converting RSS to HTML is simple, as you will see in Chapter 9, and other RSS-based sites rapidly appeared across the Web. Sites such as *slashdot.org* incorporated RSS feeds as replacements for their own homegrown headline formats, and developers of all the major scripting languages devised simple ways to read and display RSS feeds. A small revolution was underway.

Technically, however, RSS had been a compromise.

The Standards Evolve

The first draft of the RSS format, as designed by Dan Libby, was a fully RDF-based data model, and people inside Netscape felt it was too complicated for end users at that time. The resultant compromise—named RSS 0.9—was not truly useful RDF, nor was it as simple as it could be.

Some felt that using RDF improperly was worse than not using it at all, so when RSS 0.91 arrived, the RDF nature of the format had been dropped. As Dan Libby explained to the rss-dev email list (*http://groups.yahoo.com/group/rss-dev/message/239*):

> At the time, the primary users of RSS (Dave Winer the most vocal among them) were asking why it needed to be so complex and why it didn't have support for various features, e.g. update frequencies. We really had no good answer, given that we weren't using RDF for any useful purpose. Further, because RDF can be expressed in XML in multiple ways, I was uncomfortable publishing a DTD for RSS 0.9, since the DTD would claim that technically valid RDF/RSS data conforming to the RDF graph model was not valid RSS. Anyway, it didn't feel "clean". The compromise was to produce RSS 0.91, which could be validated with any validating XML parser, and which incorporated much of Userland's vocabulary, thus removing most (I think) of Dave's major objections. I felt slightly bad about this, but given actual usage at the time, I felt it better suited the needs of its users: simplicity, correctness, and a larger vocabulary, without RDF baggage.

RSS 0.91, which incorporated some features from Userland Software's Scripting-News format, was completely RDF-free. So, as would become a habit whenever a new version of RSS was released, the meaning of the RSS acronym was changed. In the RSS 0.91 Specification, Dave Winer explained:

> There is no consensus on what RSS stands for, so it's not an acronym, it's a name. Later versions of this spec may say it's an acronym, and hopefully this won't break too many applications.

A great deal of research into RDF continued, however. Indeed, Netscape's RSS development team was always keen to use it. Their original specification (the one that was watered down to produce RSS 0.9), was published on the insistence of Dan Libby, and, although it has long since gone from the Netscape servers, you can find it in the Internet Archive:

> *http://web.archive.org/web/20001204123600/http://my.netscape.com/publish/help/futures.html*

Netscape, however, was never to release any new versions—the RSS team was disbanded as the My Netscape Network was closed. So, when work began on a new version of RSS, it was left to the development community in general to sort out. They quickly broke into two camps.

The first camp, led by O'Reilly's Rael Dornfest, wanted to introduce some form of extensibility to the standard. The ability to add new features, perhaps through modularization, necessitated such complexities as XML namespaces and the reintroduction of RDF, as envisioned by the Netscape team.

However, the second camp, led by Dave Winer, the CEO of Userland Software and keeper of the RSS 0.91 standard, feared that this would add a level of complexity unwelcome among users and wanted to keep RSS as simple as possible.

The First Fork

In December 2000, after a great deal of heated discussion, RSS 1.0 was released. It embraced the use of modules, XML namespaces, and a return to a full RDF data model. Two weeks later, Dave Winer released RSS 0.92 as a rebuttal of the RDF alternative. The standard thus forked.

And that was how it remained for two years—two standards: RSS 0.92 as the simple, entry-level specification, and RSS 1.0 as the more complex, but ultimately more feature-packed specification. And, of course, some people still used RSS 0.91.

For the users of RSS feeds, this fork was not a major worry, because the two standards remained compatible. Even parsers specifically built to parse only RSS, rather than XML in general, can usually read simple examples of either version with equal ease, although the RDF implications go straight over the head of all but specifically designed RDF parsers.

All this, however, was changing.

The Second Fork

In the late summer of 2002, the RSS community forked again, perhaps irretrievably. Ironically enough, the fork came from an effort to merge the 0.9x and 1.0 strands from the previous fork and create an RSS 2.0 that would satisfy both camps.

Once again, the argument quickly settled into two sides. On one side, Dave Winer and a few others continued to believe in the importance of simplicity above all else, and regarded RDF as a technology that had yet to show any value within RSS. Winer also, for his own reasons, did not want the discussion over RSS 2.0 to take place on the traditional email lists. Rather, he wanted people to express their points of view in their weblogs, to which he would link his own at *http://www.scripting.com*.

On the other side, the members of the rss-dev mailing list, the place where RSS 1.0 had been born and nurtured to maturity, still wanted to include RDF with the specification—albeit in various simplified forms—and hold the discussion on a publicly-archived, centralized mailing list that would not be subject to Winer's filtering.

In many ways, both of these things happened. After a great deal of acrimony, Userland released a specification that they called RSS 2.0 and declared RSS frozen. That this was done without acknowledging, much less taking into account, the increasing concerns—both technical and social—of the rss-dev and RDF communities at large caused much unhappiness.

So, after RSS 2.0's release on the September 16, 2002, the rss-dev list started discussions on a possible name change to their own new, RSS 1.0–based specification. This would go hand-in-hand with a complete retooling of the specification, based on a totally open discussion and a rethink of the use of RDF. At the time of this writing, neither a new name nor the syntax of the new format have been decided, and the reader is advised to look to the Web for further news.

As it stands, therefore, the versioning number system of RSS is misleading. Taken chronologically, 0.9 was based on RDF, 0.91 was not, 1.0 was, 0.92 was not, and now 2.0 is not, but whatever 1.0 becomes probably will be. It should be noted that there is an RSS 3.0, proposed by Aaron Swartz as part of long rss-dev in-joke. (The joke culminated with a proposal to have RSS 4.0 expressed entirely through the medium of interpretive dance.) Search engine results finding these specifications are therefore wrong, though dryly funny.

For feed publishers, the two strands each have advantages and disadvantages. The first is perhaps simpler to use, whereas the second can—if both the publisher and the user have the wherewithal to allow it—provide a much richer set of information. We will go into each of the feed standards in Chapter 3.

Future Developments

As with most Internet standards, the two versions of RSS are continually being examined for revision. For the purposes of this book, these upgrades need not necessarily concern us: specification upgrades are always designed to be backward-compatible, and RSS feeds designed with the specifications in this book should work for the foreseeable future. Given that they are in XML, converting them to a new standard will also be simple, and methods for doing so will undoubtedly be provided should such a situation arise.

There are differences in the extensibility approaches of the two RSS forks. Since the September 2002 release of RSS 2.0, the core specifications of both RSS 1.0 and RSS 2.0 provide module-based extensibility. Anyone can add new elements or features. We will explore the differences in Chapter 3.

Desktop Headlines

RSS was, and is, by no means limited to the Web. Portal sites, at least in the broadband-free, nonwireless end of the twentieth century, always suffered from one thing: having to be online. There was no way for a My Netscape user, for example, to browse his headlines at his leisure without racking up expensive connectivity fees. In many countries, Internet access through a dial-up connection is still paid for by the minute. Also, the portal sites quite sensibly limited the number of feeds to which you could subscribe: a user with more than a few interests quickly found his headline habit could not be satisfied if he was limited to being online.

So, in early 1999, desktop-based headline viewers, such as Carmen's Headline Viewer, came into play. Users can download hundreds of RSS feeds at a time and browse them at their leisure. Quicker and offering more variety than RSS portals, these readers are becoming increasingly sophisticated. Chapter 10 provides more details.

Then, with the growing popularity of RSS feeds—over 4,000 in the first year—there inevitably came a need for directories.

Registries, Aggregators, and Search Engines

It's all very well being able to convert RSS feeds to a form readable within a web site, but where do you find these feeds in the first place? By the turn of the century, thousands of sites offered RSS feeds, but due to a lack of either a standardized address or an automatic system of resource discovery, users were dependent on finding feeds through a site's advertising.

Registries were, and are still, one good answer. Sites that list the details of thousands of feeds, tested and categorized for ease of use, these services are growing in size and sophistication. At the time of this writing, *Syndic8.com*, for example, will soon break the 10,000-feed mark. We'll discuss registries more fully in Chapter 10.

Aggregators, on the other hand, add an additional layer of usability to RSS feeds. By grouping feeds together and allowing a filtering of headlines, they allow the creation of a kind of meta-feed. For example, O'Reilly's Meerkat service (*http://www.oreillynet.com/meerkat*) allows an RSS feed of all the stories on a certain subject that have appeared over a set time to be created within any of the other feeds it monitors. Note that some people use the word *aggregator* to indicate a desktop reader client. This book does not.

Search engines are also starting to realize the usefulness of RSS feeds. Sites such as The Snewp (*http://www.snewp.com*) limit their indexing efforts solely to RSS feeds. RSS's concentrating nature gives the index a far greater signal-to-noise ratio than if it had to trawl every page in the site. Combined with Publish and Subscribe (see Chapter 12) it promises to allow extremely up-to-date search engine results. These results can, of course, be given in RSS itself.

Corporate Intranets

RSS's major success within the My Netscape Network has been replicated internally in many corporations. Indeed, many companies make their living acting as aggregators solely for the corporate market. By combining search engines and aggregated feeds into intranets, employees are able to track news sites for mentions of their company or related industries. Combined with knowledge management techniques, RSS feeds can be a major part of a corporation's internal information flow.

RSS on Other Platforms

RSS is not limited to web pages—far from it: its format is specifically designed to be a halfway house to any other human-readable or machine-processable format. Because of this flexibility, RSS feeds have been popping up on many services. For example, instant messaging services are perfectly suited to delivering headlines to users, as is the Short Message Service (SMS) for GSM-based mobile phones. By acting as the data-carrying glue between the content providers, third-party service providers, and the end user, RSS can provide a very simple way of creating thousands of services extremely rapidly. If it can receive text, you can use RSS somewhere along the line. We'll discuss this in Chapter 9.

Why Syndicate Your Content?

The advantages of using other people's feeds are obvious, but what about supplying your own? There are at least eight reasons to do so:

1. It increases traffic to your site.
2. It builds brand awareness for your site.
3. It can help with search engine rankings.
4. It helps cement relationships within a community of sites.
5. It improves the site/user relationship.
6. With additional technologies, it allows others to give additional features to your service—update-notification via instant messaging, for example.
7. It makes the Internet an altogether richer place, pushing semantic technology along.
8. It gives you a good excuse to play with some cool stuff.

There you are: social, spiritual, and mercenary reasons to provide an RSS feed for your site.

Legal Implications

The copyright implications for RSS feeds are quite simple. There are two choices for feed publishers, and these reflect on the user.

First, the publisher can decide that the feed must be licensed in some way. In this case, only authorized users can use the feed. It is good manners on the part of the publisher to make it as obvious as possible that this is the case—by providing a copyright notice in an XML comment, at least, and preferably by making it difficult for unauthorized users to get to the feed. Registering a pay-only feed with all the aggregators is asking for trouble.

Second, and most commonly, the publisher can decide that the RSS feed is entirely free to use. In this case, it is only polite for the publishers of public RSS feeds to consider the feed entirely in the public domain—free to be used by anyone, for anything. This might sound a little radical to the average company vice president, but remember: there is nothing in the RSS feed that is not, in some way, in the actual source information in the first place. It is rather futile to get upset that someone might not be using your headlines in the company-approved font, or committing a similar infraction, and somewhat against the spirit of the exercise.

Screen scraping a site to create a feed, by writing a script to read the site-specific layout, is a different matter. It has already been legally proven, in U.S. courts at least (in the Ticketmaster versus Tickets.com case of October 1999 to March 2000), that linking to a page is not in itself a breach of copyright. And one could argue, perhaps less convincingly, that reproducing headlines and excerpts from a site comes under fairuse guidelines for review purposes. However, it is extremely bad form to continue scraping a site if the site owner asks you to stop. This is not encouraged at all. Instead, try to evangelize RSS to the site owner, and get him to start a proper feed. Buy him this book: it's great for gifts!

If You Are Being Scraped

If you are being scraped heavily and want to stop it, there are four ways to do so. First, scrapers should obey the *robots.txt* directive—setting a *robots.txt* file in the root directory of your site should control things. Second, you can contact the scraper and ask them to stop. If they are professional they will do so immediately. Third, you can block the IP address of the scraper, although this is sometimes rather like herding cats— scrapers can move around.

The fourth and best way is to make an RSS feed of your own. We'll show how to do this in Chapter 2.

CHAPTER 2

Content-Syndication Architecture

Talent is always conscious of its own abundance,
and does not object to sharing.
—Alexander Solzhenitsyn

In this chapter, we'll look at how RSS feeds are structured: both the feed itself and the way RSS fits into the whole web publishing picture. First, let's look at the structure of publishing on the Web.

Information Flow and Other Metaphors

Publishing on the Web can be visualized as a flow of information. Ultimately, information goes from the brain of the writer to the brain of the reader, but we don't want to concern ourselves with the biological bits right now. Let's assume that whatever content you have created is safely digitized and located on a computer.

The job now is to serve this file to your readers. If you have written your content directly in HTML and uploaded it into the correct directory on your server, this step is already done.

Most people, however, rely on some form of *Content Management System* (CMS). The definition of CMS is quite fluid. Software vendors will say that a real CMS must be a multithousand-dollar application running on expensive hardware, others will point to free web-based weblogging services such as Blogger, and still others will say that a CMS is anything that takes raw content and does something with it to present it to the public—this can include plain human intervention with a text editor and some patience.

Whichever camp you fall into, your CMS will most likely have the structure shown in Figure 2-1. Here we see that the raw content is held in a repository, then passed through some form of transformation, and finally served to the end user in the correct format. This process can take any of the following paths:

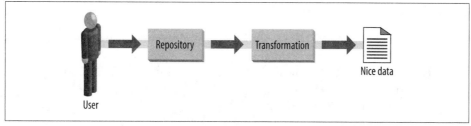

Figure 2-1. An outline of a theoretical CMS

- XML document → XLST transformation → XHTML document
- Database → Perl script → HTML document
- Plain text → Active Server Pages → HTML document
- Author's brain → NotePad → HTML document

Of course, we can easily add more than one repository:

- Plain text + XML → Perl script → HTML document

With Content Management Systems of any worth, the transformation step can be replicated. Not only can we take more than one input, but we can also create more than one output from the content. In this way, we can produce both HTML and an RSS feed as shown in Figure 2-2.

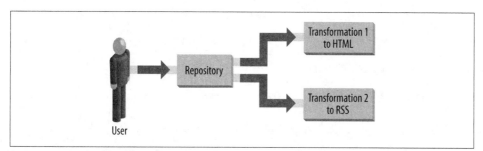

Figure 2-2. A CMS producing HTML and an RSS feed

In the popular weblogging CMSs, such as Movable Type, the transformations are made with templates containing variables. The CMS replaces the variables with the correct values and saves the static file in the correct path on the web server.

Other CMSs may run the translation stage on the fly, with script-driven XSLT or PHP transformations creating the requested document. In this case, the final document may never be saved to disk at all.

It must be said that it is perfectly OK for a CMS to produce RSS exclusively. There are many situations in which you might want to create an RSS feed only. This is not a problem—indeed, it probably indicates something quite innovative.

And at the Other End

No one wants to read raw RSS: the end user will always do something with a feed before consuming it. For the original use of RSS, to provide headlines on another site, this means using the RSS feed as input to an end user's parsing system, which will transform the RSS into something more readable. For example, the Meerkat system will transform the following RSS:

```
<?xml version="1.0"?>
<rss version="0.91">

<channel>
<title>Meerkat: An Open Wire Service</title>
<link>http://meerkat.oreillynet.com/</link>
<description>Meerkat is a Web-based syndicated content reader </description>
<language>en-us</language>

<image>
<title>Meerkat Powered!</title>
<url>http://meerkat.oreillynet.com/icons/meerkat-powered.jpg</url>
<link>http://meerkat.oreillynet.com/</link>
</image>

<item>
<title>The First Item</title>
<link>http://www.oreilly.com/example/001.html</link>
<description>This is the first item.</description>
</item>

<item>
<title>The Second Item</title>
<link>http://www.oreilly.com/example/002.html</link>
<description>This is the second item.</description>
</item>

<item>
<title>The Third Item</title>
<link>http://www.oreilly.com/example/003.html</link>
<description>This is the third item.</description>
</item>

</channel>
</rss>
```

into the screenshot shown in Figure 2-3.

Structuring the Feed Itself

RSS feeds have their own internal structure. It is good to understand it now, because it allows you to see how your CMS can create an RSS feed in the most painless way. (Remember, if you don't have a CMS, you can still create RSS files with a simple text editor.)

Figure 2-3. A screenshot of an RSS 0.91 feed transformed into HTML

At its most basic, a feed consists of a channel, with its own attributes, an image, and a number of items contained within the channel, each with their own individual attributes, like this:

- Channel (title, description, URL, creation date, etc.)
- Image
- Item (title, description, URL, etc.)
- Item (title, description, URL, etc.)
- Item (title, description, URL, etc.)

At their heart, these items inside an RSS feed are simple links to other resources, with varying amounts of description associated with each item. There are subtleties to each RSS standard's version of what a "description" actually is and how much meta-data can be given, and there are differing limits placed on which resources can be linked, but the basic aim is always the same.

For this reason, RSS feeds are always used with systems in which the content can be segmented into discrete sections or objects that can be linked.

News sites are good examples of this. News stories usually are broken into sections: headline, dateline, byline, body text, and so on, and some of these sections naturally map onto RSS fields. Weblogs are also good examples—their content grows in easily discernable chunks, each usually with a definable link, title, description, and so on.

Therefore, when working to create RSS feeds it pays to think about how the different fields within your existing content can be reused. Indeed, with all markup languages converging on XML compliance, we foresee a CMS that holds stories in a database that can produce a heavily detailed master record, and then produces an RSS feed, XHTML documents for various devices, WML for mobile phones, and so on, all with appropriate levels of detail for their medium.

This technique also shows one reason behind the push from HTML to XHTML for web-page authoring. Separating the layout from the actual data allows for the data in the master record to be unencumbered with layout details; the data can then be transformed into different formats for different uses. This transformation works both ways, as we'll discuss in the next section.

This is not to say that RSS feeds can only be used to represent big lumps of structured information. Many people are now using RSS—RSS 1.0, specifically—as a conduit for many different types of object. Events, software patches, streaming audio information, television schedules, and address books can all be encoded as RSS. We'll discuss this in detail in Chapter 7.

Serving RSS

Serving an RSS feed is simple. By far, the most common way to serve RSS is to use an ordinary web server. The feed is treated as any other text document and requested and delivered over HTTP.

Setting the Correct MIME Types

Whatever file extension you choose for your RSS feed (and although there is no standard, the RSS 1.0 specification suggests either *.xml* or *.rdf*), you should set up your server to deliver the correct MIME type with the file. At the time of this writing, there are efforts being made to create an RSS-specific MIME type. Consult the online development lists for the latest news, but in the meantime you should be using application/rss+xml.

For Apache, this is done by adding the following line to the *httpd.conf* file:

```
AddType application/rss+xml .rdf .xml
```

RSS, however, does not prescribe the transport mechanism. Feeds can be delivered over anything from FTP to Jabber, the XML-based messaging platform.

Consuming the Feed

For a standard that started out as an add-on to a simple portal web page, RSS has come a long way in terms of user clients. RSS feeds are still being used for web page creation, but they are also being wired into desktop newsreaders, search engines, instant messaging services, and content systems for mobile phone–based services, such as the Short Message Service (SMS).

Whatever the client, the feed is requested and retrieved over the transport method of choice and delivered to a parser. RSS parsers come in various flavors: from the full-on XML parsers, down to the RSS-specific quick-and-dirty versions (perhaps in a scripting language such as Perl) that rely on regular expressions to filter the content.

This is not the book to explain the actual parsing process in theory, and we should leave the practice to later chapters, but it will suffice to say that there are two ways of doing it:

Straightforward parsing

Taking values from within elements and applying them somewhere else. In this way you can build other documents, or you can apply the data within other applications.

Transformation

Using XSLT to transform the RSS into another flavor of XML—XHTML, for example.

Chapters 1 and 2 have provided a general overview of content syndication with RSS. In Chapter 3, we'll look at the different feed standards in more detail.

The Main Standards

*The nice thing about standards is that there are so
many of them to choose from.*
—Andrew S. Tanenbaum

In this short chapter, we will summarize the most commonly used XML syndication
standards, namely:

- RSS 0.91
- RSS 0.92
- RSS 2.0 and modules
- RSS 1.0 and modules

With these four main threads, each expanded on in later chapters, we run the
entire gamut of syndication possibilities: from the simple "channel and 15 URLs"
of RSS 0.91 to the "unlimited number of entire articles and massive amounts of
metadata" combination of RSS 1.0 and modules.

RSS 0.91

The oldest and most established RSS standard still in use, RSS 0.91 was originally
released by Netscape's RSS team, led by Dan Libby, in July 1999. It was later refined
and further documented by Netscape, with Userland Software's Dave Winer. It is
based on a combination of Netscape's RSS 0.90 and Userland's own older Scripting-
News 2.0b1 format. Neither of those formats are used in any meaningful way today,
but RSS 0.91 continues. At the time of this writing, Syndic8—one of the largest RSS
aggregators on the web—has 55% of its feeds declaring themselves as RSS 0.91.
While later versions of the 0.9x standard build on this original spec in many useful
ways, 0.91 is a good place for the RSS practitioner to start. Figure 3-1 shows a tree
representation of RSS 0.91.

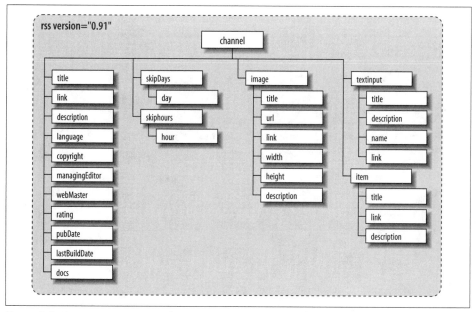

Figure 3-1. A tree representation of RSS 0.91

The Specification in Summary

- XML-based.
- Consists of one channel, containing up to 15 items.
- Each item has a title, a description, and a URL.
- Limited metadata, only applying to the channel.
- Pull-based: the user must request the feed.
- Feeds can contain an optional text entry box.

Example 3-1 is an example of RSS 0.91.

Example 3-1. An example of RSS 0.91

```
<?xml version="1.0" encoding="ISO-8859-1" ?>
<rss version="0.91">
<channel>
  <title>RSS0.91 Example</title>
  <link>http://www.exampleurl.com/example/index.html</link>
  <description>This is an example RSS0.91 feed</description>
<language>en-gb</language>
  <copyright>Copyright 2002, Oreilly and Associates.</copyright>
  <managingEditor>editor@exampleurl.com</managingEditor>
  <webMaster>webmaster@exampleurl.com</webMaster>
  <rating></rating>
  <pubDate>03 Apr 02 1500 GMT</pubDate>
  <lastBuildDate>03 Apr 02 1500 GMT</lastBuildDate>
  <docs>http://backend.userland.com/rss091</docs>
  <skipDays>
```

Example 3-1. An example of RSS 0.91 (continued)

```
    <day>Monday</day>
  </skipDays>
  <skipHours>
    <hour>20</hour>
</skipHours>
  <image>
    <title>RSS0.91 Example</title>
    <url>http://www.exampleurl.com/example/images/logo.gif</url>
    <link>http://www.exampleurl.com/example/index.html</link>
    <width>88</width>
    <height>31</height>
    <description>Computer Books, Conferences, Online Publishing</description>
  </image>

  <textInput>
    <title>
    <description>
    <name>
    <link>
  </textInput>

  <item>
    <title>The First Item</title>
    <link>http://www.exampleurl.com/example/001.html</link>
    <description>This is the first item.</description>
  </item>

  <item>
    <title>The Second Item</title>
    <link>http://www.exampleurl.com/example/002.html</link>
    <description>This is the second item.</description>
  </item>

  <item>
    <title>The Third Item</title>
    <link>http://www.exampleurl.com/example/003.html</link>
    <description>This is the third item.</description>
  </item>
</channel>
</rss>
```

RSS 0.92

RSS 0.92 arrived on Christmas Day 2000. Written by Userland Software's Dave Winer, it expanded on 0.91 with five additional elements and a rethink of various restrictions placed on string length. According to Syndic8, 30% of publicly available RSS feeds declare themselves as 0.92. This may or may not be meaningful: 0.91 feeds are also valid as 0.92 feeds, and many declared 0.92 feeds may not use any of the additional elements or features. Nevertheless, the additional elements do provide richer metadata and the ability to use the Publish and Subscribe feature, as described in Chapter 12. Figure 3-2 shows a tree representation of RSS 0.92.

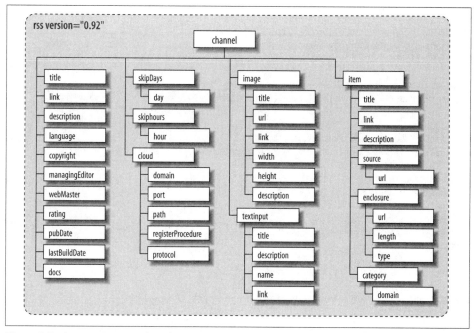

Figure 3-2. A tree representation of RSS 0.92

The Specification in Summary

- XML-based.
- One channel, with an unlimited number of items.
- Each item may have a title, description, and URL, as well as a source, category, and enclosure.
- Richer metadata—now pertaining to the item, as well as the channel.
- Primarily pull-based, but gives facilities to enable Publish and Subscribe.

Example 3-2 is an example of RSS 0.92.

Example 3-2. An example of RSS 0.92

```
<?xml version="1.0"?>
<rss version="0.92">
<channel>
  <title>RSS0.92 Example</title>
  <link>http://www.exampleurl.com/example/index.html</link>
  <description>This is an example RSS0.91 feed</description>
  <language>en-gb</language>
  <copyright>Copyright 2002, Oreilly and Associates.</copyright>
  <managingEditor>editor@exampleurl.com</managingEditor>
  <webMaster>webmaster@exampleurl.com</webMaster>
  <rating> </rating>
  <pubDate>03 Apr 02 1500 GMT</pubDate>
  <lastBuildDate>03 Apr 02 1500 GMT</lastBuildDate>
```

Example 3-2. An example of RSS 0.92 (continued)

```
<docs>http://backend.userland.com/rss091</docs>
<skipDays><day>Monday</day></skipDays>
<skipHours><hour>20</hour></skipHours>

<cloud domain="http://www.exampleurl.com" port="80" path="/RPC2"
registerProcedure="pleaseNotify" protocol="XML-RPC" />

<image>
  <title>RSS0.91 Example</title>
  <url>http://www.exampleurl.com/example/images/logo.gif</url>
  <link>http://www.exampleurl.com/example/index.html</link>
  <width>88</width>
  <height>31</height>
  <description>The World's Leading Technical Publisher</description>
</image>

<textInput>
  <title>Search</title>
  <description>Search the Archives</description>
  <name>query</name>
  <link>http://www.exampleurl.com/example/search.cgi</link>
</textInput>

<item>
  <title>The First Item</title>
  <link>http://www.exampleurl.com/example/001.html</link>
  <description>This is the first item.</description>
  <source url="http://www.anothersite.com/index.xml">Another Site</source>
  <enclosure url="http://www.exampleurl.com/example/001.mp3" length="543210" type"audio/
mpeg"/>
  <category domain="http://www.dmoz.org">Business/Industries/Publishing/Publishers/
Nonfiction/Business/O'Reilly_and_Associates/</category>
</item>

<item>
  <title>The Second Item</title>
  <link>http://www.exampleurl.com/example/002.html</link>
  <description>This is the second item.</description>
<source url="http://www.anothersite.com/index.xml">Another Site</source>
  <enclosure url="http://www.exampleurl.com/example/002.mp3" length="543210" type"audio/
mpeg"/>
  <category domain="http://www.dmoz.org">Business/Industries/Publishing/Publishers/
Nonfiction/Business/O'Reilly_and_Associates/</category>
</item>

<item>
  <title>The Third Item</title>
  <link>http://www.exampleurl.com/example/003.html</link>
  <description>This is the third item.</description>
<source url="http://www.anothersite.com/index.xml">Another Site</source>
  <enclosure url="http://www.exampleurl.com/example/003.mp3" length="543210" type"audio/
mpeg"/>
```

Example 3-2. An example of RSS 0.92 (continued)

```
    <category domain="http://www.dmoz.org">Business/Industries/Publishing/Publishers/
Nonfiction/Business/O'Reilly_and_Associates/</category>
  </item>

</channel>
</rss>
```

RSS 2.0

With RSS 2.0, Dave Winer and Userland Software declared the simpler strand of the RSS specification frozen. Small point releases (2.0.1, 2.0.2, etc.) might be made to clarify matters, but for all intents and purposes, development of simple RSS ended with Version 2.0.

This is not to say that RSS 2.0 cannot be extended, however. Taking its cue from the RSS 1.0 community's use of XML namespaces, RSS 2.0 can be extended by the use of modules. Figure 3-3 shows a tree representation of RSS 2.0.

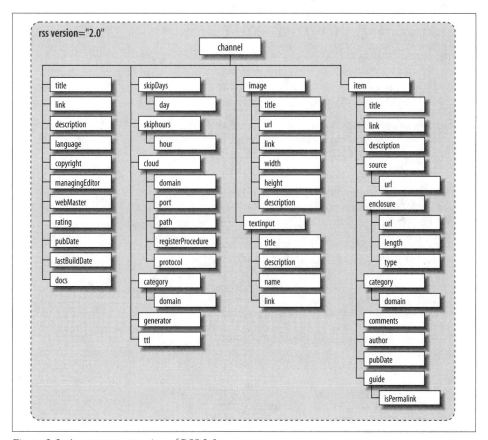

Figure 3-3. A tree representation of RSS 2.0

The Specification in Summary

- XML-based, but in a more complex form than in previous versions.
- Modularized, providing massive extensibility but also additional complexity.
- Based on (and the last of) the simple RSS strand.

Example 3-3 is an example of RSS 2.0.

Example 3-3. An example of RSS 2.0

```
<rss version="2.0" xmlns:dc="http://purl.org/dc/elements/1.1/">
<channel>
  <title>RSS2.0Example</title>
  <link>http://www.exampleurl.com/example/index.html</link>
  <description>This is an example RSS 2.0 feed</description>
  <language>en-gb</language>
  <copyright>Copyright 2002, Oreilly and Associates.</copyright>
  <managingEditor>example@exampleurl.com</managingEditor>
  <webMaster>webmaster@exampleurl.com</webMaster>
  <rating> </rating>
  <pubDate>03 Apr 02 1500 GMT</pubDate>
  <lastBuildDate>03 Apr 02 1500 GMT</lastBuildDate>
  <docs>http://backend.userland.com/rss</docs>
  <skipDays><day>Monday</day></skipDays>
  <skipHours><hour>20</hour></skipHours>
  <category  domain="http://www.dmoz.org">Business/Industries/Publishing/Publishers/
Nonfiction/Business/O'Reilly_and_Associates/</category>
  <generator>NewsAggregator'o'Matic</generator>
  <ttl>30<ttl>
  <cloud domain="http://www.exampleurl.com" port="80" path="/RPC2"
registerProcedure="pleaseNotify" protocol="XML-RPC" />

  <image>
    <title>RSS2.0 Example</title>
    <url>http://www.exampleurl.com/example/images/logo.gif</url>
    <link>http://www.exampleurl.com/example/index.html</link>
    <width>88</width>
    <height>31</height>
    <description>The World's Leading Technical Publisher</description>
  </image>

  <textInput>
    <title>Search</title>
    <description>Search the Archives</description>
    <name>query</name>
    <link>http://www.exampleurl.com/example/search.cgi</link>
  </textInput>

  <item>
    <title>The First Item</title>
    <link>http://www.exampleurl.com/example/001.html</link>
    <description>This is the first item.</description>
    <dc:creator>A.N. Author</dc:creator>
```

Example 3-3. An example of RSS 2.0 (continued)

```
      <source url="http://www.anothersite.com/index.xml">Another Site</source>
      <enclosure url="http://www.exampleurl.com/example/001.mp3" length="543210" type"audio/
mpeg"/>
      <category domain="http://www.dmoz.org">Business/Industries/Publishing/Publishers/
Nonfiction/Business/O'Reilly_and_Associates/</category>
      <comments>http://www.exampleurl.com/comments/001.html</comments>
      <author>Ben Hammersley</author>
      <pubDate>Sat, 01 Jan 2002 0:00:01 GMT</pubDate>
      <guid isPermaLink="true">http://www.exampleurl.com/example/001.html</guid>
    </item>

    <item>
      <title>The Second Item</title>
      <link>http://www.exampleurl.com/example/002.html</link>
      <description>This is the second item.</description>
      <dc:creator>A.N. Author</dc:creator>
      <source url="http://www.anothersite.com/index.xml">Another Site</source>
      <enclosure url="http://www.exampleurl.com/example/002.mp3" length="543210" type"audio/
mpeg"/>
      <category domain="http://www.dmoz.org">Business/Industries/Publishing/Publishers/
Nonfiction/Business/O'Reilly_and_Associates/</category>
      <comments>http://www.exampleurl.com/comments/002.html</comments>
      <author>Ben Hammersley</author>
      <pubDate>Sun, 02 Jan 2002 0:00:01 GMT</pubDate>
      <guid isPermaLink="true">http://www.exampleurl.com/example/002.html</guid>
    </item>

    <item>
      <title>The Third Item</title>
      <link>http://www.exampleurl.com/example/003.html</link>
      <description>This is the third item.</description>
      <dc:creator>A.N. Author</dc:creator>
      <source url="http://www.anothersite.com/index.xml">Another Site</source>
      <enclosure url="http://www.exampleurl.com/example/003.mp3" length="543210" type"audio/
mpeg"/>
      <category domain="http://www.dmoz.org">Business/Industries/Publishing/Publishers/
Nonfiction/Business/O'Reilly_and_Associates/</category>
      <comments>http://www.exampleurl.com/comments/003.html</comments>
      <author>Ben Hammersley</author>
      <pubDate>Mon, 03 Jan 2002 0:00:01 GMT</pubDate>
      <guid isPermaLink="true">http://www.exampleurl.com/example/003.html</guid>
    </item>

</channel>
</rss>
```

RSS 1.0

With RSS 1.0, released two weeks before 0.92, RSS reclaimed its RDF roots and took a jump into the more complex end of XML technology. By adding RDF, namespaces, and modularization, RSS 1.0 both gives and takes away: what it loses in simplicity, it gains in extensibility and improved support for metadata. The Dublin Core metadata set is introduced at both the item level and the channel level. At the time of this writing there are over 14 additional sets of elements available as modules to the base specification, providing support for listing objects as diverse as streaming media and real-world events. Figure 3-4 shows a tree representation of RSS 1.0.

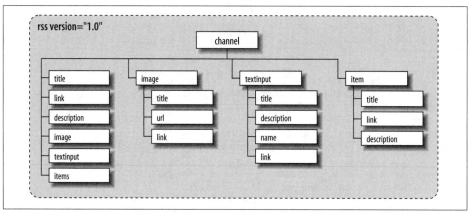

Figure 3-4. A tree representation of RSS 1.0

The Specification in Summary

- XML-based, but in a more complex form than in previous versions.
- RDF-based, providing much richer metadata.
- Modularized, providing massive extensibility but also additional complexity.
- Pull-based, but with features to allow Publish and Subscribe.

Example 3-4 is an example of RSS 1.0 using four optional modules.

Example 3-4. An example of RSS 1.0 using four optional modules

```
<?xml version="1.0" encoding="utf-8"?>
<rdf:RDF
  xmlns:rdf="http://www.w3.org/1999/02/22-rdf-syntax-ns#"
  xmlns:dc="http://purl.org/dc/elements/1.1/"
  xmlns:sy="http://purl.org/rss/1.0/modules/syndication/"
  xmlns:co="http://purl.org/rss/1.0/modules/company/"
  xmlns:ti="http://purl.org/rss/1.0/modules/textinput/"
  xmlns="http://purl.org/rss/1.0/"
>

<channel rdf:about="http://meerkat.oreillynet.com/?_fl=rss1.0">
  <title>Meerkat</title>
  <link>http://meerkat.oreillynet.com</link>
  <description>Meerkat: An Open Wire Service</description>
```

Example 3-4. An example of RSS 1.0 using four optional modules (continued)

```
    <dc:publisher>The O'Reilly Network</dc:publisher>
    <dc:creator>Rael Dornfest (mailto:rael@exampleurl.com)</dc:creator>
    <dc:rights>Copyright &#169; 2000 O'Reilly &amp; Associates, Inc.</dc:rights>
    <dc:date>2000-01-01T12:00+00:00</dc:date>
    <sy:updatePeriod>hourly</sy:updatePeriod>
    <sy:updateFrequency>2</sy:updateFrequency>
    <sy:updateBase>2000-01-01T12:00+00:00</sy:updateBase>

    <image rdf:resource="http://meerkat.oreillynet.com/icons/meerkat-powered.jpg" />
    <textinput rdf:resource="http://meerkat.oreillynet.com" />

    <items>
      <rdf:Seq>
        <rdf:li resource="http://c.moreover.com/click/here.pl?r123" />
      </rdf:Seq>
    </items>
  </channel>

  <image rdf:about="http://meerkat.oreillynet.com/icons/meerkat-powered.jpg">
    <title>Meerkat Powered!</title>
    <url>http://meerkat.oreillynet.com/icons/meerkat-powered.jpg</url>
    <link>http://meerkat.oreillynet.com</link>
  </image>

  <textinput rdf:about="http://meerkat.oreillynet.com">
    <title>Search Meerkat</title>
    <description>Search Meerkat's RSS Database...</description>
    <name>s</name>
    <link>http://meerkat.oreillynet.com/</link>
    <ti:function>search</ti:function>
    <ti:inputType>regex</ti:inputType>
  </textinput>

  <item rdf:about="http://c.moreover.com/click/here.pl?r123">
    <title>XML: A Disruptive Technology</title>
    <link>http://c.moreover.com/click/here.pl?r123</link>
    <dc:description>This the description of the article</dc:description>
    <dc:publisher>The O'Reilly Network</dc:publisher>
    <dc:creator>Simon St.Laurent (mailto:simonstl@simonstl.com)</dc:creator>
    <dc:rights>Copyright &#169; 2000 O'Reilly &amp; Associates, Inc.</dc:rights>
    <dc:subject>XML</dc:subject>
    <co:name>XML.com</co:name>
    <co:market>NASDAQ</co:market>
    <co:symbol>XML</co:symbol>
  </item>
</rdf:RDF>
```

RSS 0.91 and 0.92 (Really Simple Syndication)

It's so simple to be happy, but so difficult to be simple.
—Gururaj Ananda Yogi

In this chapter we examine the RSS 0.91, 0.92, and 2.0 specifications in detail. We also show how to create your own feeds and use those created by others.

RSS 0.91

The version documented in this section is based on the Userland document of April 2000 (currently found at *http://backend.userland.com/rss091*). Its author, Dave Winer, did not invent any new practices with this specification, but he did codify RSS in a far more precise way than the Netscape original (at *http://my.netscape.com/publish/formats/rss-spec-0.91.html*), based on common practice at the time. Primarily, the new codification imposed limits on the number of characters allowed within each element.

The only major difference between the Userland spec and the original Netscape write-up is that the Userland version lacks a document type definition (DTD) declaration. In fact, Netscape RSS 0.91 is the only RSS version with an official DTD, so most RSS parsers are used to dealing without one. Including the declaration is therefore a matter of personal preference (though it must be noted that useful character entities such as ™ cannot be used without it). Example 4-1 provides a DTD declaration for those who wish to use one.

Example 4-1. The top of an RSS 0.91 document, with a DTD declaration

```
<?xml version="1.0"?>
<!DOCTYPE rss PUBLIC "-//Netscape Communications//DTD RSS 0.91//EN" "http://my.netscape.
com/publish/formats/rss-0.91.dtd">
<rss version="0.91">
```

The Basic Structure

The top level of an RSS 0.91 document is the `<rss version="0.91">` element. This is followed by a single `channel` element. The `channel` element contains the entire feed contents and all associated metadata.

Required channel Subelements

There are five required subelements of `channel` within RSS 0.91:

title
> The name of the feed. In most cases, this is the same name as the associated web site. It can have a maximum of 100 characters.

link
> A URL pointing to the associated web site. It can have a maximum of 500 characters.

description
> Some words to describe your channel. This section cannot contain anything other than plain text (no HTML or other markup is allowed).

language
> The code for the language in which the feed is written. A full list of these codes appears in Appendix A.

image
> An element that contains subelements to describe the feed's accompanying icon. It has three required and two optional subelements:
>
> url
>> The URL of a GIF, JPG, or PNG image that corresponds to the feed. It can have a maximum of 500 characters, and it is required.
>
> title
>> A description of the image, usually used within the ALT attribute of HTML's `<img>` tag. It can have 100 characters, and it is required.
>
> link
>> The URL to which the image should be linked. This is usually the same as the channel-level `link`. It can have 500 characters, and it is required.
>
> width *and* height
>> The width and height of the icon, in pixels. The icons should be a maximum of 144 pixels wide by 400 pixels high. The emergent standard is 88 pixels wide by 31 pixels high. Both of these elements are optional.

Optional channel Subelements

There are ten optional `channel` subelements of RSS 0.91. Technically speaking, you can leave these out altogether. However, you are encouraged to add them. Much of this stuff is static—the content of the element never changes. Placing it into your RSS template, or adding another line to a script, is little work for the additional value of your feed's metadata. This is especially true for the first three subelements listed here:

copyright
> A copyright notice for the content in the feed. It can have a maximum of 10 characters.

managingEditor
> The email address of the person to contact for editorial enquiries. It is suggested that this is in the format *name@example.com* (*FirstName LastName*). It can have a maximum of 100 characters.

webMaster
> The email address of the webmaster for this feed. It can have a maximum of 100 characters.

rating
> The PICS rating for the feed. The maximum length is 500 characters. More information on PICS can be found at *http://www.w3.org/PICS/*.

pubDate
> The publication date of the content within the feed. For example, a daily morning newspaper publishes at a certain time early every morning. Technically, any information in the feed should not be displayed until after the publication date. Few RSS readers take any notice of this element in this way. Nevertheless, it should be in the format outlined in RFC 822. This element is also demonstrated in Example 3-2.

lastBuildDate
> The date and time, RFC 822–style, that the feed last changed.

docs
> A URL that points to an explanation of the standard, for future reference. This should point to either *http://backend.userland.com/rss091* or *http://my.netscape. com/publish/formats/rss-spec-0.91.html*.

skipDays *and* skipHours
> A set of elements that can control when a feed user reads the feed. skipDays can contain up to seven day subelements: Monday, Tuesday, Wednesday, Thursday, Friday, Saturday, or Sunday. skipHours contains up to 24 hour subelements, the numbers 1–24, representing the time in Greenwich Mean Time (GMT). The client should not retrieve the feed during any day or hour listed within these two elements. For example usage, see Example 3-2.

textInput
> An element that gives RSS feeds the ability to display a small text box and Submit button and associate them with a CGI application. Many RSS parsers support this feature, and many sites use it to offer archive searching or email newsletter sign-ups, for example. textInput has four required subelements:

title
> The label for the Submit button. It can have a maximum of 100 characters.

description
> Text to explain what the textInput actually does. It can have a maximum of 500 characters.

name
> The name of the text object that is passed to the CGI script. It can have a maximum of 20 characters.

link
> The URL of the CGI script. It can have a maximum of 500 characters.

item Elements

RSS 0.91 can take up to 15 item elements. The item element is at the heart of RSS, containing the primary content of the feed. Technically, item elements are optional, but a syndication feed with no items is just a glorified link. Not having any items does not mean the feed is invalid; it just means that the feed may be extremely boring.

item takes two mandatory subelements and one optional subelement:

title
> The title of the story. The maximum length is 100 characters.

link
> The URL of the story. The maximuml length is 500 characters.

description
> A synopsis of the story. This is optional and can have a maximum of 500 characters. The description can contain plain text only (no HTML).

Special Notes for RSS 0.91

The link and url elements can begin with only http:// or ftp://. Note that https://, file:, mailto:, news:, and javascript: are not permitted.

Also not permitted inside any element within RSS 0.91 is any form of HTML. Even entity-encoded HTML is forbidden.

Example 4-2 shows the complete Userland RSS 0.91 specification in action.

Example 4-2. The complete Userland RSS 0.91 specification in action

```
<?xml version="1.0" encoding="ISO-8859-1" ?>
<rss version="0.91">
<channel>
  <title>RSS0.91 Example</title>
  <link>http://www.oreilly.com/example/index.html</link>
  <description>This is an example RSS0.91 feed</description>
  <language>en-gb</language>
```

```
    <copyright>Copyright 2002, Oreilly and Associates.</copyright>
    <managingEditor>editor@oreilly.com</managingEditor>
    <webMaster>webmaster@oreilly.com</webMaster>
<rating> <!-- See the text --> </rating>
    <pubDate>03 Apr 02 1500 GMT</pubDate>
    <lastBuildDate>03 Apr 02 1500 GMT</lastBuildDate>
    <docs>http://backend.userland.com/rss091</docs>
    <skipDays>
      <day>Monday</day>
    </skipDays>
    <skipHours>
      <hour>20</hour>
    </skipHours>

    <image>
      <title>RSS0.91 Example</title>
      <url>http://www.oreilly.com/example/images/logo.gif</url>
      <link>http://www.oreilly.com/example/index.html</link>
      <width>88</width>
      <height>31</height>
      <description>The World's Leading Technical Publisher</description>
    </image>

    <textInput>
      <title>Search</title>
      <description>Search the Archives</description>
      <name>query</name>
      <link>http://www.oreilly.com/example/search.cgi</link>
    </textInput>

    <item>
      <title>The First Item</title>
      <link>http://www.oreilly.com/example/001.html</link>
      <description>This is the first item.</description>
    </item>

    <item>
      <title>The Second Item</title>
      <link>http://www.oreilly.com/example/002.html</link>
      <description>This is the second item.</description>
    </item>

    <item>
      <title>The Third Item</title>
      <link>http://www.oreilly.com/example/003.html</link>
      <description>This is the third item.</description>
    </item>

</channel>
</rss>
```

RSS 0.92

RSS 0.92 followed 0.91 in December 2000. It is a historic curiosity that RSS 0.92 actually followed RSS 1.0 by two weeks. By this time, Netscape's interest in all things RSS had waned, and the job of formalizing the latest developments in the simpler side of RSS was taken up by Userland's Dave Winer, building on his previous role of elucidating the RSS 0.91 specification. The 0.92 specification builds extensively on 0.91 and is upwardly compatible with it. Therefore, all 0.91 files are also valid 0.92 files.

Changes to Existing Elements

- `<rss version="0.91">` becomes `<rss version="0.92">`.
- All character limits are now removed. Elements can be as long as you like.
- You can have as many item elements as you like.
- All subelements of item are optional.
- language is now optional.

New Elements to RSS 0.92

RSS 0.92 also introduced four new elements into RSS:

`<source url="">`
> An optional subelement of item. It should contain the name of the RSS feed of the site from which the item is derived, and the attribute url should be the URL of the other site's RSS feed.

`<enclosure url="" length="" type=""/>`
> An optional subelement of item used to describe a file associated with an item. It has no content, but it takes three attributes: url is the URL of the enclosure, length is its size in bytes, and type is the standard MIME type for the enclosure.

`<category domain="">`
> An optional subelement of item that takes one attribute, domain. The value of category should be a forward slash–separated string that identifies a hierarchical location in a taxonomy represented by the domain attribute. See Example 4-3 for an example.

`<cloud domain="" port="" path="" registerProcedure="" protocol="" />`
> The `<cloud/>` element is an optional subelement of the channel element. It takes no value, but it has five mandatory attributes: domain, path, port, registerProcedure, and protocol. These attributes provide details that allow for the Publish and Subscribe function, as described in Chapter 12.

Example 4-3 demonstrates these elements in action.

Example 4-3. An example of RSS 0.92, with two items

```
<?xml version="1.0" encoding="ISO-8859-1" ?>
<rss version="0.92">
<channel>
  <title>RSS0.92 Example</title>
  <link>http://www.oreilly.com/example/index.html</link>
  <description>This is an example RSS0.91 feed</description>
  <language>en-gb</language>
  <copyright>Copyright 2002, Oreilly and Associates.</copyright>
  <managingEditor>editor@oreilly.com</managingEditor>
  <webMaster>webmaster@oreilly.com</webMaster>
<rating> <!-- See the text --> </rating>
  <pubDate>03 Apr 02 1500 GMT</pubDate>
  <lastBuildDate>03 Apr 02 1500 GMT</lastBuildDate>
  <docs>http://backend.userland.com/rss091</docs>
  <skipDays>
    <day>Monday</day>
  </skipDays>
  <skipHours>
    <hour>20</hour>
  </skipHours>
  <cloud domain="http://www.oreilly.com" port="80" path="/RPC2"
registerProcedure="pleaseNotify" protocol="xml-rpc" />
  <image>
    <title>RSS0.91 Example</title>
    <url>http://www.oreilly.com/example/images/logo.gif</url>
    <link>http://www.oreilly.com/example/index.html</link>
    <width>88</width>
    <height>31</height>
    <description>The World's Leading Technical Publisher</description>
  </image>
  <textInput>
    <title>Search</title>
    <description>Search the Archives</description>
    <name>query</name>
    <link>http://www.oreilly.com/example/search.cgi</link>
  </textInput>

  <item>
    <title>The First Item</title>
    <link>http://www.oreilly.com/example/001.html</link>
    <description>This is the first item.</description>
    <source url="http://www.anothersite.com/index.xml">Another Site</source>
    <enclosure url="http://www.oreilly.com/001.mp3" length="54321" type"audio/mpeg"/>
    <category domain="http://www.dmoz.org"> Business/Industries/Publishing/Publishers/
Nonfiction/</category>
  </item>

  <item>
    <title>The Second Item</title>
    <link>http://www.oreilly.com/example/002.html</link>
    <description>This is the second item.</description>
```

Example 4-3. An example of RSS 0.92, with two items (continued)

```
<source url="http://www.anothersite.com/index.xml">Another Site</source>
    <enclosure url="http://www.oreilly.com/002.mp3" length="54321" type"audio/mpeg"/>
<category domain="http://www.dmoz.org">
Business/Industries/Publishing/Publishers/Nonfiction/</category>
  </item>
</channel>
</rss>
```

Including HTML Within a Feed

Whether the description element within RSS 0.92, 2.0, and 1.0 may contain HTML is a matter of great debate. In my opinion, it should not, for both practical and philosophical reasons. Practically speaking, including HTML markup requires the client software to have the ability to parse or filter it. While this is fine with many desktop agents, it is restricting for developers looking for other uses of the data. This brings us to the philosophical aspect. RSS's second use, after providing headlines and content to desktop readers and sites, is to provide indexable metadata. By combining presentation and content (i.e., by including HTML markup within the description element), we risk breaking this feature.

Creating RSS 0.9x Feeds

RSS 0.91 and 0.92 feeds are created in the same way—the additional elements found in 0.92 are well handled by the existing RSS tools.

Of course, you can always hand-code your RSS feed. Doing so certainly gets you on top of the standard, but it's neither convenient, quick, nor recommended. Ordinarily, feeds are created by a small program in one of the scripting languages: Perl, PHP, Python, etc. Many CMSs already create RSS feeds automatically, but you may want to create a feed in another context. Hey, you might even write your own CMS!

There are various ways to create a feed, all of which are used in real life:

XML transformation
> Running a transformation on an XML master document to convert the relevant parts into RSS. This technique is used in Apache Axkit-based systems, for example.

Templates
> Substituting values within a RSS feed template. This technique is used within the Movable Type weblogging platform, for example.

An RSS-specific module or class
> Used within hundreds of little ad hoc scripts across the Net, for example.

We'll look at all three of these methods, but let's start with the third, using an RSS-specific module. In this case, it's Perl's XML::RSS.

Creating RSS with Perl Using XML::RSS

Jonathan Eisenzopf's XML::RSS module for Perl is one of the key tools in the Perl RSS world. It is built on top of XML::Parser—the basis for many Perl XML modules—and it is object-oriented. Actually, XML::RSS also supports both creating RSS 1.0 and parsing existing feeds, but in this section we will deal only with its 0.91 creation capabilities. Currently, it does not support the additional elements within RSS 0.92.

Example 4-4 shows a simple Perl script that creates the feed shown in Example 4-5.

Example 4-4. A sample XML::RSS script

```perl
#!/usr/local/bin/perl -w

## Chapter 4, Example 1.
## Create an example RSS 0.91 feed

use XML::RSS;

my $rss = new XML::RSS (version => '0.91');

$rss->channel(title        => 'The Title of the Feed',
            link           => 'http://www.oreilly.com/example/',
            language       => 'en',
            description    => 'An example feed created by XML::RSS',
            lastBuildDate  => 'Tue, 04 Jun 2002 16:20:26 GMT',
            docs           => 'http://backend.userland.com/rss092',
            );

$rss->image(title       => 'Oreilly',
            url         => 'http://meerkat.oreillynet.com/icons/meerkat-powered.jpg',
            link        => 'http://www.oreilly.com/example/',
            width       => 88,
            height      => 31,
            description => 'A nice logo for the feed'
            );

$rss->textinput(title => "Search",
            description => "Search the site",
            name    => "query",
            link    => "http://www.oreilly.com/example/search.cgi"
            );

$rss->add_item( title => "Example Entry 1",
            link  => "http://www.oreilly.com/example/entry1",
             description => 'blah blah',
            );

$rss->add_item( title => "Example Entry 2",
            link  => "http://www.oreilly.com/example/entry2",
             description => 'blah blah'
            );
```

Example 4-4. A sample XML::RSS script (continued)

```
$rss->add_item( title => "Example Entry 3",
                link  => "http://www.oreilly.com/example/entry3",
                 description => 'blah blah'
              );

$rss->save("example.rss");
```

Example 4-5. The resultant RSS 0.91 feed

```
<?xml version="1.0" encoding="UTF-8"?>

<!DOCTYPE rss PUBLIC "-//Netscape Communications//DTD RSS 0.91//EN"
           "http://my.netscape.com/publish/formats/rss-0.91.dtd">

<rss version="0.91">

<channel>
<title>The Title of the Feed</title>
<link>http://www.oreilly.com/example/</link>
<description>An example feed created by XML::RSS</description>
<language>en</language>
<lastBuildDate>Tue, 04 Jun 2002 16:20:26</lastBuildDate>
<docs>http://backend.userland.com/rss092</docs>

<image>
<title>Oreilly</title>
<url>http://meerkat.oreillynet.com/icons/meerkat-powered.jpg</url>
<link>http://www.oreilly.com/example/</link>
<width>88</width>
<height>31</height>
<description>A nice logo for the feed</description>
</image>

<item>
<title>Example Entry 1</title>
<link>http://www.oreilly.com/example/entry1</link>
<description>blah blah</description>
</item>

<item>
<title>Example Entry 2</title>
<link>http://www.oreilly.com/example/entry2</link>
<description>blah blah</description>
</item>

<item>
<title>Example Entry 3</title>
<link>http://www.oreilly.com/example/entry3</link>
<description>blah blah</description>
</item>

<textinput>
```

Example 4-5. The resultant RSS 0.91 feed (continued)

```
<title>Search</title>
<description>Search the site</description>
<name>query</name>
<link>http://www.oreilly.com/example/search.cgi</link>
</textinput>

</channel>
</rss>
```

After the required Perl module declaration, we create a new instance of XML::RSS, like so:

```
my $rss = new XML::RSS (version => '0.91');
```

The new method function returns a reference to the new XML::RSS object. The function can take three arguments, two of which we are interested in here:

```
new XML::RSS (version=>$version, encoding=>$encoding);
```

The version attribute refers to the version of RSS you want to make (either '0.91' or '1.0'), and the encoding attribute sets the encoding of the XML declaration. The default encoding is UTF-8.

The rest of the script is quite self-explanatory. The methods channel, image, textinput, and add_item all add new elements and associated values to the feed you are creating, and the $rss->save method saves the created feed as a file.

In Example 4-4, we're passing known strings to the module. Therefore, it is not of much use as a script; we need to add a more dynamic form of data, or the feed will be very boring indeed.

Creating an RSS feed with the Google SOAP API

In the absence of a generalized publishing system to play with, let's use Google's SOAP API. This web-services interface was released with much fanfare in April 2002, and at the time of this writing it is still an experimental affair. It may even be defunct by the time you read this book, but you'll get the idea.

The Google API requires a developer's key. This is readily available (again, at the time of this writing) from *http://www.google.com/apis*—I have left it out of the code here, as daily usage is limited and I'm fond of my own. You will also need to grab Google's WSDL file, which the SOAP::Lite module requires.

The script in Example 4-6 is designed to be run from a web browser. It takes two parameters—the query and the Google API key—so the URL would look something like this:

http://example.org/googlerss.cgi?q=queryHere&k=YourVeryOwnGoogleKeyHere

Example 4-6. googlerss.cgi Google API to RSS using Perl

```perl
#!/usr/local/bin/perl -w
use strict;
use SOAP::Lite;
use XML::RSS;
use CGI qw(:standard);
use HTML::Entities ();

# Set up the query term from the cgi input
my $query = param("q");
my $key   = param("k");

# Initialise the SOAP interface
my $service = SOAP::Lite -> service('http://api.google.com/GoogleSearch.wsdl');

# Run the search
my $result = $service -> doGoogleSearch ($key, $query, 0, 10, "false", "", "false",
"", "latin1", "latin1");

# Create the new RSS object
my $rss = new XML::RSS (version => '0.91');

# Add in the RSS channel data
$rss->channel( title => "Google Search for $query",
               link => "http://www.google.com/search?q=$query",
               description => "Google search for $query",
              language => "en",
              );

#Add in the required image
$rss->image(title       => 'Google2RSS',
            url         => 'http://www.example.org/icons/google2rss.jpg',
            link        => 'http://www.google.com/search?q=$query',
            width       => 88,
            height      => 31,
            description => 'Google2RSS'
            );

# Create each of the items
foreach my $element (@{$result->{'resultElements'}}) {
        $rss->add_item(
               title => HTML::Entities::encode($element->{'title'}),
               link  => HTML::Entities::encode($element->{'URL'})
               );
        }

# print out the RSS
print header('application/xml+rss'), $rss->as_string;
```

Example 4-7 shows the RSS file created by the script in Example 4-6.

Example 4-7. The resultant RSS file from the Google script, searching for RSS

```
<?xml version="1.0" encoding="UTF-8"?>

<!DOCTYPE rss PUBLIC "-//Netscape Communications//DTD RSS 0.91//EN"
            "http://my.netscape.com/publish/formats/rss-0.91.dtd">

<rss version="0.91">
<channel>
<title>Google Search for RSS</title>
<link>http://www.google.com/search?q=RSS</link>
<description>Google search for RSS</description>
<image>
<title>Google2RSS</title>
<url>http://www.example.org/icons/google2rss.jpg</url>
<link>http://www.google.com/search?q=$query</link>
<width>88</width>
<height>31</height>
<description>Google2RSS</description>
</image>
<item>
<title>MAPS &lt;b&gt;RSS&lt;/b&gt;</title>
<link>http://work-rss.mail-abuse.org/rss/</link>
</item>
<item>
<title>Yahoo! Groups</title>
<link>http://www.purl.org/rss/1.0/</link>
</item>
<item>
<title>&lt;b&gt;RSS&lt;/b&gt; 0.92</title>
<link>http://backend.userland.com/rss092</link>
</item>
<item>
<title>&lt;b&gt;RSS&lt;/b&gt; 0.91</title>
<link>http://backend.userland.com/stories/rss091</link>
</item>
<item>
<title>Royal Statistical Society</title>
<link>http://www.rss.org.uk/</link>
</item>
<item>
<title>Latest &lt;b&gt;RSS&lt;/b&gt; News (&lt;b&gt;RSS&lt;/b&gt; Info)</title>
<link>http://blogspace.com/rss/</link>
</item>
<item>
<title>Yahoo! Groups</title>
<link>http://groups.yahoo.com/group/rss-dev/files/specification.html</link>
</item>
<item>
<title>Yahoo! Groups : &lt;b&gt;rss&lt;/b&gt;-dev</title>
<link>http://groups.yahoo.com/group/rss-dev/</link>
</item>
<item>
```

```
<title>Yahoo! Groups</title>
<link>http://groups.yahoo.com/files/rss-dev/specification.html</link>
</item>
<item>
<title>O'Reilly Network: &lt;b&gt;RSS&lt;/b&gt; DevCenter</title>
<link>http://www.oreillynet.com/rss/</link>
</item>
</channel>
</rss>
```

Walking through the script in Example 4-6, we see it loads the required modules and then sets up the CGI parameters. The SOAP interface is initialized, and the query is sent via the method doGoogleSearch.

At this point, $result contains the array of results returned by Google. We leave it there for a moment and initialize XML::RSS as before. We add the required channel and image details, in this case using the $query string to make the description more interesting.

Google's SOAP API returns only ten results by default, so there is no need to add any limit to the number of item elements in the Google results. A simple foreach loop is enough to deal with the results.

But beware! Google's results contain HTML that has not been entity-encoded: we have to whiz the relevant data through HTML::Entity::encode, or the angle brackets will come out unencoded. Unencoded brackets are not allowed in any form of RSS. (For a complete run-down of correct XML form, see Appendix A.)

After that, it's really just a matter of returning the RSS in the correct manner. Note that we give the returned file a MIME type of application/xml+rss—the emergent standard.

So there it is: a dynamically created RSS feed from a SOAP interface. Other inputs could be included, obviously. For example, we could include a few lines to add a lastBuildDate.

When we move on to RSS 1.0, we'll look at building RSS feeds from multiple data sources, but for that we will have to wait for Chapter 6.

Because of its relatively limited nature, RSS 0.9x tends to be used for simple feeds of simple content. Therefore, RSS 0.9x is usually created automatically by the CMS (blogging software is a prime example).

Once You Have Created Your Simple RSS Feed

Once you have created your feed, there are just one or two more things to do. None of these are mandatory, but they are all so simple, and give so much to the richness of the Net, that you are encouraged to invest the little time needed.

Publish a Link

Place a link to the RSS feed on your page! Many people forget to do this and wonder why, after looking at their server logs, no one is subscribed to their feed. There are standard icons emerging from each of the news aggregators and desktop readers— some of these are freely available for this use, but even a simple text link is better than nothing at all.

Registering with Aggregators

Chapter 10 deals with news aggregators in more detail, so for now we'll look only at the postcreation chores. Registering your feed at the major aggregators will help people and automatic services find your information. For example, most of the desktop news readers available today will use the lists of feeds available at Syndic8 as a menu of feeds available to their users. Being part of this is a good thing. Here are a few of the major aggregators and their URLs:

Syndic8
> *http://www.syndic8.com/suggest_start.php*

NewsIsFree
> *http://www.newsisfree.com/contact.php*

Userland
> *http://aggregator.userland.com/register*

Once that's done, you need to edit the HTML of your front page (the page that your RSS feed links to from its `link` element).

Metadata for the Main Page

Your front page needs some metadata within it. First, we have the line that will allow for automatic discovery of your RSS feed. Enter this between the `head` elements within your page:

```
<link rel="alternate" type="application/rss+xml" title="RSS" href="url/to/rss/file">
```

This allows search engines, browsers, and desktop news readers to detect if the page they are looking at is represented by an RSS feed. It is an automatic version of placing a link or an icon on the page.

Syndic8 has a few other built-in features that aid with its cataloging and require some metadata to be added to your page. These features deal with the geographical origin of the feed and its subject's place within the Open Directory at *http://www.dmoz.org*. If you are registering your feed with Open Directory, it is worthwhile to add these lines:

```
<META NAME="dc.creator.e-mail" CONTENT="yourname@yourdomain.com">
<META NAME="dc.creator.name" CONTENT="Your Name">
```

Then find the correct place within the Open Directory (*http://www.dmoz.org*) and add it to your site's page, like so (if your site is not in the Open Directory, take this opportunity to submit it!):

```
<META NAME="dmoz.id" CONTENT="Computers/Internet/On_the_Web/Weblogs/Tools">
```

Now visit the Getty Thesaurus of Geographical Names (TGN), at *http://www.getty. edu/research/tools/vocabulary/tgn/*, and find the location that best represents your web site's location. Make a note of the name of the place, the name of the nation, the latitude, the longitude, and the TGN number.

Then go to Appendix B of this book and find the country code of your nation. Use this information to add the following lines to your site (replace my information with yours):

```
<meta name="tgn.id" content="7011781" />
<meta name="tgn.name" content="London" />
<meta name="tgn.nation" content="United Kingdom" />

<meta name="geo.position" content="51.500;-0.167" />
<meta name="geo.placename" content="London, England" />
<meta name="geo.country" content="UK" />
```

Now post a message to the Syndic8 mailing list (*syndic8@yahoogroups.com*) asking for a Syndic8 editor to flick the proverbial metadata switch on your feed. People will now be able to search for you by location and subject.

## CHAPTER 5

Richer Metadata and RDF

Every public action which is not customary, either is
wrong, or, if it is right, is a dangerous precedent.
It follows that nothing should ever be done
for the first time.
—Francis M. Cornford

The feeds we've seen so far are very simple. They provide little information beyond what is needed for the instant gratification of displaying the feed in a human-readable form. Of course, this isn't such a bad deal—many people only want to display the feeds as they come.

Others, however, are more ambitious in their plans for the RSS feeds they use, and for this they require a far richer set of metadata. In this chapter, we look at metadata and give a basic overview of the Resource Descriptive Framework (RDF). This will prepare us for Chapter 6 and the pleasures of RSS 1.0—the RDF-based RSS standard.

Metadata in RSS 0.9x

As all good tutorials on the subject will tell you, metadata is data about data. In the case of RSS 0.92, this includes the name of the author of the feed, the date the channel was last updated, and so on. In Example 5-1, the bold code is the metadata. You could remove this data, and the feed itself would still both parse and be useful to the reader when displayed as HTML. The metadata is in the background, silent, but meaningful to those who can see it.

Example 5-1. The metadata within an RSS 0.92 feed

```
<rss version="0.92">
<channel>
  <title>RSS0.92 Example</title>
  <link>http://www.oreilly.com/example/index.html</link>
  <description>This is an example RSS0.91 feed</description>
  <language>en-gb</language>
```

Example 5-1. The metadata within an RSS 0.92 feed (continued)

```
    <copyright>Copyright 2002, Oreilly and Associates.</copyright>
    <managingEditor>editor@oreilly.com</managingEditor>
    <webMaster>webmaster@oreilly.com</webMaster>
    <pubDate>03 Apr 02 1500 GMT</pubDate>
    <lastBuildDate>03 Apr 02 1500 GMT</lastBuildDate>
    <docs>http://backend.userland.com/rss091</docs>
    <skipDays>
      <day>Monday</day>
    </skipDays>
    <skipHours>
      <hour>20</hour>
    </skipHours>
    <cloud domain="http://www.oreilly.com" port="80" path="/RPC2"
registerProcedure="pleaseNotify" protocol="XML-RPC" />

    <image>
      <title>RSS0.91 Example</title>
      <url>http://www.oreilly.com/example/images/logo.gif</url>
      <link>http://www.oreilly.com/example/index.html</link>
      <width>88</width>
      <height>31</height>
      <description>The World's Leading Technical Publisher</description>
    </image>
    <textInput>
      <title>Search</title>
      <description>Search the Archives</description>
      <name>query</name>
      <link>http://www.oreilly.com/example/search.cgi</link>
    </textInput>

    <item>
      <title>The First Item</title>
      <link>http://www.oreilly.com/example/001.html</link>
      <description>This is the first item.</description>
      <source url="http://www.anothersite.com/index.xml">Another Site</source>
      <enclosure url="http://www.oreilly.com/001.mp3" length="54321" type"audio/mpeg"/>
<category domain="http://www.dmoz.org">
Business/Industries/Publishing/Publishers/Nonfiction/</category>
    </item>

    <item>
      <title>The Second Item</title>
      <link>http://www.oreilly.com/example/002.html</link>
      <description>This is the second item.</description>
      <source url="http://www.anothersite.com/index.xml">Another ;Site</source>
      <enclosure url="http://www.oreilly.com/002.mp3" length="54321"
type"audio/mpeg"/>
      <category domain="http://www.dmoz.org">
      Business/Industries/Publishing/Publishers/Nonfiction/</category>
    </item>
  </channel>
</rss>
```

With this sort of simple metadata, written in the grammar of RSS 0.92's XML format, we are describing simple statements. Take the first line of metadata in Example 5-1, for example. Focusing on the language aspect, we see:

```
<channel>
...
<language>en-gb</language>
...
</channel>
```

Here we see the language element with a value of en-gb. The language element is a subelement of channel, so a simple translation of the XML into English could read, "The object called channel has a subelement called language whose value is en-gb."

This phrase is grammatically and semantically correct, but it lacks a certain poetry. We can rewrite it with something more friendly: "The channel's language is en-gb."

Now that's more like it. We've created a statement of fact from the metadata: "The language of the channel is British English."

So far, so easy, you say. Well, you're quite right; metadata is all about making statements. With the simple metadata present in RSS 0.9x, we do it all the time:

```
<language>en-gb</language>
<copyright>Copyright 2002, O'Reilly and Associates.</copyright>
<managingEditor>editor@oreilly.com</managingEditor>
<webMaster>webmaster@oreilly.com</webMaster>
<pubDate>03 Apr 02 1500 GMT</pubDate>
<lastBuildDate>03 Apr 02 1500 GMT</lastBuildDate>
```

From this section, we see the feed is in English, it is copyright 2002, O'Reilly & Associates, the managing editor is *editor@oreilly.com*, and so on.

You will notice, alas, that all is not perfect with this syntax. For example, the managing editor is defined as *editor@oreilly.com*. To you and me, it is obvious that this is an email address for a person, and we can act accordingly, but to a machine—a search engine, for example—it is a general email address at best and just a string at worst. Either way, no one can tell anything at all about the managing editor. Herein lies a problem.

Let's recap. The simple metadata found in RSS 0.9x makes a simple statement based on its element, the element's value, and the place of the element within the document. We know the language element refers to the channel that is one level above it within the XML document. We also know that in our example the value of language is en-gb, and by understanding what the element and its value mean we can make the statement that the channel is written in British English.

Going back to our childhood grammar classes, we can see that this is a simple subject/predicate/object sentence:

The channel (subject) has the language (predicate) British English (object).

This sort of statement is called a *triple*. Remember this word—we'll need it later. Now, these simple triples work well for most things within RSS 0.9x, but they somewhat limit us to raw data values: things such as dates and language codes that are unambiguous and easily understood. Triples do not help us one bit when we're talking about abstract concepts, such as subjects, or when we're referring to other entities, such as people. Plus, and this is key, without human interaction, the combination of an arbitrary element name, value, and position within the document would be meaningless. If we disregard our ability to read English, we find we cannot tell what any of the element names refer to, and we cannot understand their values. As it stands, RSS 0.9x's metadata cannot be understood by machines, and the triple, though elegant, is very limited when you take the human out of the equation. Without machine comprehension, we lose a great deal of potential utility from our RSS feeds.

To start rectifying this situation, we need to define exactly what every word in the statement means. To do this, we must introduce the Uniform Resource Identifier (URI).

Using URIs in RSS

The URI is a string of characters that identifies a resource. This resource can be anything that has an identity, whether it is tangible or not: a person, a book, a standard, a web site, a service, an email address, and so on. For example:

`mailto:ben@benhammersley.com`
> The URI for me

`http://www.w3.org/1999/xhtml`
> The URI for the concept of XHTML

`pop://pop.example.org`
> The URI for an example POP mailbox

You'll notice that these look very similar to URLs—the standard hyperlinks. You're right; URLs are a subset of URIs. There are, however, some major differences between the two.

Primarily, even though many URIs are named after, and closely resemble, network-contactable URLs, this does not mean that the resources they identify are retrievable via that network method: a person can be represented by a URI that looks like a URL, but pointing a browser at it will not retrieve the person. A concept—the XML standard, for example—has its own URI that starts with `http://`, but typing it into your address bar will not download the XML standard into your machine.

A URI simply provides a unique identifier for the resource, whatever it is. Granted, wherever possible, the URI will give you something useful (documentation on the resource, usually) if it is treated like a URL, but this is not in any way necessary.

Now, by allowing resources to be defined, we can make our metadata more robust. Let's reconsider the managingEditor example:

```
<managingEditor>editor@oreilly.com</managingEditor>
```

At the moment, we can't make any form of definitive statement about this, bar what we understand from being able to read English. We can't say for sure what managingEditor actually means (what context is this in?), nor can we understand what the value denotes. Is it an email address we may freely contact, or is it something else? We just can't tell.

If we can assign URIs to each of the resources in this statement, we can give it more meaning:

```
<rdf:RDF xmlns:rdf="http://www.w3.org/1999/02/22-rdf-syntax-ns#"
         xmlns:RSS091="http://purl.org/rss/1.0/modules/rss091#"
         xmlns:rss="http://purl.org/rss/1.0/">

  <rss:channel rdf:about="http://www.example.org/example.rss">
    <RSS091:managingEditor>editor@oreilly.com</RSS091:managingEditor>
  </rss:channel>

</rdf:RDF>
```

In this example, we introduce a few more concepts, which we'll discuss in the next section. In the meantime, if you look at the emphasized code, you'll see that the channel gains a URI, denoted by the rdf:about="" attribute, and the managingEditor element becomes RSS091:managingEditor.

This immediately gives more context to the metadata. For one, the channel is uniquely defined. Second, the managingEditor element is associated with a concept of RSS091, which itself is given a URI to identify it uniquely. Third, the concept of a channel is associated with its own URI. From this information, we can make the following assertion:

> The channel (where the concept of channel is identified by the URI http://purl.org/rss/1.0/, and the channel itself is identified by the URI http://www.example.org/example.rss) has an attribute called managingEditor (which is part of a concept as defined by the URI http://purl.org/rss/1.0/modules/rss091#), whose value is editor@oreilly.com.

Because we can know what the managingEditor element means in the context of the resource represented by the URI http://purl.org/rss/1.0/modules/rss091# (it's the guy in charge of the site the feed is from, but you'll have to wait until Chapter 7 to see why), we can now understand what the statement means. Even better than that, we can start to make definitive statements about the metadata within a document, and hence about the document itself. We, and other machines, can definitively state that the managing editor of this feed has the email address *editor@oreilly.com*, because we've defined all the terms we are using. There is no ambiguity as to what each phrase means or to what it refers.

You can't have failed to notice the additional lines of code within the example. This was your first look at RDF. Much of the rest of this book deals with RDF, so let's take a look at it in some detail.

Resource Description Framework

This system of defining everything with URIs, and using this to describe the relationships between things, has been formalized in a system known as the Resource Description Framework (RDF). In this section, we'll look at enough RDF to give us a head start on the rest of the book. For a much deeper insight into RDF, take a look at Shelley Powers' *Practical RDF* (O'Reilly).

Because RDF is quite abstract—its ability to be written in different ways notwithstanding—in this chapter we are going to look at what the RDF developers call the "data model," which we can call "the really simple version, in pictures."

Resources, PropertyTypes, and Properties

As before, within the data model anything (an object, a person, a document, a concept, a section of a document, etc.) can have a URI. In RDF we call anything addressable with a URI a *resource*.

Some resources can be used as properties of other resources. For example, the concept of "Author" has a URI of its own (all concepts can), and other resources can have a property of "author". Such resources are called *PropertyTypes*.

A *property* is the combination of a resource, a PropertyType, and a value. For example, "The Author of *Content Syndication with RSS* is Ben Hammersley." The value can be a string ("Ben Hammersley" in the previous example), or it can be another resource—for example, "Ben Hammersley (resource) has a home page (PropertyType) at *http://www.benhammersley.com* (resource)."

Nodes and Arcs

RDF's data model uses diagrams, called *RDF graphs*, to show the relationships between resources, PropertyTypes, and properties. Within these diagrams, the RDF world is split into nodes and arcs.

The resources and the values are the nodes, identified by their URIs. The PropertyTypes are the arcs, representing connections between nodes. The arcs themselves are also described by a URI.

Figure 5-1 is an RDF graph that shows the previous `managingEditor` example as three nodes, connected by two arcs—two separate RDF triples. By convention, the subject is at the blunt end of the arrow, the property (or predicate) is the arrow itself, and the object is at the pointy end of the arrow.

Figure 5-1. A simple RDF graph

In Figure 5-1, the subject node on the left, representing the URI http://www.example.org/example.rss, has a relationship with the object node on the right, representing the URI editor@oreilly.com, and this relationship is defined by the URI http://purl.org/rss/1.0/modules/rss091#managingEditor. The subject node also has a relationship with another object node, representing the URI http://purl.org/rss/1.0/channel, and that relationship is defined by the URI http://www.w3.org/199/02/22-rdf-syntax-ns#type.

What makes things interesting with RDF is that, as we've said before, a node can be both a subject and an object in a chain of node, arc, node, arc, node, and so on (or, to put it another way, resource, PropertyType, resource, PropertyType, resource, and so on). Consider the graph in Figure 5-2.

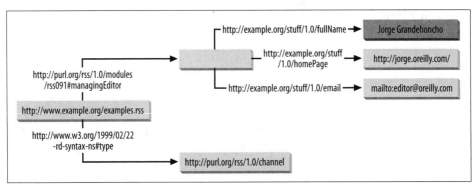

Figure 5-2. Taking a triple further

In this example, we've taken the RDF graph a step further. We've created a resource to represent the managing editor (you'll notice that the managing editor resource itself is anonymous—we have not defined it with a URI yet, hence the empty rectangle—this is not a problem), but given resources of its own, with PropertyType arcs whose URIs represent the managing editor's full name, home page, and email address.

This allows us to make some definitive statements:

> The channel (where the concept of "channel" is identified by the URI http://purl.org/rss/1.0/ and the channel itself is identified by the URI http://www.example.org/example.rss) has a resource called managingEditor (which is part of a concept defined by the URI http://purl.org/rss/1.0/modules/rss091#), which in turn has one resource

of its own, identified as a "home page" in the context of the URI http://example.org/stuff/1.0/, which is itself identified with the URI http://jorge.oreilly.com/. It also has two properties, fullName and email, both in the context of the URI http://example.org/stuff/1.0/, with the values Jorge Grandehoncho and mailto:editor@oreilly.com, respectively.

Or to put it simply:

This channel has a managing editor whose name is Jorge Grandehoncho, whose home page is http://jorge.oreilly.com/, and whose email address is editor@oreilly.com.

You should bear two things in mind. First, the continuation of the RDF graph need not be constrained to one RDF document. The preceding example can be extended by including more RDF data at the network-retrievable version of the resource's URIs. So, while the RDF data for this book may refer to me solely by author, PropertyType, and a URI, the RDF at that URI could also refer to other things I have written, and those articles could contain RDF data that refers to the subjects of the articles. This distributed nature of RDF allows for vast fields of statements to be made definitively, and every additional set of RDF data increases the power of the whole considerably.

Second, and this will become key in Chapter 7, because the PropertyTypes—the possible relationships between nodes—are represented by a URI, anyone can develop a set of elements. RDF vocabularies, therefore, can be developed to describe anything. And, as long as the URI is unique, RDF parsers will not get confused. Your descriptive powers, therefore, are endless—either an RDF vocabulary exists, or it is simple to make up your own.

Outside the scope of this book, there are also various languages for describing RDF vocabularies, or *ontologies*.

Fitting RDF with RSS

This system for creating definitive statements from metadata fits perfectly with the aims of RSS. RSS feeds are, at their core, collections of resources with implicit relationships, and RDF is designed to describe these relationships. Also, and most powerfully, RDF makes these relationships explicit in a way that allows for them to be used.

For example, the RDF graph can be travelled in any direction. The statement "This document (subject/resource) was written (predicate/PropertyType) by Ben Hammersley (object/resource)" can be read from the other end of the graph: "Ben Hammersley (subject/resource) wrote (predicate/PropertyType) this document (object/resource)."

So, you can query a database of RDF-based documents for "all the documents written by Ben Hammersley." If more triples are declared within the documents, you can query for "all the documents written by the man with the email address *ben@benhammersley.com*," or even "all the documents written by the man with the email address *ben@benhammersley.com*, and which are on the subject of dates." To take it even further, you can query for "all the documents written by the man with the email address *ben@benhammersley.com*, and which are on the subject of dates (in the context of small fruits, but not romantic encounters)." By taking different paths through an RDF graph, we can extract all sorts of data quite easily.

The ability of RDF to allow complex querying is one definite attraction, but the implications go further than that. Because RDF works just as well distributed as in a database, publishing an RDF version of RSS provides a remarkably useful entry point for the RDF world to access your site. Also, because the RDF vocabularies are easily definable, anyone can invent one. This makes RDF both wide ranging and fast growing, but in a way that does not require a single standards overlord. In the language of RSS 1.0, RDF is *extensible*.

RDF in XML

In preparation for Chapter 6, we need to look at how RDF is written in XML.

The Root Element

In all the examples in this book, I have given the RDF attributes a prefix of `rdf:`. This is not necessary in many RDF documents, but it is the way they appear in RSS 1.0. For the sake of clarity, we will leave them in here too. Therefore, for reasons we will discuss in Chapter 6, the root element of an RDF document is:

```
<rdf:RDF xmlns:rdf="http://www.w3.org/1999/02/22-rdf-syntax-ns#">
 . . .
</rdf:RDF>
```

As we will see in Chapter 6, the root element can also contain the URIs of additional RDF vocabularies. In the following examples, we will use elements from the RSS 1.0 vocabulary.

<element rdf:about="URI OF ELEMENT">

The `rdf:about` attribute defines the URI for the element that contains it. Remember, it is like the subject in a sentence—everything else refers to it. For example:

```
<rdf:RDF xmlns:rdf="http://www.w3.org/1999/02/22-rdf-syntax-ns#"
         xmlns="http://purl.org/rss/1.0/"
>
<channel rdf:about="http://www.example.org/">
 . . .
</channel>
</rdf:RDF>
```

means the channel resource is identified by the URI http://www.example.org/. Or, more to the point, everything within the channel element is referred to by http://www.example.org.

The contents of the element then describe the object referred to by the URI:

```
<rdf:RDF xmlns:rdf="http://www.w3.org/1999/02/22-rdf-syntax-ns#">
        xmlns="http://purl.org/rss/1.0/" >
<channel rdf:about="http://www.example.org">
<title>Sausages are tasty for breakfast</title>
<channel>
</rdf:RDF>
```

In this example, the resource channel identified by the URI http://www.example.org has a PropertyType title whose value is Sausages are tasty for breakfast.

Remember, RDF describes the relationship between resources, their attributes, and other resources. You have to define all the resources, and the relationship Property-Types, before the RDF is valid and meaningful. The different objects are distinguished by unique URIs. So, every resource must have an rdf:about attribute when it is described.

<element rdf:resource="URI" />

Sometimes, the value of a property is another resource. To describe this, we cannot just use the URI of the resource as the value of the element describing the Property-Type, because nothing identifies it as a URI and not just a string or a hyperlink. Instead, we must use the rdf:resource attribute:

```
<rdf:RDF xmlns:rdf="http://www.w3.org/1999/02/22-rdf-syntax-ns#">
        xmlns="http://purl.org/rss/1.0/" >

<channel rdf:about="http://www.example.org">
<title>Sausages are tasty for breakfast</title>
<image rdf:resource="http://www.example.org/picture.jpg" />
</channel>

</rdf:RDF>
```

In this example, the channel resource has a PropertyType image whose value is a resource, http://www.example.org/picture.jpg.

If we then want to describe the image itself, we need to create a description using the rdf:about attribute, as follows:

```
<rdf:RDF xmlns:rdf="http://www.w3.org/1999/02/22-rdf-syntax-ns#">
        xmlns="http://purl.org/rss/1.0/">

<channel rdf:about="http://www.example.org">
<title>Sausages are tasty for breakfast</title>
<image rdf:resource="http://www.example.org/picture.jpg" />
</channel>
```

```
<image rdf:about="http://www.example.org/picture.jpg">
<title>A picture of some sausages</title>
</image>

</rdf:RDF>
```

So now we begin to see the way RDF documents are structured. In this example, every concept, object, or thing is defined with reference to a URI. Figure 5-3 shows this example as an RDF graph, using the data model. Table 5-1 shows the relationships between subjects, predicates, and objects in Figure 5-3.

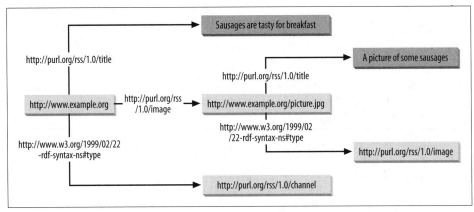

Figure 5-3. An RDF graph of the continuing example

Table 5-1. The relationship illustrated in Figure 5-3

Subject	Predicate	Object
http://www.example.org	http://purl.org/rss/1.0/title	Sausages are tasty for breakfast
http://www.example.org	http://purl.org/rss/1.0/image	http://www.example.org/picture.jpg
http://www.example.org	http://www.w3.org/1999/02/22-rdf-syntax-ns#type	http://purl.org/rss/1.0/channel
http://www.example.org/picture.jpg	http://purl.org/rss/1.0/title	A picture of some sausages
http://www.example.org/picture.jpg	http://www.w3.org/1999/02/22-rdf-syntax-ns#type	http://purl.org/rss/1.0/image

RDF Containers

We've seen that RDF resources can also be used as properties with the use of the rdf:resource attribute. But what if we need to list more than one resource? For this, we need to introduce RDF containers. There are three to choose from, each with its own purpose.

rdf:Bag

rdf:Bag is used to denote an unordered list of resources. It is used like this:

```
<rdf:Bag>
  <rdf:li rdf:resource="URI" />
  <rdf:li rdf:resource="URI" />
  <rdf:li rdf:resource="URI" />
</rdf:Bag>
```

As you can see, each list item within the `rdf:Bag` is denoted with an `rdf:li` element, which takes the `rdf:resource` attribute. The order of the list items is unimportant and is ignored.

rdf:Seq

`rdf:Seq` is used to denote an ordered list of resources. The syntax is similar to `rdf:Bag`, but the order of the list is considered important:

```
<rdf:Seq>
  <rdf:li rdf:resource="URI Number 1" />
  <rdf:li rdf:resource="URI Number 2" />
  <rdf:li rdf:resource="URI Number 3" />
</rdf:Seq>
```

rdf:Alt

`rdf:Alt` is used to describe a list of alternatives. The order is unimportant, except that the first list item is considered the default. The list items can contain other attributes to differentiate between them. For example, the `xml:lang` attribute denotes the language of the resource:

```
<rdf:Alt>
  <rdf:li xml:lang="en" rdf:resource="URI of English Version" />
  <rdf:li xml:lang="fr" rdf:resource="URI of French Version" />
  <rdf:li xml:lang="de" rdf:resource="URI of German Version" />
</rdf:Alt>
```

So, to continue our example, let's give the `channel` some items. Example 5-2 shows the first stage: we declare the items as resources connected to the `channel`.

Example 5-3 includes the `items` themselves. Note how the URIs match correctly, and pay attention to the position of the `items` and `item` elements with respect to the `channel`.

Example 5-2. A document with references to items

```
<rdf:RDF xmlns:rdf="http://www.w3.org/1999/02/22-rdf-syntax-ns#">
        xmlns="http://purl.org/rss/1.0/">
<channel rdf:about="http://www.example.org">
  <title>Sausages are tasty for breakfast</title>
  <image rdf:resource="http://www.example.org/picture.jpg" />

  <items>
    <rdf:Seq>
      <rdf:li rdf:resource="http://www.example.org/item1"/>
      <rdf:li rdf:resource="http://www.example.org/item2"/>
```

Example 5-2. A document with references to items (continued)

```
    <rdf:li rdf:resource="http://www.example.org/item3"/>
  </rdf:Seq>
 </items>
</channel>

<image rdf:about="http://www.example.org/picture.jpg">
  <title>A picture of some sausages</title>
</image>

</rdf:RDF>
```

Example 5-3. A document with the detailed items themselves

```
<rdf:RDF xmlns:rdf="http://www.w3.org/1999/02/22-rdf-syntax-ns#">
        xmlns="http://purl.org/rss/1.0/">
<channel rdf:about="http://www.example.org">
  <title>Sausages are tasty for breakfast</title>
  <image rdf:resource="http://www.example.org/picture.jpg" />

  <items>
    <rdf:Seq>
      <rdf:li rdf:resource="http://www.example.org/item1"/>
      <rdf:li rdf:resource="http://www.example.org/item2"/>
      <rdf:li rdf:resource="http://www.example.org/item3"/>
    </rdf:Seq>
  </items>
</channel>

<image rdf:about="http://www.example.org/picture.jpg">
  <title>A picture of some sausages</title>
</image>

<item rdf:about=" http://www.example.org/item1">
<title>This is item 1</title>
</item>

<item rdf:about=" http://www.example.org/item2">
<title>This is item 2/title>
</item>

<item rdf:about=" http://www.example.org/item3>
<title>This is item 3/title>
</item>

</rdf:RDF>
```

Do you see the resemblance between Example 5-3 and a RSS 0.92 document? In this section, we have made something very close to RSS depicted using RDF. This leads us to Chapter 6, where we will meet RSS 1.0, which is exactly that: RSS written as an RDF document.

RSS 1.0 (RDF Site Summary)

Live in fragments no longer. Only connect, and the
beast and the monk, robbed of the isolation that is life
to either, will die.
—E. M. Forster, *Howards End*

Now that we're steeped in metadata and RDF syntax, it's time to move on to RSS 1.0. This standard, released in December 2000, brought about two major changes to the RSS world: the reintroduction of RDF and with it an introduction of *namespaces*.

The reintroduction of RDF requires key changes in the syntax of RSS, but it also introduces the advantages and concepts we dealt with in Chapter 5. Namespaces are the XML solution to the classic language problem of one word meaning two things in different contexts. Take "windows," for example. In the context of houses, "windows" are holes in the wall through which we can look. In the context of computers, "Windows" is a trademark of the Microsoft Corporation and refers to their range of operating systems. The context within which the name has a particular meaning is called its namespace.

In XML, we can distinguish between the two meanings by assigning a namespace and placing the namespace's name in front of the element name, separated by a colon, like this:

```
<computing:windows>This is an operating system</computing:windows>
```

```
<building:windows>This is a hole in a wall</building:windows>
```

Namespaces solve two problems. First, they allow you to distinguish between different meanings for words that are spelled the same way, which means you can use useful words more than once for different meanings. Second, they allow you to group together words that are related to each other—using a computer to look through an XML document for all elements with a certain namespace is easy.

RSS 1.0 uses namespaces to allow for *modularization*. The modularization of RSS 1.0 means that developers can add new features to RSS 1.0 documents without changing the core specification. In RDF terms, this means we have included another vocabulary.

Modularization has great advantages over RSS 0.9x's method for including new elements. For starters, anyone can create a module: there are no standards issues or any need for approval, bar making sure that the namespace you use has not been used before. And, it means RSS 1.0 is potentially far more powerful that RSS 0.9x, with modules adding features for syndicating details of streaming media, Wikis, real-world events, and much more, not to mention the simplicity of adding the hundreds of vocabularies that already exist in the RDF community.

We'll look at many different modules in Chapter 7, but in the meantime, Example 6-1 shows a sample RSS 1.0 document that uses four additional modules: Dublin Core, Syndication, Company, and Text Input.

Example 6-1. A sample RSS 1.0 document

```
<?xml version="1.0" encoding="utf-8"?>

<rdf:RDF  xmlns="http://purl.org/rss/1.0/"
  xmlns:rdf="http://www.w3.org/1999/02/22-rdf-syntax-ns#"
  xmlns:dc="http://purl.org/dc/elements/1.1/"
  xmlns:sy="http://purl.org/rss/1.0/modules/syndication/"
  xmlns:co="http://purl.org/rss/1.0/modules/company/"
  xmlns:ti="http://purl.org/rss/1.0/modules/textinput/"
>

<channel rdf:about="http://meerkat.oreillynet.com/?_fl=rss1.0">
  <title>Meerkat</title>
  <link>http://meerkat.oreillynet.com</link>
  <description>Meerkat: An Open Wire Service</description>
  <dc:publisher>The O'Reilly Network</dc:publisher>
  <dc:creator>Rael Dornfest (mailto:rael@oreilly.com)</dc:creator>
  <dc:rights>Copyright &#169; 2000 O'Reilly &amp; Associates, Inc.</dc:rights>
  <dc:date>2000-01-01T12:00+00:00</dc:date>
  <sy:updatePeriod>hourly</sy:updatePeriod>
  <sy:updateFrequency>2</sy:updateFrequency>
  <sy:updateBase>2000-01-01T12:00+00:00</sy:updateBase>

  <image rdf:resource="http://meerkat.oreillynet.com/icons/meerkat-powered.jpg" />
  <textinput rdf:resource="http://meerkat.oreillynet.com" />

  <items>
    <rdf:Seq>
      <rdf:li rdf:resource="http://c.moreover.com/click/here.pl?r123" />
    </rdf:Seq>
  </items>
</channel>

<image rdf:about="http://meerkat.oreillynet.com/icons/meerkat-powered.jpg">
  <title>Meerkat Powered!</title>
  <url>http://meerkat.oreillynet.com/icons/meerkat-powered.jpg</url>
  <link>http://meerkat.oreillynet.com</link>
</image>

<textinput rdf:about="http://meerkat.oreillynet.com">
  <title>Search Meerkat</title>
```

Example 6-1. A sample RSS 1.0 document (continued)

```
    <description>Search Meerkat's RSS Database...</description>
    <name>s</name>
    <link>http://meerkat.oreillynet.com/</link>
    <ti:function>search</ti:function>
    <ti:inputType>regex</ti:inputType>
</textinput>

<item rdf:about="http://c.moreover.com/click/here.pl?r123">
    <title>XML: A Disruptive Technology</title>
    <link>http://c.moreover.com/click/here.pl?r123</link>
    <dc:description>This the description of the article</dc:description>
    <dc:publisher>The O'Reilly Network</dc:publisher>
    <dc:creator>Simon St.Laurent (mailto:simonstl@simonstl.com)</dc:creator>
    <dc:rights>Copyright &#169; 2000 O'Reilly &amp; Associates, Inc.</dc:rights>
    <dc:subject>XML</dc:subject>
    <co:name>XML.com</co:name>
    <co:market>NASDAQ</co:market>
    <co:symbol>XML</co:symbol>
</item>
</rdf:RDF>
```

Walking Through an RSS 1.0 document

At first glance, RSS 1.0 can look very complicated indeed. It isn't really, and breaking an example down into chunks can help a great deal, so that's what we're going to do now.

In sidebars throughout this section, we'll also examine RDF in XML syntax in general. An RSS 1.0 document is also a valid RDF document (though the reverse is not always true, and you must not forget that RDF has many different ways of being written).

Example 6-1 is a simple RSS 1.0 feed with one item, an image, and a text-input section. The first line includes the standard XML declaration, declaring the document's encoding to be UTF-8:

```
<?xml version="1.0" encoding="utf-8"?>
```

The root element (the first line) is also the place we declare the additional namespaces that are used in the document, telling the parser that we are also going to be using the vocabularies represented by these certain URIs. The required line already declares the namespace for all the core elements of RSS 1.0—the elements that appear without a colon—and the namespace for RDF:

```
<rdf:RDF xmlns="http://purl.org/rss/1.0/"
    xmlns:rdf="http://www.w3.org/1999/02/22-rdf-syntax-ns#"
    xmlns:dc="http://purl.org/dc/elements/1.1/"
    xmlns:sy="http://purl.org/rss/1.0/modules/syndication/"
    xmlns:co="http://purl.org/rss/1.0/modules/company/"
    xmlns:ti="http://purl.org/rss/1.0/modules/textinput/"
    >
```

Namespaces are represented by URIs. Nothing special needs to be at the namespace's URI (though by convention there is usually some documentation about the module): the only requirement is that the URI and the namespace are unique to each other. The syntax of a namespace declaration is simple and can be read aloud for greater understanding. For example, the line `xmlns:dc="http://purl.org/dc/elements/1.1/` is read as follows: "the XML namespace `dc` is associated with the URI `http://purl.org/dc/elements/1.1`."

Every namespace used in the RSS 1.0 document must be declared in the root element. For documents with many namespaces, this element can look very untidy, but a judicious application of spaces and new lines can make it easier to read.

Reformatting for Fun and Profit

RSS 1.0 documents can look absolutely forbidding. The first few lines can contain more colons, URIs, and weird acronyms than a bad day on the O'Reilly Network.

So, it can help a great deal if you load the suspect file into a text editor and have a good go at reformatting it before you try to work out what is going on. Once you've done this to a few feeds, you do get to see the underlying structure, and a good concept of RSS 1.0's inner workings will hopefully appear in your head.

Now let's look at the channel element:

```
<channel rdf:about="http://meerkat.oreillynet.com/?_fl=rss1.0">
  <title>Meerkat</title>
  <link>http://meerkat.oreillynet.com</link>
  <description>Meerkat: An Open Wire Service</description>
  <dc:publisher>The O'Reilly Network</dc:publisher>
  <dc:creator>Rael Dornfest (mailto:rael@oreilly.com)</dc:creator>
  <dc:rights>Copyright &#169; 2000 O'Reilly &amp; Associates, Inc.</dc:rights>
  <dc:date>2000-01-01T12:00+00:00</dc:date>
  <sy:updatePeriod>hourly</sy:updatePeriod>
  <sy:updateFrequency>2</sy:updateFrequency>
  <sy:updateBase>2000-01-01T12:00+00:00</sy:updateBase>
```

In the first half of the channel element, we start to see the main differences in structure between RSS 0.9x and RSS 1.0. First, every top-level element (channel, item, image, text input) has an `rdf:about` attribute. This denotes the URI of that resource in the scope of RDF.

Second, we start to see subelements of the channel using namespaces. In this example, we see `dc:` and `sy:` (the Dublin Core and Syndication modules) in use.

Next comes a major departure from RSS 0.9x. The `image` and `textinput` elements of RSS 1.0 are not contained within the `channel`. Rather, `channel` contains a pointer to their objects, which are elsewhere in the RSS 1.0 document, at the same level as `channel`. The pointers are RDF notation, using the `rdf:resource` attribute:

```
<image rdf:resource="http://meerkat.oreillynet.com/icons/meerkat-powered.jpg" />
<textinput rdf:resource="http://meerkat.oreillynet.com" />
```

In the same way, within RSS 1.0 (unlike RSS 0.9x), channel does not contain any
item elements. It does, however, contain an items element within which sits an RDF
list of all the item elements that exist within the whole document. Again, these are
simply pointers that provide the correct RDF descriptions:

```
<items>
  <rdf:Seq>
    <rdf:li rdf:resource="http://c.moreover.com/click/here.pl?r123" />
  </rdf:Seq>
</items>

</channel>
```

Note that the channel element is closed here. Unlike RSS 0.9x, in RSS 1.0 channel
does not encompass the entire document. Once it has defined its own metadata and
pointed to the items, image, and textinput objects, its job is done.

The image, textinput, and item elements are similar to the RSS 0.9x equivalents, differing only in that they declare the rdf:about attribute, as previously discussed, and
allow for additional namespaced subelements from the optional modules:

```
<image rdf:about="http://meerkat.oreillynet.com/icons/meerkat-powered.jpg">
  <title>Meerkat Powered!</title>
  <url>http://meerkat.oreillynet.com/icons/meerkat-powered.jpg</url>
  <link>http://meerkat.oreillynet.com</link>
</image>

<textinput rdf:about="http://meerkat.oreillynet.com">
  <title>Search Meerkat</title>
  <description>Search Meerkat's RSS Database...</description>
  <name>s</name>
  <link>http://meerkat.oreillynet.com/</link>
  <ti:function>search</ti:function>
  <ti:inputType>regex</ti:inputType>
</textinput>

<item rdf:about="http://c.moreover.com/click/here.pl?r123">
  <title>XML: A Disruptive Technology</title>
  <link>http://c.moreover.com/click/here.pl?r123</link>
  <dc:description>This the description of the article</dc:description>
  <dc:publisher>The O'Reilly Network</dc:publisher>
  <dc:creator>Simon St.Laurent (mailto:simonstl@simonstl.com)</dc:creator>
  <dc:rights>Copyright &#169; 2000 O'Reilly &amp; Associates, Inc.</dc:rights>
  <dc:subject>XML</dc:subject>
  <co:name>XML.com</co:name>
  <co:market>NASDAQ</co:market>
  <co:symbol>XML</co:symbol>
</item>
</rdf:RDF>
```

The Specification in Detail

This section is based on the RSS 1.0 Specification, Version 1.3.4, dated 30 May 2001. The full document is available at *http://purl.org/rss/1.0/spec*.

The Basic Structure

As we've seen, RSS 1.0's structure differs from the earlier versions of RSS by bringing the item, image, and textinput elements to the same level as channel. Examples 6-2 and 6-3 show this difference in their basic structures.

Example 6-2. The basic structure of RSS 0.9x

```
<rss>
<channel>
    <image/>
    <textinput/>
    <item/>
    <item/>
    <item/>
</channel>
</rss>
```

Example 6-3. The basic structure of RSS 1.0

```
<rdf>
  <channel/>
  <image/>
  <textinput/>
  <item/>
  <item/>
  <item/>
</rdf>
```

This difference both results from, and necessitates, the use of RDF notation to define the relationships between the elements.

The Root Element

The root element of an RSS 1.0 document is always built upon this line:

```
<rdf:RDF xmlns="http://purl.org/rss/1.0/"
         xmlns:rdf="http://www.w3.org/1999/02/22-rdf-syntax-ns#">
```

Any additional namespace declarations are inserted within this line. When designing your feed, and again after creating it, it is worth checking that all the namespaces you have used have been declared in the root element.

<channel rdf:about=""> (a Subelement of rdf:RDF)

The next level begins with the required channel element. This element must look like this:

```
<channel rdf:about="URI THAT IDENTIFIES THE CHANNEL">

subelements here

</content>
```

The contents of the rdf:about attribute must represent the feed itself. The specification states that this may be either the URL of the feed itself or the URL of the site it represents. Common usage seems to favor the URL of the feed itself—i.e., the URI.

Required subelements of channel

channel can contain many subelements. The additional modules, detailed in Chapter 7, define about 30 optional additions to these core subelements:

title
> The title of the feed, with a suggested maximum of 40 characters

description
> A summary of the feed, with a suggested maximum of 400 characters

link
> The URL of the site the feed represents

The following elements are required only if the feed contains the objects to which they refer. RSS 1.0 does not require an image, text input, or even any items to be present. However, the feed will be very dull indeed without at least one of these elements:

<image rdf:resource="URI OF THE IMAGE" />
> This line creates the RDF relationship between the channel and any <image> within the RSS 1.0 feed. The URI within the rdf:resource must therefore be the same as the URI within the rdf:about element (which we'll discuss later) contained within the image element (i.e., the URL of the image file itself).

<textinput rdf:resource="URI OF THE TEXT INPUT" />
> This line creates the RDF relationship between the channel and any <textinput> element within the feed. The URI within the rdf:resource must, again, be the same as the URI within the rdf:about element of the textinput element later in the feed. This URL should be the URL to which a text-input submission will be directed.

items
> The items element is tremendously important and pleasingly simple-yet-complicated-looking. It defines the RDF relationship between the channel and any

item found within the RSS 1.0 document. The URIs should be the same as the `rdf:resource` attribute of each of the items later in the document, so they should be identical to the value of the `link` subelement of the `item` element, if possible. For example:

```
<items>
<rdf:Seq>
<rdf:li resource="URI OF ITEM 1" />
<rdf:li resource="URI OF ITEM 2" />
...
</rdf:Seq>
</items>
```

<image rdf:resource=""> (a Subelement of rdf:RDF)

Unlike RSS 0.9x, there is no requirement for an image to be associated with an RSS 1.0 feed. This is because RSS 1.0 is not restricted to uses that involve plain-and-simple parsing into HTML. Mandating an image would be superfluous on these occasions.

Nevertheless, `image` is still used a great deal. According to the specification, "this image should be of a format supported by the majority of web browsers. While the later 0.91 specification allowed for a width of 1–144 and height of 1–400, convention (and the 0.9 specification) dictate 88×31."

This element takes the `rdf:resource` attribute. This attribute should be the URL of the image file, and it should be mirrored within the `image` subelement of `channel`.

The element also takes three mandatory subelements, in addition to the optional subelements available through the modules that we will discuss in Chapter 7. The mandatory subelements are:

title
> The alternative text (`alt` attribute) associated with the channel's image tag when rendered as HTML. Text should be no more than 40 characters.

url
> The URL of the image file. This also appears within the `rdf:resource` attribute and is mirrored within the `<image>` subelement of the `<channel>`.

link
> The URL to which the image file will link when the feed is rendered in HTML. This link usually is to the page the feed represents, so it is usually identical to the `link` subelement of `channel`.

<textinput rdf:about=""> (a Subelement of rdf:RDF)

This element, like its RSS 0.9x counterpart, provides a method of describing a form of input for delivering data to a URL that can deal with an HTTP GET request (a CGI script, for example). It's entirely optional, however, as the specification states:

The field is typically used as a search box or subscription form—among others. While this is of some use when RSS documents are rendered as channels and accompanied by human readable title and description, the ambiguity in automatic determination of meaning of this overloaded element renders it otherwise not particularly useful. RSS 1.0 therefore suggests either deprecation or augmentation with some form of resource discovery of this element in future versions while maintaining it for backward compatibility with RSS 0.9.

Nevertheless, it is still used. It takes an `rdf:about` attribute, which should point to the URL contained within its own `link` subelement, and requires four mandatory subelements:

title
> The label for the Submit button. It has a maximum of 40 characters.

description
> Text to explain what the `textinput` actually does. It has a maximum of 100 characters.

name
> The name of the text object that is passed to the CGI script. It has a maximum of 500 characters.

link
> The URL of the CGI script. It has a maximum of 500 characters.

`<item rdf:about="">` (a Subelement of rdf:RDF)

The `item` subelement is where the real work gets done. Like its RSS 0.9x namesake, the `item` subelement contains the details of each of the URLs listed within the feed, along with metadata, description, and so on. Unlike RSS 0.9x, however, RSS 1.0's `item` can point to many different things—basically anything that can be represented by a URL, even if it is not an ordinary page.

Because of this capability, the `item` subelement is the one most affected by the use of optional modules. We'll deal with those in Chapter 7, so for now we'll look at its own core subelements:

title
> The title of the object. The maximum length is 100 characters.

link
> The URL of the object. The maximum is 500 characters.

description
> A synopsis of the object. This element is optional. The maximum length is 500 characters and it must be plain text only (no HTML).

Creating RSS 1.0 Feeds

Despite the additional complexity of the RDF attributes, the methods for creating RSS 1.0 feeds are similar to those used to create RSS 0.9x feeds (discussed in Chapter 4).

Creating RSS 1.0 with Perl

The XML::RSS module we used in Chapter 4 also works for RSS 1.0, with a few changes to the scripts. Example 6-4 shows a sample script to produce the feed shown in Example 6-5.

Example 6-4. Creating RSS 1.0 with Perl

```perl
#!/usr/local/bin/perl -w

use XML::RSS;

my $rss = new XML::RSS (version => '1.0');

$rss->channel(title        => "The Title of the Feed",
            link           => "http://www.oreilly.com/example/",
            description     => "The description of the Feed",
        dc => {
            date        => "2000-08-23T07:00+00:00",
            subject     => "Linux Software",
            creator     => "scoop@freshmeat.net",
            publisher   => "scoop@freshmeat.net",
            rights      => "Copyright 1999, Freshmeat.net",
            language    => "en-us",
            },
            );

$rss->image(title        => "Oreilly",
            url          => "http://meerkat.oreillynet.com/icons/meerkat-powered.jpg",
            link         => "http://www.oreilly.com/example/",
        dc => {
                creator  => "G. Raphics (graphics at freshmeat.net)",
            },
            );

$rss->textinput(title => "Search",
                description => "Search the site",
                name   => "query",
                link   => "http://www.oreilly.com/example/search.cgi"
                );

$rss->add_item( title => "Example Entry 1",
                link  => "http://www.oreilly.com/example/entry1",
                 description => 'blah blah',
        dc => {
```

Example 6-4. Creating RSS 1.0 with Perl (continued)

```
                subject     => "Software",
              },
              );


$rss->add_item( title => "Example Entry 2",
                link  => "http://www.oreilly.com/example/entry2",
                 description => 'blah blah'
              );


$rss->add_item( title => "Example Entry 3",
                link  => "http://www.oreilly.com/example/entry3",
                 description => 'blah blah'
              );


$rss->save("example.rdf");
```

Example 6-5. The RSS feed produced by Example 6-4

```
<?xml version="1.0"?>


<rdf:RDF  xmlns="http://purl.org/rss/1.0/"
xmlns:rdf="http://www.w3.org/1999/02/22-rdf-syntax-ns#"
xmlns:dc="http://purl.org/dc/elements/1.1/"
>


<channel rdf:about="http://www.oreilly.com/example/example.rdf">
<title>The title of the feed</title>
<link>http://www.oreilly.com/example/</link>
<description>The description of the feed</description>
<dc:language>en-us</language>
<dc:date>2000-08-23T07:00+00:00</dc:date>
<dc:subject>Linux Software</dc:subject>
<dc:creator>scoop@freshmeat.net</dc:creator>
<dc:publisher>scoop@freshmeat.net</dc:publisher>
<dc:rights>Copyright 1999, Freshmeat.net</dc:rights>


<image rdf:resource="http://meerkat.oreillynet.com/icons/meerkat-powered.jpg"/ >
<textinput rdf:resource="http://www.oreilly.com/example/search.cgi"/>


<items>
<rdf:Seq>
<rdf:li rdf:resource="http://www.oreilly.com/example/entry1" />
<rdf:li rdf:resource="http://www.oreilly.com/example/entry2" />
<rdf:li rdf:resource="http://www.oreilly.com/example/entry3" />
</rdf:Seq>
</items>


</channel>


<image rdf:about="http://meerkat.oreillynet.com/icons/meerkat-powered.jpg">
<title>Oreilly</title>
<url>http://meerkat.oreillynet.com/icons/meerkat-powered.jpg</url>
<link>http://www.oreilly.com/example</link>
```

Example 6-5. The RSS feed produced by Example 6-4 (continued)

```
<dc:creator>G.Raphics (graphics at freshmeat.net)</dc:creator>
</image>

<textinput rdf:about="http://www.oreilly.com/example/search.cgi">
<description>Search the Site</description>
<name>query</name>
<link>http://www.oreilly.com/example/search.cgi</link>
</textinput>

<item rdf:about="http://www.oreilly.com/example/entry1">
<title>Example Entry 1</title>
<description>blah blah</description>
<link>http://www.oreilly.com/example/entry1</link>
<dc:subject>Software</dc:subject>
</item>

<item rdf:about="http://www.oreilly.com/example/entry2">
<title>Las Ramblings</title>
<description>blah blah</description>
<link>http://www.oreilly.com/example/entry2</link>
</item>

<item rdf:about="http://www.oreilly.com/example/entry3">
<title>Example Entry 3</title>
<description>blah blah</description>
<link>http://www.oreilly.com/example/entry3</link>
</item>
```

The differences between making RSS 0.91 and RSS 1.0 with XML::RSS are slight. Just make sure you declare the correct version, like so:

```
my $rss = new XML::RSS (version => '1.0');
```

The module takes care of itself, for the most part. If you use other namespaces, you must surround them with their namespace prefix. In this section, the script adds six elements that are part of the Dublin Core module into the channel section of the feed:

```
$rss->channel(title        => "The Title of the Feed",
             link          => "http://www.oreilly.com/example/",
             description   => "The description of the Feed",
         dc => {
             date     => "2000-08-23T07:00+00:00",
             subject  => "Linux Software",
             },
             );
```

XML::RSS comes with built-in support for the Dublin Core, Syndication, and Taxonomy modules. You can easily add support for any other module:

```
$rss->add_module(prefix=>'my', uri=>'http://purl.org/my/rss/module/');
```

This line does two things. First, it makes the module add the correct namespace declaration into the root element of the document (in this case, it adds the line xmlns:my=http://purl.org/my/rss/module/, but you should replace the prefix and the URI with the correct ones for your module), and second, it allows you to use the same syntax as the preceding Dublin Core example to add your elements to the feed:

```
$rss->channel(title        => "The Title of the Feed",
              link         => "http://www.oreilly.com/example/",
              description  => "The description of the Feed",
      dc => {
              date       => "2000-08-23T07:00+00:00"
              subject    => "Software",
              },
      my => {
              element    => 'value',
              },
              );
```

The rest of the script is identical to the RSS 0.91 creation script using the same module.

Creating RSS Feeds from Amazon.com's Web Service

To put what we've discussed to use, we can now create an RSS 1.0 feed from an external data source. One increasingly popular source, in addition to the Google API discussed in Chapter 4, is provided by Amazon.com, the online retailer. In July 2002, Amazon.com released a set of web services that allow developers to query their database using either SOAP, or XML over HTTP (also known as REST).

We used SOAP in Chapter 4, so this time we'll look at XML over HTTP. By passing a correctly formed URL to the Amazon.com server, we receive in return an XML document containing details of the books for which we've searched. For example, passing the URL:

http://xml.amazon.com/onca/xml?v=1.0&t=webservices-20&devt=DEVELOPERKEY&KeywordSearch=bananas&mode=books&type=lite&page=1&f=xml

will return an XML document, which begins like this:

```
<?xml version="1.0" encoding="UTF-8"?>
<!DOCTYPE ProductInfo PUBLIC "-//Amazon.com //DTD  Amazon Product Info//EN" "http://
xml.amazon.com/schemas/dev-lite.dtd">
<ProductInfo xmlns:xsi="http://www.w3.org/2001/XMLSchema-instance" xsi:
noNamespaceSchemaLocation="http://xml.amazon.com/schemas/dev-lite.xsd">

<Details url="http://www.amazon.com/exec/obidos/redirect?tag=webservices-
20%26creative=D3PEW6MKWJIULE%26camp=2025%26link_code=xm2%26path=ASIN/0140547444">
  <Asin>0140547444</Asin>
  <ProductName>The Day the Teacher Went Bananas</ProductName>
  <Catalog>Book</Catalog>
  <Authors>
    <Author>James Howe</Author>
    <Author>Lillian Hoban</Author>
```

```
  </Authors>
  <ReleaseDate>August, 1992</ReleaseDate>
  <Manufacturer>Puffin</Manufacturer>
  <ImageUrlSmall>
  http://images.amazon.com/images/P/0140547444.01.THUMBZZZ.jpg
  </ImageUrlSmall>
  <ImageUrlMedium>
http://images.amazon.com/images/P/0140547444.01.MZZZZZZZ.jpg
</ImageUrlMedium>
<ImageUrlLarge>
http://images.amazon.com/images/P/0140547444.01.LZZZZZZZ.jpg
</ImageUrlLarge>
  <ListPrice>$5.99</ListPrice>
  <OurPrice>$5.99</OurPrice>
  <UsedPrice>$3.35</UsedPrice>
</Details>

. . .

</ProductInfo>
```

Note that I have removed my developer's token from the URL (get your own from Amazon.com) and have truncated all but one Details element for the sake of space.

Looking at the resultant XML, we can immediately see potential ways to map Amazon.com's ProductInfo document standard over to RSS 1.0. Here's the document again, with the values explained within:

```
<?xml version="1.0" encoding="UTF-8"?>
<!DOCTYPE ProductInfo PUBLIC "-//Amazon.com //DTD  Amazon Product Info//EN" "http://
xml.amazon.com/schemas/dev-lite.dtd">
<ProductInfo xmlns:xsi="http://www.w3.org/2001/XMLSchema-instance" xsi:
noNamespaceSchemaLocation="http://xml.amazon.com/schemas/dev-lite.xsd">

<Details url="URL TO BOOK'S PAGE ON AMAZON.COM">
  <Asin>THE BOOK'S ASIN NUMBER</Asin>
  <ProductName>THE NAME OF THE BOOK</ProductName>
  <Catalog>THE CATALOG ON AMAZON THE SEARCH RESULT CAME FROM</Catalog>
  <Authors>
    <Author>AUTHOR NAME</Author>
    <Author>AUTHOR NAME</Author>
  </Authors>
  <ReleaseDate>RELEASE DATE (Month, Year)</ReleaseDate>
  <Manufacturer>THE NAME OF THE PUBLISHER</Manufacturer>
  <ImageUrlSmall>URL TO THUMBNAIL IMAGE</ImageUrlSmall>
  <ImageUrlMedium>URL TO MEDIUM SIZED IMAGE</ImageUrlMedium>
<ImageUrlLarge>URL TO LARGE IMAGE</ImageUrlLarge>
  <ListPrice>THE LIST PRICE OF THE BOOK ($dd.cc)</ListPrice>
  <OurPrice>AMAZON'S PRICE OF THE BOOK ($dd.cc)</OurPrice>
  <UsedPrice>AMAZON'S PRICE FOR THE BOOK SECOND HAND ($dd.cc)</UsedPrice>
</Details>

. . .

</ProductInfo>
```

This document would map nicely to an RSS 1.0 document, like so:

```
<?xml version="1.0"?>
<rdf:RDF xmlns:rdf="http://www.w3.org/1999/02/22-rdf-syntax-ns#"
  xmlns:dc="http://purl.org/dc/elements/1.1/"
  xmlns="http://purl.org/rss/1.0/">
<channel rdf:about="SEARCH URL">
  <title>Amazon Search Results for XXX</title>
  <link>LINK TO WEBSITE VERSION OF SEARCH</link>
  <description>Amazon Search Results for XXX</description>
  <dc:publisher>Amazon Inc</dc:publisher>
  <items>
    <rdf:Seq>
      <rdf:li resource="URI OF FIRST BOOK" />
      <rdf:li resource="URI OF SECOND BOOK" />
      <rdf:li resource="URI OF THIRD BOOK" />
      . . .
    </rdf:Seq>
  </items>
</channel>
<item rdf:about="URI OF BOOK">
  <title>TITLE OF BOOK</title>
  <link>URL of BOOK WITHIN AMAZON SITE</link>
  <description>TITLE OF THE BOOK, by AUTHOR, priced PRICE</description>
  <dc:publisher>THE NAME OF THE PUBLISHER</dc:publisher>
  <dc:creator>AUTHOR NAME</dc:creator>
  <dc:date>RELEASE DATE</dc:date>
</item>
</rdf:RDF>
```

You can see that with some imagination we can carry all the information over from the Amazon.com document to an RSS 1.0 equivalent. In this example, we have used the Dublin Core module to provide us with some more useful elements. Other data sources might require other modules. Chapter 7 goes into these in detail.

We can convert the Amazon.com XML feed into RSS 1.0 by loading the XML, parsing it, retrieving the data, and creating a new RSS document with the resulting variables.

XML to data to RSS

In Chapter 4, we retrieved data from Google using a SOAP query. In this example, we'll leave out SOAP entirely and simply retrieve the XML as we would anything else on the Web. The script will take two parameters, as before—the developer's token and the search term.

We are also going to point to specific URLs on the Amazon.com site, so we need to work out how Amazon.com creates these. At the time of this writing, the search box on their site is an HTTP POST request—the parameters do not show up in the resulting URL. Thus, we can't make the link element of the channel correspond directly to the search that creates the feed. For simplicity's sake, we'll make it point to *http://www.amazon.com*.

The item link element can point directly to a URL, however. The ASIN number (an Amazon.com-specific coding, which for books is the same as the ISBN standard) we retrieve from the Amazon.com XML is used like this:

```
http://www.amazon.com/exec/obidos/ASIN/ASIN-NUMBER-HERE/
```

Furthermore, whereas the Perl SOAP module we used returns the result as an array, here we retrieve the XML directly. It needs to be parsed first to make the RSS creation easier. We'll use XML::Simple, which is—oddly enough—a simple XML parser.

Example 6-6 shows the entire source of *amazonrss.cgi*. This is run from the browser, and takes two parameters: q equals the search term, and t equals the Amazon.com developer's token. For example:

```
http://URL/amazonrss.cgi?q=QUERY&t=TOKEN
```

Example 6-6. Amazonrss.cgi

```perl
#!/usr/bin/perl -w
use strict;
use XML::RSS;
use LWP::Simple qw(get);
use XML::Simple;
use CGI qw(:all);

# Set up the query term from the cgi input
my $query = param("q");
my $token = param("t");

# Run the search
my $result = get('http://xml.amazon.com/onca/xml?v=1.0&t=webservices-20&dev-t='.$token.
'&KeywordSearch='.$query.'&mode=books&type=lite&page=1&f=xml');

# Parse the XML
my $xml = XMLin($result);

# Create the new RSS object
my $rss = new XML::RSS (version => '1.0');

# Add in the RSS channel data
$rss->channel(  title  => "Amazon Search for $query",
                link => "http://www.amazon.com",
                description => "Amazon search results for $query",
        dc => {
                publisher      => "Amazon.com",
              },
            );

# Create each of the items
foreach my $element (@{$xml->{'Details'}}) {
```

Example 6-6. Amazonrss.cgi (continued)

```perl
    $rss->add_item(
            title    => $element->{'ProductName'},
            link     => "http://www.amazon.com/exec/obidos/ASIN/".$element->{'Asin'},
    dc => {
            publisher    => "Amazon.com",
            creator      => $element->{'Authors'}->{'Author'},
            date         => $element->{'ReleaseDate'},
        },
            );
    }

print "Content-type: application/xml+rss\n\n";
print $rss->as_string;
```

CHAPTER 7

RSS 1.0 Modules

How can one conceive of a one-party system in a
country that has 246 varieties of cheese?
—Charles de Gaulle

The modularization of RSS 1.0 was the second major change that the standard underwent. While the reintroduction of RDF allows you to create graphs of the relationships between RSS items and their attributes, modularization gives you many more attributes to play with in the first place. By using modules, RSS 1.0 can be extended without having to rewrite the core specification and without having to get consensus from the entire RSS community.

RSS 1.0 modules are easy to use. You simply declare the namespace in the root element and then use the new elements in the way the module author intended. In this chapter, we will look at how to use 19 different modules, and then we'll show you how to write your own.

Module Status

According to the specification, "Modules are classified as Proposed until accepted as Standard by members of the RSS-DEV working group or a sub-membership thereof focused on the area addressed by the module."

Currently, there are only 3 modules classified as Standard—Dublin Core, Syndication, and Content—and at least 16 that are Proposed. The Proposed classifications, however, should not stop you from using the modules—it indicates only the lack of a schedule for voting on the modules, not a lack of merit. These modules may well be accepted as Standard in the future. So, to reflect this, here are the current modules, in alphabetical order.

mod_admin

The Administration module, written by Aaron Swartz and Ken Macleod, provides information on the feed's owner and the toolkit used to produce it. This helps the RSS user work with his provider to get things right, and it helps the RSS community at large to identify problems with certain systems.

Recommended Usage

It is good manners to include this module as a matter of course. The data is not dynamically created, so it can be included within a template and just left to do its job.

Namespace

The namespace prefix for this module is admin:, which should point to http://webns.net/mvcb/. Therefore, the root element and the RSS 1.0 module containing mod_admin should look like this:

```
<rdf:RDF xmlns:rdf="http://www.w3.org/1999/02/22-rdf-syntax-ns#"
         xmlns="http://purl.org/rss/1.0/"
         xmlns:admin="http://webns.net/mvcb/">
```

Elements

The mod_admin elements occur as subelements of channel only. They consist of:

`<admin:errorReportsTo rdf:resource="URI"/>`

> The URI is typically a mailto: URL for contacting the feed administrator to report technical errors.

`<admin:generatorAgent rdf:resource="URI"/>`

> The URI is the home page of the software used to generate the feed. If possible, this should be a page that specifies a version number within the URI.

Example

Example 7-1. mod_admin in the channel element

```
<?xml version="1.0" encoding="utf-8"?>
<rdf:RDF xmlns:rdf="http://www.w3.org/1999/02/22-rdf-syntax-ns#"
         xmlns="http://purl.org/rss/1.0/"
         xmlns:admin="http://webns.net/mvcb/">
  <channel rdf:about="http://rss.benhammersley.com/index.rdf">
    <title>Content Syndication with RSS</title>
    <link>http://rss.benhammersley.com</link>
    <description>Content Syndication with RSS, the blog</description>
    <admin:errorReportsTo rdf:resource="mailto:ben@benhammersley.com"/>
    <admin:generatorAgent rdf:resource="http://www.movabletype.org/?v=2.1"/>
...
```

mod_aggregation

The Aggregation module plays a small but useful part in the life cycle of information passing through the Web. It allows news aggregators, such as Meerkat, Snewp, and so on (all covered in Chapter 12) to display the sources of their items. These services gather items from many other sources and group them by subject. mod_aggregation allows us to know where they originated.

This, of course, works over generations: as long as the mod_aggregation elements are respected, a Meerkat feed that uses a Snewp item from a Moreover feed that is itself an aggregation (for example) will still have the original source credited. As long as the mod_aggregation elements are left in place, the information is preserved. There is not, as yet, any feature for describing an aggregation history, however. You only know about the primary source.

Aggregators are the only people generating these elements—if you're building such a system, consider including them. The act of parsing such elements, however, is good for everyone. One can easily envisage an HTML representation of an RSS 1.0 feed with a "link via x" section. This is already done manually by many weblog owners, so why not include the feature in your RSS parsing scripts?

Namespace

mod_aggregation takes ag: as its prefix and http://purl.org/rss/modules/aggregation as its identifying URI. Therefore, an RSS 1.0 root element that uses it should look like this:

```
<?xml version="1.0"?>
<rdf:RDF xmlns:rdf="http://www.w3.org/1999/02/22-rdf-syntax-ns#"
         xmlns="http://purl.org/rss/1.0/"
         xmlns:ag="http://purl.org/rss/1.0/modules/aggregation/" >
```

Elements

mod_aggregation's elements are all subelements of item. There are three, and they are all mandatory if you are using the module:

ag:source
> The name of the source of the item (no character limit).

ag:sourceURL
> The URL of the source of the item (no character limit).

ag:timestamp
> The time the item was published by the original source, in the ISO 8601 standard (ccyy-mm-ddThh:mm:ss+hh:mm).

Example

Example 7-2. mod_aggregation in action

```xml
<?xml version="1.0"?>
<rdf:RDF xmlns:rdf="http://www.w3.org/1999/02/22-rdf-syntax-ns#"
        xmlns="http://purl.org/rss/1.0/"
        xmlns:ag="http://purl.org/rss/1.0/modules/aggregation/"
>

  <channel rdf:about="http://meerkat.oreillynet.com/?_fl=rss1.0">
    <title>Meerkat</title>
    <link>http://meerkat.oreillynet.com</link>
    <description>Meerkat: An Open Wire Service</description>
  </channel>

  <items>
    <rdf:Seq>
      <rdf:li rdf:resource="http://c.moreover.com/click/here.pl?r123" />
    </rdf:Seq>
  </items>

  <item rdf:about="http://c.moreover.com/click/here.pl?r123" >
    <title>XML: A Disruptive Technology</title>
<link>http://c.moreover.com/click/here.pl?r123</link>
    <description>
    XML is placing increasingly heavy loads on the existing technical
    infrastructure of the Internet.
    </description>
    <ag:source>XML.com</ag:source>
    <ag:sourceURL>http://www.xml.com</ag:sourceURL>
    <ag:timestamp>2000-01-01T12:00+00:00</ag:timestamp>
  </item>
</rdf:RDF>
```

mod_annotation

mod_annotation is the smallest module. It consists of one element, which refers to a URL where a discussion of the item is being held. It might point to a discussion group, a commenting service, Usenet, an Annotea service, etc.

For sites that host such discussions, the addition of this module into the RSS feed should be simple and worthwhile. Weblogs, for example, might only need to point the element to the URL of the main entry page for a particular item.

If you want to parse this module into HTML, you should, as with many of these modules, have no problems simply assigning a separate div or span for the contents of the element, wrapping it within an <a href="*URL*">, and formatting it as you wish. This would probably only make sense if your parser is also taking notice of either the description element or the data provided by mod_content, simply because it is hard to have a discussion based solely on a headline.

Namespace

mod_annotation is identified by the namespace prefix annotate: and the URI http://purl.org/rss/1.0/modules/annotate/. Hence, the root element looks like this:

```
<rdf:RDF xmlns:rdf="http://www.w3.org/1999/02/22-rdf-syntax-ns#"
        xmlns="http://purl.org/rss/1.0/"
        xmlns:annotate="http://purl.org/rss/1.0/modules/annotate/"
    >
```

Element

There's only one element, a subelement of item, and here it is:

```
<annotate:reference rdf:resource="URL" />
```
The URL points to a discussion on the item.

However, this element can also take subelements of its own from the Dublin Core modules, mod_dublincore and mod_DCTerms. We'll cover these modules soon, but Example 7-4 will give you an idea.

Do you see how the namespaces system works? In Example 7-3, we have a feed using only the mod_annotation system. We've added one additional namespace and used the element correctly. In Example 7-4, we want to use another module to describe something in terms that the currently available elements cannot. So we decide upon mod_dublincore, add in the namespace declaration, and go ahead.

Also notice that in Example 7-3 annotate is a one-line element, with a closing />, whereas in Example 7-4 annotate contains the mod_dublincore elements before closing. This means that the mod_dublincore elements refer to annotate, not to the item or channel. As we'll see, mod_dublincore can get addictive, and you might find yourself describing everything in your feed. This is not bad at all, but it may get confusing. By paying attention to which elements are within which, you can see what is happening.

Examples

Example 7-3. mod_annotation with additional mod_dublincore data

```
<rdf:RDF xmlns:rdf="http://www.w3.org/1999/02/22-rdf-syntax-ns#"
        xmlns="http://purl.org/rss/1.0/"
        xmlns:annotate="http://purl.org/rss/1.0/modules/annotate/"
>

<item rdf:about="http://www.example.com/item1">
    <title>RSS 0.9 or RSS 1.0...Discuss</title>
    <link>http://www.example.com/item1</link>
    <annotate:reference rdf:resource="http://www.example.com/discuss/item1"/>
</item>
```

Example 7-4. mod_annotation inside an item element

```
<rdf:RDF xmlns:rdf="http://www.w3.org/1999/02/22-rdf-syntax-ns#"
        xmlns="http://purl.org/rss/1.0/"
        xmlns:annotate="http://purl.org/rss/1.0/modules/annotate/"
```

Example 7-4. mod_annotation inside an item element (continued)

```
        xmlns:dc="http://purl.org/dc/elements/1.1/"
>

. . .


<item rdf:about="http://www.example.com/item1">
    <title>RSS 0.9 or RSS 1.0...Discuss</title>
    <link>http://www.example.com/item1</link>
<annotate:reference rdf:resource="http://www.example.com/discuss/item1">
      <dc:subject>XML</dc:subject>
   <dc:description>A discussion group on the subject in hand</dc:description>
</annotate>
</item>
```

mod_audio

mod_audio is the first of the RSS 1.0 modules we have seen that points at something other than a text page. It is specifically designed for the syndication of MP3 files—its elements matching those of the ID3 tag standard—but it can be used for any audio format.

It was designed by Brian Aker, who also wrote the mp3 module for the Apache web server. That Apache module not only streams MP3s from a server, but also creates RSS playlists.

If you're syndicating audio, or pointing at feeds that are syndicating audio, this is a must. Also, consider using mod_streaming, the module for streaming.

Namespace

mod_audio uses the prefix audio: and is indentified by the URI http://media.tangent.org/rss/1.0/. Hence:

```
<rdf:RDF xmlns:rdf="http://www.w3.org/1999/02/22-rdf-syntax-ns#"
         xmlns="http://purl.org/rss/1.0/"
         xmlns:audio="http://media.tangent.org/rss/1.0/" >
```

Elements

mod_audio elements are all subelements of item. None of them are mandatory to the module, but you should make an effort to include as many as possible per track.

audio:songname
: The title of the song.

audio:artist
: The name of the artist.

audio:album
: The name of the album.

audio:year
> The year of the track.

audio:comment
> Any text comment on the track.

audio:genre
> The genre of the track (should match genre_id).

audio:recording_time
> The length of the track in seconds.

audio:bitrate
> The bitrate of the track, in kbps.

audio:track
> The number of the track on the album.

audio:genre_id
> The genre ID number, as defined by the ID3 standard.

audio:price
> The price of the track, if you're selling it.

Example

Example 7-5. An item using mod_audio

```
<item rdf:about="http://www.example.com/boyband.mp3" >
    <title>BoyBand's Latest Track!</title>
    <description>The latest track from the fab five.</description>
    <link>http://www.example.com/boyband.mp3</link>
    <audio:songname>One Likes to Get Funky</audio:songname>
    <audio:artist>BoyBand</audio:artist>
    <audio:album>Not Just Another</audio:album>
    <audio:year>2005</audio:year>
    <audio:genre>Top 40</audio:genre>
    <audio:genre_id>60</audio:genre_id>
</item>
```

Applications

It could be said that some of these elements are superfluous, since they can be replaced by other elements (for example, audio:songname could be replaced by title). This is true in many cases, but it is much neater to use a simple MP3 tag-reading script to generate the RSS and map ID3 elements across directly. There are many ID3 tag-reading libraries available, including Chris Nandor's MP3::Info for Perl.

mod_changedpage

mod_changedpage does for RSS 1.0 what the cloud element does for RSS 0.9x—it introduces a form of Publish and Subscribe. We'll discuss Publish and Subscribe in detail in Chapter 12, but basically it enables a system in which you can "subscribe" to a feed and be notified when something new is published.

mod_changedpage uses only one element, which points to a *changedPage server*. Users wishing to be told when the feed has updated send an HTTP POST request of a certain format to this server. Upon updating, this server sends a similar POST request back to the user. The user's client then knows about the update. Again, Chapter 12 examines this in detail.

Namespace

mod_changedpage takes the namespace prefix cp: and is identified by the URI http://my.theinfo.org/changed/1.0/rss/. Hence, its declaration looks like this:

```
<rdf:RDF xmlns:rdf="http://www.w3.org/1999/02/22-rdf-syntax-ns#"
        xmlns="http://purl.org/rss/1.0/"
        xmlns:cp="http://my.theinfo.org/changed/1.0/rss/">
```

Element

mod_changedpage takes only one element, a subelement of channel:

```
<cp:server rdf:resource="URL" />
```
    The URL is the address of the changedPage server.

Example

Example 7-6. mod_changedpage in the channel

```
<?xml version="1.0" encoding="utf-8"?>

<rdf:RDF  xmlns:rdf="http://www.w3.org/1999/02/22-rdf-syntax-ns#"
        xmlns=http://purl.org/rss/1.0/
          xmlns:cp="http://my.theinfo.org/changed/1.0/rss/"
>

<channel rdf:about="http://meerkat.oreillynet.com/?_fl=rss1.0">
  <title>Meerkat</title>
  <link>http://meerkat.oreillynet.com</link>
  <description>Meerkat: An Open Wire Service</description>
<cp:server rdf:resource="http://example.org/changedPage" />
</channel>
...
```

mod_company

mod_company allows RSS feeds to deliver business news metadata. Like mod_audio, this is another example of RSS 1.0 stretching the bounds of RSS functionality; this module could lead to RSS being used as a specialist business news vehicle rather than just a generalized list of links.

Namespace

mod_company takes the namespace prefix company: and is identified by the URI http://purl.org/rss/1.0/modules/company. By now you'll realize that this means the root element of a RSS 1.0 document containing mod_company will resemble this:

```
<rdf:RDF xmlns:rdf="http://www.w3.org/1999/02/22-rdf-syntax-ns#"
         xmlns="http://purl.org/rss/1.0/"
         xmlns:company="http://purl.org/rss/1.0/modules/company/">
```

Elements

mod_company provides four elements, all of which are subelements of item. None of them are defined as mandatory, but there's little hassle and much reward in including all of them.

company:name
> The name of the company.

company:symbol
> The ticker symbol of the company's stock.

company:market
> The abbreviation of the market in which the stock is traded.

company:category
> The category of the company, expressed using the Taxonomy module. For more details, see "mod_taxonomy" later in this chapter.

Example

Example 7-7. mod_company being used within an item

```
<item rdf:about="http://www.example.com/financial_news/00001.html">
    <title>Cisco Stock moves either up or down!</title>
<description>A brief story about a thing happening today</description>
<link>http://www.example.com/financial_news/00001.html<link>
    <company:symbol>CSCO</company:symbol>
    <company:market>NASDAQ</company:market>
    <company:name>Cisco Systems Inc.</company:name>
    <company:category>
    <taxo:topic rdf:resource="http://dmoz.org/Computers/Data_Communications/Vendors/
Manufacturers/">
    </company:category>
</item>
```

mod_content

mod_content is perhaps the most misunderstood module of all. Its purpose is not only to allow for much richer content—the entire site, images and all, for example—to be included within a RSS 1.0 item, but also to give a complete RDF description of this content. Now, not only can we make RDF graphs from channel to item, but we can also make them from item to an image within an item. An RDF query of "Find all the feeds that point to articles accompanied by a picture of an elephant" can now be executed easily, as mod_content provides not just the content itself, but the relationship metadata as well. It can also be used to split the object to which an item points into smaller sections, from the standpoint of an RDF parser.

The syntax for this can look a little long-winded—RDF is rather verbose when written in XML—and, because of this, mod_content feeds can often look scary. They're not really, and reformatting them in a text editor can give you an idea of what is happening. Despite this apparent complexity, it is one of the only modules to have been officially accepted by the rss-dev working group.

It must be noted that mod_content is not to be confused with the core specification's description subelement of item. Some RSS 1.0 feeds use description to contain the content the item represents. While this may be common practice with RSS 0.9x users, RSS 1.0 users may wish to do it properly. description is for a description of the content; mod_content is for the content itself.

Namespaces

mod_content is identified by the namespace prefix content: and the URI http://purl. org/rss/1.0/modules/content/. Hence, the root element looks like this:

```
<rdf:RDF  xmlns:rdf="http://www.w3.org/1999/02/22-rdf-syntax-ns#"
          xmlns="http://purl.org/rss/1.0/"
          xmlns:content="http://purl.org/rss/1.0/modules/content/">
```

Elements

mod_content is slightly more complex than the other modules—it has a specific structure that must be followed. It consists of one element with various subelements that have important attributes of their own, some of which are mandatory, while others are not.

The first element, content:items, is a subelement of item. It consists of an rdf:Bag that contains as many content:items as needed, each enveloped in an rdf:li element, as shown in Example 7-8.

Example 7-8. The basic structure of a mod_content items

```
<item>
...
<content:items>
```

Example 7-8. The basic structure of a mod_content items (continued)

```
<rdf:Bag>
  <rdf:li>
      <content:item rdf:about=""/>
  </rdf:li>
  <rdf:li>
      <content:item />
  </rdf:li>
</rdf:Bag>
</content:items>
</item>
```

Notice that one of the content:item elements in Example 7-8 has an rdf:about attribute, but the other does not. This difference is to show that if the content is available on the Web at a specific address, the rdf:about attribute contains the URI of the content, including any part of the content that is directly addressable (an image, for example). Hence, a deeper level of RDF relationship is declared.

Now, you will also notice that the content:item element in Example 7-8 is empty. This is not much use, so we'll look into filling it. Content, as you know, can come in many formats: plain text, HTML 4.0, XHTML 1.1, and so on. What you do with such content depends on its format, so mod_content needs to be able to describe the format. It does this with a content:format subelement.

This element takes one attribute, rdf:resource, which points to a URI that represents the format of the content. Basically, this attribute declares the namespace of the content. For example, for XHTML 1.0 Strict, the URI is http://www.w3.org/TR/ xhtml1/DTD/xhtml1-strict. The URI for HTML 4.0 is http://www.w3.org/TR/html4/. Further examples can be found in the RDDL natures document at *http://www.rddl. org/natures/*.

The content:format element is required. If you don't include it, you force anyone parsing your feed to guess your content's format.

Because you have declared the format of the content:item using an RDF declaration, you must now envelop the actual content inside an rdf:value element. Example 7-9 shows a simple version.

Example 7-9. A simple version of a mod_content item

```
<item>
...
<content:items>
  <rdf:Bag>
    <rdf:li>
      <content:item>
      <content:format rdf:resource="http://www.w3.org/TR/html4/" />
        <rdf:value>
          <![CDATA[<em>This is<strong>very</em> cool</strong>.]]>
        </rdf:value>
```

Example 7-9. A simple version of a mod_content item (continued)

```
      </content:item>
  </rdf:li>
  </rdf:Bag>
  </content:items>
```

Example 7-9 shows a single `item` containing a single `content:item`, containing a line of HTML 4.0 that reads `<em>This is<strong>very</em> cool</strong>`. Note that the HTML content is encased in a `CDATA` section. As with all XML (see Appendix A for details), non-XML-compliant content must be wrapped away in this manner inside an RSS feed.

HTML, however, is not the only content type, and newer content types are fully XML-compliant. XHTML, for example, does not need to be wrapped away, as long as the parser is made aware that the contents of the `rdf:value` element can be treated accordingly. For this, we use `rdf:value`'s optional range of attributes, `rdf:parseType` and `xmlns`. Example 7-10 shows the same content as Example 7-9, but reformatted into XHTML. Note the differences in bold.

Example 7-10. A simple version of a mod_content item, with XHTML

```
<item>
...
<content:items>
  <rdf:Bag>
    <rdf:li>
      <content:item>
      <content:format rdf:resource="http://www.w3.org/1999/xhtml"/>
       <content:encoding rdf:resource="http://www.w3.org/TR/REC-xml#dt-wellformed" />
        <rdf:value rdf:parseType="Literal" xmlns="http://www.w3.org/1999/xhtml">
          <em>This is <strong>very</strong> </em> <strong>cool</strong>.
        </rdf:value>
      </content:item>
  </rdf:li>
  </rdf:Bag>
  </content:items>
```

In Example 7-10, we've told the `rdf:value` element that its contents are both parsable of the namespace represented by the URI `http://www.w3.org/1999/xhtml`. We declare all of this to prevent RDF parsers from getting confused. We humans, of course, are anything but.

The content itself is now well-formed XML. To show this, we can include a new subelement of `content:item`, the optional `content:encoding`. This points to the `rdf:resource` of the URI of well-formed XML, `http://www.w3.org/TR/REC-xml#dt-wellformed`.

If no `content:encoding` is present, we assume that the content is plain character data, either enclosed in a `CDATA` section or surrounded by escaped characters such as `&lt;b&gt;`.

In summary:

content:items
: Contains a subelement of rdf:Bag.

rdf:Bag
: Contains one or more subelements of rdf:li.

rdf:li
: Contains a mandatory subelement of content:item.

content:item
: Takes the mandatory subelements content:format and rdf:value, and the optional subelement content:encoding. content:item must take the attribute rdf:about="*URI*" if the object can be directly addressed.

  content:format
  : Takes the attribute rdf:about="*URI*", where the URI represents the format of the the content.

  rdf:value
  : Contains the actual content. It can take two attributes. If its content is well-formed XML, it must take the attributes rdf:Parsetype="literal" and xmlns="http://www.w3.org/1999/xhtml".

  content:encoding
  : Takes the attribute rdf:about="*URI*", where the URI represents the format in which the content is encoded.

Examples

Example 7-11. A fully mod_contented item

```
<item rdf:about="http://example.org/item/">
 <title>The Example Item</title>
 <link>http://example.org/item/</link>
 <description>I am an example item</description>
 <content:items>
  <rdf:Bag>

   <rdf:li>
    <content:item>
    <content:format rdf:resource="http://www.w3.org/1999/xhtml" />
    <content:encoding rdf:resource="http://www.w3.org/TR/REC-xml#dt-wellformed" />
     <rdf:value rdf:parseType="Literal" xmlns="http://www.w3.org/1999/xhtml">
      <em>This is a <strong>very cool</strong> example of mod_content</em>
     </rdf:value>
    </content:item>
   </rdf:li>

   <rdf:li>
    <content:item>
     <content:format rdf:resource="http://www.w3.org/TR/html4/" />
```

Example 7-11. A fully mod_contented item (continued)

```
    <rdf:value>
     <![CDATA[You can include content in lots of formats. <a
      href="http://www.oreillynet.com">links</a> too. ]]>
     </rdf:value>
    </content:item>
   </rdf:li>


  </rdf:Bag>
 </content:items>
</item>
```

It may either amuse or terrify you to realize that as content:item can contain any XML-formatted content, it can itself contain other RSS feeds. This might be of use for a RSS tutorial website, syndicating its lessons. Here, in Example 7-12, is an early version of this very section of this book, represented as an item, stopping right here to prevent a spiral of recursion.

Example 7-12. This page, formatted into an RSS 1.0 item

```
<item rdf:about="http://example.org/item/">
<title>Examples</title>
<description>The text of the first part of the Examples section of the mod_content bit of
chapter 7 of Content Syndication with XML and RSS</description>

<content:items>
<rdf:Bag>

<rdf:li>
<content:item>
<content:format rdf:resource="http://www.w3.org/TR/html4/" />
<rdf:value>
<![CDATA[ <h2>Examples</h2>]]>
</rdf:value>
</content:item>
</rdf:li>

<rdf:li>
<content:item>
<content:format rdf:resource="http://purl.org/rss/1.0/" />
<content:encoding rdf:resource="http://www.w3.org/TR/REC-xml#dt-wellformed" />
<rdf:value rdf:parseType="Literal"
         xmlns="http://purl.org/rss/1.0/"
         xmlns:rdf="http://www.w3.org/1999/02/22-rdf-syntax-ns#"
         xmlns:content="http://purl.org/rss/1.0/modules/content/">
<item rdf:about="http://example.org/item/"><title>The Example Item</title>
<link>http://example.org/item/</link><description>I am an example item</description>
<content:items><rdf:Bag><rdf:li><content:item><content:format rdf:resource="http://www.w3.
org/1999/xhtml" /><content:encoding rdf:resource="http://www.w3.org/TR/REC-xml#dt-
wellformed" /><rdf:value rdf:parseType="Literal" xmlns="http://www.w3.org/1999/xhtml"><em>
This is a <strong>very cool</strong> example of mod_content</em></rdf:value></content:
item>
```

Example 7-12. This page, formatted into an RSS 1.0 item (continued)

```
</rdf:li><rdf:li><content:item><content:format rdf:resource="http://www.w3.org/TR/html4/"
/><rdf:value><![CDATA[You can include content in lots of formats. <a href="http://www.
oreillynet.com">links</a> too. ]]>
</rdf:value></content:item></rdf:li></rdf:Bag></content:items></item>
</rdf:value>
</content:item>
</rdf:li>

<rdf:li>
<content:item>
<content:format rdf:resource="http://www.w3.org/TR/html4/" />
<rdf:value><![CDATA[ <p><i> Example 7.12 A fully mod_contented &lt;item&gt;</i></p><p> It
may either amuse or terrify you to realize that as &lt;content:item&gt; can contain any
XML-formatted content, it can itself contain other RSS feeds. This might be of use for a
RSS tutorial website, syndicating its lessons. Here, in example 7.13, is this very section
of this book, represented as an &lt;item&gt;, stopping right here to prevent a spiral of
recursion.</p>]]>
</rdf:value>
</content:item>
</rdf:li>
</rdf:Bag>
</content:items>
</item>
```

mod_dublincore

The second of the Standard modules to be examined in this chapter, mod_dublincore
is the most-used of all the RSS 1.0 modules. It allows an RSS 1.0 feed to express the
additional metadata formalized by the Dublin Core Metadata Initiative. Chapter 5
discusses this initiative in detail, so let's move on to the details of the module itself.

Namespace

mod_dublincore is identified by the prefix dc: and the URI http://purl.org/dc/
elements/1.1/. So, in the grand tradition, the root element appears as:

```
<rdf:RDF xmlns:rdf="http://www.w3.org/1999/02/22-rdf-syntax-ns#"
         xmlns="http://purl.org/rss/1.0/"
         xmlns:dc="http://purl.org/dc/elements/1.1/"
    >
```

Elements

mod_dublincore can be used in two ways: the simpler and the more RDF-based.

In either usage, mod_dublincore elements are entirely optional and can be applied to
the channel, an item, an image, a textinput element, or all of them, as liberally as you
wish, as long as the information you are relating makes sense. It is rather addictive, I
must say, and I encourage you to put Dublin Core metadata all over your feeds.
Here's what we can include:

`dc:title`
> The title of the item.

`dc:creator`
> The name of the creator of the item (i.e., a person, organization, or system). If the creator is a person, this information is customarily in the format *Firstname Lastname* (*email@domain.com*).

`dc:subject`
> The subject of the item.

`dc:description`
> A brief description of the item.

`dc:publisher`
> The name of the publisher, either a person or an organization. If the publisher is a person, this information is customarily in the format *Firstname Lastname* (*email@domain.com*).

`dc:contributor`
> The name of a contributor, customarily in the format *Firstname Lastname* (*email@domain.com*).

`dc:date`
> The publishing date, in the W3CDTF format (e.g., `2000-01-01T12:00+00:00`).

`dc:type`
> The nature of the item, taken from the list of Dublin Core types at *http://dublincore.org/documents/dcmi-type-vocabulary/*:
>
> *Collection*
>> A collection is an aggregation of items, described as a group; its parts can be described and navigated separately (for example, a weblog).
>
> *Dataset*
>> A dataset is information encoded in a defined structure (for example, lists, tables, and databases), intended to be useful for direct machine processing.
>
> *Event*
>> According to the official definition of the Dublin Core authors, an event is a nonpersistent, time-based occurrence. Examples include any exhibition, webcast, conference, workshop, open-day, performance, battle, trial, wedding, tea-party, conflagration, or orgy. The soon-to-be-described mod_event has a lot to do with this sort of thing.
>
> *Image*
>> They are worth a thousand words, you know.
>
> *Interactive resource*
>> The official Dublin Core definition of an interactive resource is "a resource which requires interaction from the user to be understood, executed, or experienced. For example—forms on web pages, applets, multimedia

learning objects, chat services, virtual reality." In the RSS world, resrouces could be either pointers to programs, or the `textinput` element itself.

Service

Technically, a service is a system that provides one or more functions of value to the end user. Assuming that just providing information doesn't count, a service could be used to point to web applications or web services, as long as you create an RSS feed that provides the necessary details (using mod_content to syndicate WSDL files, for example).

Software

You know what software is. In this case, it is distinguished from an interactive resource by being downloadable, rather than run on a remote server.

Sound

Officially, a sound is a resource with content primarily intended to be rendered as audio.

Text

Plain text content.

`dc:format`

This differs from `dc:type` by a degree of sophistication. Whereas `dc:type` provides a top-level indication of the feed's nature, `dc:format` should point to the exact MIME type of the content itself.

`dc:identifier`

The identifier should be an unambiguous reference to the resource within a given context. So, in RSS 1.0 terms, this is the same as the item's `rdf:about` attribute.

`dc:source`

In RSS 1.0 terms, this element can do the same job as the `ag:sourceURL` of the mod_aggregation module. It should point to an unambiguous reference of the source of the item. Unlike the `ag:sourceURL` element, however, `dc:source` is not restricted to URLs. Any sufficiently unambiguous reference works (ISBN numbers, for example).

`dc:language`

The language in which the item is written, using the standard language code, as covered in Appendix B.

`dc:relation`

The URI of a related resource. See mod_DCTerms later in this chapter for more details.

`dc:coverage`

According to the Dublin Core authors, "Coverage will typically include spatial location (a place name or geographic coordinates), temporal period (a period label, date, or date range), or jurisdiction (such as a named administrative entity). Recommended best practice is to select a value from a controlled vocabulary (for example, the Thesaurus of Geographic Names [TGN]) and that, where appropriate, named places or time periods be used in preference to numeric identifiers such as sets of coordinates or date ranges."

dc:rights

This element should contain any copyright, copyleft, public domain, or similar declaration. The absence of this element does not imply anything whatsoever.

The more complex version of mod_dublincore adds RDF and the mod_taxonomy module to give a richer meaning to dc:subject. For example, dc:subject can be used simply like this:

```
<dc:subject>World Cup</dc:subject>
```

or combined with a definition of a topic, in a richer RDF version:

```
<dc:subject>
  <rdf:Description>
    <taxo:topic rdf:resource="http://dmoz.org/Sports/Soccer/" />
    <rdf:value>World Cup</rdf:value>
  </rdf:Description>
</dc:subject>
```

This not only defines the subject, but also provides it with a wider contextual meaning. In this example, we're saying the subject is "the World Cup of soccer" (or more correctly, we're saying that "this item is on the subject represented by the term 'World Cup' in the context provided by the URI http://dmoz.org/Sports/Soccer".) After all, there is more than one World Cup. This approach is a especially useful for describing homonyms, such as:

```
<dc:subject>
  <rdf:Description>
    <taxo:topic rdf:resource="http://dmoz.org/Business/Industries/Food_and_Related_
Products/Beverages/Soft_Drinks" />
    <rdf:value>Coke</rdf:value>
  </rdf:Description>
</dc:subject>
```

as opposed to:

```
<dc:subject>
  <rdf:Description>
    <taxo:topic rdf:resource="http://dmoz.org/Health/Addictions/Substance_Abuse/
Illegal_Drugs/" />
    <rdf:value>Coke</rdf:value>
  </rdf:Description>
</dc:subject>
```

Example

Example 7-13. An RSS 1.0 feed with mod_dublincore

```
<?xml version="1.0" encoding="utf-8"?>
<rdf:RDF xmlns:rdf="http://www.w3.org/1999/02/22-rdf-syntax-ns#"
  xmlns="http://purl.org/rss/1.0/"
```

Example 7-13. An RSS 1.0 feed with mod_dublincore (continued)

```
  xmlns:dc="http://purl.org/dc/elements/1.1/"
>

<channel rdf:about="http://meerkat.oreillynet.com/?_fl=rss1.0">
  <title>Meerkat</title>
  <link>http://meerkat.oreillynet.com</link>
  <description>Meerkat: An Open Wire Service</description>
  <dc:publisher>The O'Reilly Network</dc:publisher>
  <dc:creator>Rael Dornfest (mailto:rael@oreilly.com)</dc:creator>
  <dc:rights>Copyright &#169; 2000 O'Reilly &amp; Associates, Inc.</dc:rights>
  <dc:date>2000-01-01T12:00+00:00</dc:date>
  <dc:type>Interactive Resource</dc:type>
  <image rdf:resource="http://meerkat.oreillynet.com/icons/meerkat-powered.jpg" />
  <textinput rdf:resource="http://meerkat.oreillynet.com" />

  <items>
    <rdf:Seq>
      <rdf:li resource="http://c.moreover.com/click/here.pl?r123" />
    </rdf:Seq>
  </items>

</channel>

<image rdf:about="http://meerkat.oreillynet.com/icons/meerkat-powered.jpg">
  <title>Meerkat Powered!</title>
  <url>http://meerkat.oreillynet.com/icons/meerkat-powered.jpg</url>
<link>http://meerkat.oreillynet.com</link>
  <dc:creator> Rael Dornfest (mailto:rael@oreilly.com)</dc:creator>
  <dc:type>image</dc:type>
</image>

<textinput rdf:about="http://meerkat.oreillynet.com">
  <title>Search Meerkat</title>
  <description>Search Meerkat's RSS Database...</description>
  <name>s</name>
  <link>http://meerkat.oreillynet.com/</link>
</textinput>

<item rdf:about="http://c.moreover.com/click/here.pl?r123">
  <title>XML: A Disruptive Technology</title>
  <link>http://c.moreover.com/click/here.pl?r123</link>
  <dc:description>This the description of the article</dc:description>
  <dc:publisher>The O'Reilly Network</dc:publisher>
  <dc:creator>Simon St.Laurent (mailto:simonstl@simonstl.com)</dc:creator>
  <dc:rights>Copyright &#169; 2000 O'Reilly &amp; Associates, Inc.</dc:rights>
  <dc:subject>XML</dc:subject>
</item>
</rdf:RDF>
```

mod_DCTerms

Once Dublin Core metadata has sunk its I-must-add-metadata-to-everything addictive nature into your very soul, you soon realize that the core terms are lacking in depth. For example, dc:relation means "is related to," but in what way? We don't know, unless we use mod_DCTerms.

mod_DCTerms introduces 28 new subelements to channel, item, image, and textinput, as appropriate. These subelements are related, within Dublin Core, to the core elements found within mod_dublincore, but mod_DCTerms does not express this relationship. For example, dcterms:created is actually a refinement of dc:date.

Namespace

mod_DCTerms takes the namespace prefix dcterms: and is identified by the URI http://purl.org/dc/terms/. So, the root element looks like this:

```
<rdf:RDF xmlns:rdf="http://www.w3.org/1999/02/22-rdf-syntax-ns#"
         xmlns="http://purl.org/rss/1.0/"
         xmlns:dcterms="http://purl.org/dc/terms/"
>
```

Elements

You have a lot to choose from with this module. As we've said, the elements can be subelements of channel, item, image, or textinput. Apply liberally and with gusto.

dcterms:alternative

An alternative title for the item. For example:

```
<title>Programming Perl</title>
<dc:title>Programming Perl</dc:title>
<dcterms:alternative>The Camel Book</dcterms:alternative>
```

dcterms:created

The date the object was created, in W3CDTF standard (YYYY-MM-DDTHH:MM:SS).

dcterms:issued

The date the object was first made available. This should be used, for backward compatibility, with dc:date, and it should contain the same value. Again, the date must be in W3CDTF format.

dcterms:modified

The date the content of the object last changed, in W3CDTF format. This can sit inside channel, item, or both.

dcterms:extent

The size of the document referred to by the section of the feed in which the element appears, in bytes.

`dcterms:medium`

The HTTP Content-Type of the object to which the parent element refers. The HTTP Content-Type is made up of the MIME type, followed optionally by the character set, denoted by the string `;charset=`. For example:

```
<dcterms:medium>text/html; charset=UTF-8</dcterms:medium>
```

Paired elements

Some of the `mod_DCterms` elements come paired together naturally. When we talk about two separate `items`, it is important to remember that the following paired elemets must work together:

`dcterms:isVersionOf` *and* `dcterms:hasVersion`

This pair of elements works together to point to different versions of an object. For example, you could use it to list versions in different languages or different formats. Their values should point to each other, should be URIs, and, for complete RDF compatibility, should be encased in an `rdf:resource` attribute. There is also nothing to stop you from providing further information about the version, via additional RDF markup, like so:

```
<dcterms:hasVersion rdf:resource="URI OF RESOURCE">
<dc:title>TITLE OF OTHER VERSION</dc:title>
</dcterms:hasVersion>
```

`dcterms:isReplacedBy` *and* `dcterms:replaces`

Used to denote an `item` that points to a more recent version of the object in question. The syntax is the same as the `dcterms:isVersionOf` pair—it takes an `rdf:resource` attribute that points to the URI of the object in question.

`dcterms:isRequiredBy` *and* `dcterms:requires`

Used to denote an object relationship in which, according to the Dublin Core specification, "the described resource requires the referenced resource to support its function, delivery, or coherence of content." As you might expect by now, this pair takes the attribute `rdf:resource` to denote the URI of the object to which you're pointing , and may be augmented by additional RDF.

`dcterms:isPartOf` *and* `dcterms:hasPart`

The `mod_DCTerms` elements have quite self-explanatory names, and this pair is no exception. It denotes objects that are subsections of other objects. It's the traditional syntax of an `rdf:resource` attribute, with the option of additional RDF within the element.

`dcterms:isReferencedBy` *and* `dcterms:references`

A pair in which one object refers to or cites the other. Its syntax is the usual drill—an `rdf:resource` attribute and some additional RDF if you're feeling generous.

`dcterms:isFormatOf` *and* `dcterms:hasFormat`

This final pair of elements denotes two objects that contain the same intellectual content but differ in format. For example, one object could be color PDF and the other could be a Word document. The syntax is the same as the other

---

paired elements, but with the additional recommendation that you include dc:format, dc:language, or another element that helps the end user tell the difference between the two separate versions. Also bear in mind that URIs must be unique, so anyone using content negotiation on their server must give different URIs for each format, whether or not it is actually necessary.

Using DCSV values

There are three mod_DCTerms elements that take a special syntax to denote a timespan. This syntax, Dublin Core Structured Values (DCSV), represents complex values together in one simple string. It takes the following format (all the attributes are optional):

```
name=ASSOCIATED NAME; start=START TIME; end=END TIME; scheme=W3C-DTF;
```

dcterms:temporal

> This element denotes any timespan of the item's subject matter. For example:
>
> ```
> <dcterms:temporal>
> name=World War 2; start=1939; end=1945; scheme=W3C-DTF;
> </dcterms:temporal>
> ```

dcterms:valid

> This denotes the timespan during which the item's contents is valid. For example:
>
> ```
> <dcterms:valid>start=20030101; end=200300201;  scheme=W3C-DTF;</dcterms:valid>
> ```

dcterms:available

> This denotes the timespan during which the object to which the item points is available (i.e., network-retrievable).

---

mod_event

mod_event really breaks RSS 1.0 out of the datacentric model and into the real world. It's purpose is to describe details of real-world events. You can then use this data in your calendar applications, display it on a page, email it, or whatever purpose you like.

According to Søren Roug, the module's author, "This specification is not a reimplementation of RFC 2445 iCalendar in RDF. In particular, it lacks such things as TODO and repeating events, and there is no intention of adding those parts to the specification."

Namespace

The events module takes the shapely ev: as its namespace prefix, and it is identified by the pleasingly regular http://purl.org/rss/1.0/modules/event/. So, the root element looks like this:

```
<?xml version="1.0" encoding="utf-8"?>

<rdf:RDF xmlns:rdf="http://www.w3.org/1999/02/22-rdf-syntax-ns#"
```

```
                         xmlns="http://purl.org/rss/1.0/"
                         xmlns:ev="http://purl.org/rss/1.0/modules/event/"
           >
```

Elements

The mod_events elements are all subelements of item. None of them are mandatory,
but common sense should prevail regarding usage: the more the better.

ev:startdate

> The time and date of the start of the event, in W3CDTF format.

ev:enddate

> The time and date of the end of the event, in W3CDTF format.

ev:location

> The location of the event. This can be a simple string or a URI, or it can be
> semantically augmented via RDF. For example:
>
> ```
>     <ev:location>At Ben's house</ev:location>
>     or
>     <ev:location>http://www.example.org/benshouse</ev:location>
>     or
>     <ev:location rdf:resource="http://www.mapquest.com">
>     <rdf:value>
>     http://www.mapquest.com/maps/map.adp?map.x=177&map.
>     y=124&mapdata=xU4YXdELrnB2xoPaJ66QjsffE4Zu%252bP6OZQy2y1Ah8EPehGZcP7zX7a3LAujflI
>     6g%252boY5z8%252b7lqnLexYmGmo96xAPLE%252bMe4H2TaNOPDMZ5pH9rjsN3owqiP9AOg8%252fOX
>     tNlI1FGCb4fddEaWl23DGyUhXfazgpROqIrCGP%252fmKvh2vwRsOlc8k9FOltIpaTc%252foiXwyvfB
>     CMSvv2EAvYEbNgn6ztUAlmEA%252bK2tqfR5jD9QRdgAOyRNovXEpgRakMia3g2jRzToO6OcbL8TDJru
>     fAn11sl6d5CQUD8xjR1nJj3ieObeWOVwRBOw8T4MSHFQLg9SoPaSN3LMG2PixeD2X5%252bs4Sg3K1JS
>     4LqmvDON%252bugHKDenLg%252b%252fxQhtVGFuhugqWLosZ%252fSo2wQ7Y%253d&click=center
>     </rdf:value>
>     </ev:location>
> ```

ev:organizer

> The name of the organizer of the event. Again, we can semantically augment this
> element to include more information. For example:
>
> ```
>     <ev:organizer>Ben Hammersley</ev:organiser>
> ```

ev:type

> According to the specification, this should be "the type of event, such as confer-
> ence, deadline, launch, project meeting. The purpose is to promote or filter out
> certain types of events that the user has a particular (lack of) interest for. Avoid
> the use of subject-specific wording. Use instead the Dublin Core subject element."

Example

Example 7-14. An RSS 1.0 feed with mod_event

```
<?xml version="1.0" encoding="utf-8"?>

<rdf:RDF xmlns:rdf="http://www.w3.org/1999/02/22-rdf-syntax-ns#"
```

Example 7-14. An RSS 1.0 feed with mod_event (continued)

```
  xmlns:ev="http://purl.org/rss/1.0/modules/event/"
  xmlns:dc="http://purl.org/dc/elements/1.1/"
  xmlns="http://purl.org/rss/1.0/"
>

  <channel rdf:about="http://events.oreilly.com/?_fl=rss1.0">
    <title>O'Reilly Events</title>
    <link>http://events.oreilly.com/</link>
    <description>O'Reilly Events</description>

    <items>
      <rdf:Seq>
        <rdf:li resource="http://conferences.oreilly.com/p2p/" />
        <rdf:li resource="http://www.oreilly.com/catalog/progxmlrpc/" />
      </rdf:Seq>
    </items>

  </channel>

  <item rdf:about="http://conferences.oreilly.com/p2p/">
    <title>The O'Reilly Peer-to-Peer and Web Services Conference</title>
    <link>http://conferences.oreilly.com/p2p/</link>
    <ev:type>conference</ev:type>
    <ev:organizer>O'Reilly</ev:organizer>
    <ev:location>Washington, DC</ev:location>
    <ev:startdate>2001-09-18</ev:startdate>
    <ev:enddate>2001-09-21</ev:enddate>
    <dc:subject>P2P</dc:subject>
  </item>
  <item rdf:about="http://www.oreilly.com/catalog/progxmlrpc/">
    <title>Programming Web Services with XML-RPC</title>
    <link>http://www.oreilly.com/catalog/progxmlrpc/</link>
    <ev:startdate>2001-06-20</ev:startdate>
    <ev:type>book release</ev:type>
    <dc:subject>XML-RPC</dc:subject>
    <dc:subject>Programming</dc:subject>
  </item>
</rdf:RDF>
```

mod_rss091

The mod_rss091 module is designed to give RSS 1.0 "sideways compatibility" with RSS 0.91. Because the three core subelements of the item element are the same in both standards, including mod_rss091 elements in your RSS 1.0 feed allows for dynamic downgrading of the feed for parsers that can't be bothered with all the RDF stuff. Because the data is rather simple and mostly static, including this module within your RSS 1.0 feed is straightforward. With this in mind, it's worth doing.

Namespace

The prefix for this module is the self-explanatory `rss091:`, and the module is represented by the URI `http://purl.org/rss/1.0/modules/rss091#`. Hence:

```
<rdf:RDF xmlns:rdf="http://www.w3.org/1999/02/22-rdf-syntax-ns#"
         xmlns="http://purl.org/rss/1.0/"
         xmlns:rss091="http://purl.org/rss/1.0/modules/rss091/"
    >
```

Elements

The `mod_rss091` elements represent the same elements within RSS 0.91. Chapter 4 provides details on each of those elements.

Subelements of channel

`rss091:language`
> The language of the feed.

`rss091:rating`
> The PICS rating of the feed.

`rss091:managingEditor`
> The managing editor of the feed.

`rss091:webmaster`
> The webmaster of the feed.

`rss091:pubDate`
> The publication date of the feed.

`rss091:lastBuildDate`
> The date of the feed's last build.

`rss091:copyright`
> The copyright notice of the feed.

`rss091:skipHours rdf:parseType="Literal"`
> The skipHours element, with correct RDF syntax.

> `rss091:hour`
> > The hours, in GMT, during which the feed *should not* be retrieved.

`rss091:skipDays rdf:parseType="Literal"`
> The skipDays element, with correct RDF syntax.

> `rss091:day`
> > The days during which a feed *should not* be retrieved (Monday is 1 and Sunday is 7).

Subelements of image

`rss091:width`
> The width of the image.

rss091:height
> The height of the image.

Subelement of item

rss091:description
> The description of the item. While this element is replicated by core RSS 1.0, it is listed here for the sake of completion.

Example

Example 7-15. RSS 1.0 feed elements using mod_rss091

```
<?xml version="1.0"?>
<rdf:RDF xmlns:rdf="http://www.w3.org/1999/02/22-rdf-syntax-ns#"
         xmlns="http://purl.org/rss/1.0/"
         xmlns:rss091="http://purl.org/rss/1.0/modules/rss091/"
>
  <channel rdf:about="http://www.xml.com/xml/news.rss">
    <title>XML.com</title>
    <link>http://xml.com/pub</link>
    <description>
    XML.com features a rich mix of information and services for the XML community.
    </description>
    <rss091:language>en-us</rss091:language>
    <rss091:rating>(PICS-1.1 "http://www.rsac.org/ratingsv01.html"
     l gen true comment "RSACi North America Server"
     for "http://www.rsac.org" on "1996.04.16T08:15-0500"
     r (n 0 s 0 v 0 l 0))</rss091:rating>
    <rss091:managingEditor>Edd Dumbill</rss091:managingEditor>
    <rss091:webmaster>(mailto:webmaster@xml.com)</rss091:webmaster>
    <rss091:pubDate>Sat, 01 Jan 2000 12:00:00 GMT</rss091:pubDate>
    <rss091:lastBuildDate>Sat, 01 Jan 2000 12:00:00 GMT</rss091:lastBuildDate>
    <rss091:skipHours rdf:parseType="Literal">
    <rss091:hour>12</rss091:hour>
    </rss091:skipHours>
    <rss091:skipDays rdf:parseType="Literal">
    <rss091:day>Thursday</rss091:day>
    </rss091:skipDays>
  </channel>

  <image rdf:about="http://xml.com/universal/images/xml_tiny.gif">
    <title>XML.com</title>
    <link>http://www.xml.com</link>
    <url>http://xml.com/universal/images/xml_tiny.gif</url>
    <rss091:width>88</rss091:width>
    <rss091:height>31</rss091:height>
    <rss091:description>XML.com...</rss091:description>
  </image>

  <item rdf:about="http://xml.com/pub/2000/08/09/xslt/xslt.html" position="1">
    <title>Processing Inclusions with XSLT</title>
    <link>http://xml.com/pub/2000/08/09/xslt/xslt.html</link>
```

Example 7-15. RSS 1.0 feed elements using mod_rss091 (continued)

```
  <rss091:description>
  Processing document inclusions with general XML tools can be
  problematic. This article proposes a way of preserving inclusion
  information through SAX-based processing.
  </rss091:description>
 </item>

</rdf:RDF>
```

mod_servicestatus

mod_servicestatus is one of the latest RSS 1.0 modules. Its purpose is to allow RSS 1.0 to display details of the status and current availability of services and servers.

You should bear in mind the difference between services and servers. One service may rely on more than one server in the back end. For the user, however, such information is irrelevant—something either works or it doesn't. With mod_servicestatus, you cannot differentiate between a virtual service and an actual physical server, but you can combine servers into services at the parsing stage. This means that one feed can be used for multiple things: a detailed display for sysadmins, and a simplified version for end users.

Namespace

The mod_servicestatus prefix is ss:, and the module is identified by the URI http://purl.org/rss/1.0/modules/servicestatus/. So, a mod_servicestatus feed will start like this:

```
<rdf:RDF xmlns:rdf="http://www.w3.org/1999/02/22-rdf-syntax-ns#"
      xmlns="http://purl.org/rss/1.0/"
        xmlns:ss="http://purl.org/rss/1.0/modules/servicestatus/"
  >
```

Elements

The first element of mod_servicestatus is a subelement of channel:

ss:aboutStats
  A URI that points to a page explaining the results and methodology being used.

All the other elements within mod_servicestatus are subelements of item. As with many modules, all of these elements are optional, but the more you include the more fun you'll have.

ss:responding
  This can be either true or false, and it refers to whether the server is responding.
ss:lastChecked
  The date and time the server was last checked, in W3CDTF format.

`ss:lastSeen`

> The date and time the server last responded, in W3CDTF format. In conjunction with `ss:lastChecked`, this enables you to work out down times.

`ss:availability`

> A figure that describes server availability. Usually a integer percentage, this should be explained in the document referenced by `ss:aboutStats`.

`ss:averageResponseTime`

> The average response time of the server, usually in seconds. This should also be explained in the `ss:aboutStats` document.

`ss:statusMessage`

> A message aimed at the end user. For example: "We know this is broken, and we're working on it," or "Please log out, pushing of the Big Red Button is imminent," or "Run for the door! Run! Run!"

Example

Example 7-16. An RSS 1.0 feed with mod_servicestatus

```
<?xml version="1.0" encoding="utf-8"?>

<rdf:RDF xmlns:rdf="http://www.w3.org/1999/02/22-rdf-syntax-ns#"
         xmlns="http://purl.org/rss/1.0/"
         xmlns:ss="http://purl.org/rss/1.0/modules/servicestatus/"
>

<channel rdf:about="http://my.organisation.com">
  <title>An Example</title>
  <description>Just an example of system statuses</description>
 <link>http://my.organisation.com</link>
<ss:aboutStats>http://my.organisation.com/status.html</ss:aboutStats>
  <items>
    <rdf:Seq>
      <rdf:li resource="http://my.organisation.com/website" />
      <rdf:li resource="http://my.organisation.com/database" />
    </rdf:Seq>
  </items>
</channel>

<item rdf:about="http://my.organisation.com/website">
  <title>Website</title>
  <link>http://my.organisation.com/website</link>
  <ss:responding>true</ss:responding>
  <ss:lastChecked>2002-05-10T19:20:30.45+01:00</ss:lastChecked>
  <ss:lastSeen>2002-05-10T19:20:30.45+01:00</ss:lastSeen>
  <ss:availability>85</ss:availability>
  <ss:averageResponseTime>5.2</ss:averageResponseTime>
</item>

<item rdf:about="http://my.organisation.com/database">
  <title>Database server</title>
```

Example 7-16. An RSS 1.0 feed with mod_servicestatus (continued)

```
    <link>http://my.organisation.com/database</link>
    <ss:responding>false</ss:responding>
    <ss:lastChecked>2002-05-10T19:20:30.45+01:00</ss:lastChecked>
    <ss:lastSeen>2002-05-09T13:43:56.24+01:00</ss:lastSeen>
    <ss:availability>77</ss:availability>
    <ss:averageResponseTime>12.2</ss:averageResponseTime>
    <ss:statusMessage>Engineers are investigating.</ss:statusMessage>
</item>

</rdf:RDF>
```

mod_slash

Slash is the software originally written to run the popular technology news site, Slashdot. It has spread quite far lately, and now hundreds of sites use it for their content management system. Slash's unique features do not fit into the core RSS 1.0 specification, so Rael Dornfest and Chris Nandor wrote this module. The features are most easily understood after a look at a Slash-based site, so go over to *http://www.slashdot.org* to see what's happening.

Namespace

The namespace prefix is slash:, and the identifying URI is http://purl.org/rss/1.0/modules/slash/. Hence:

```
    <rdf:RDF xmlns:rdf="http://www.w3.org/1999/02/22-rdf-syntax-ns#"
            xmlns="http://purl.org/rss/1.0/"
            xmlns:slash="http://purl.org/rss/1.0/modules/slash/"
    >
```

Elements

All the mod_slash elements are subelements of item. They are all mandatory.

slash:section
> The title of the section in which the article appears.

slash:department
> The title of the department in which the article appears (in most Slash sites, this title is a joke).

slash:comments
> The number of comments attached to an article.

slash:hit_parade
> A comma-separated list of the number of comments displayable at each karma threshold (this will make sense to you if you look at a Slash-based site). There should be seven figures, matching karma thresholds of −1, 0, 1, 2, 3, 4, and 5.

Example

Example 7-17. An item element containing mod_slash

```
<item rdf:about="http://slashdot.org/article.pl?sid=02/07/01/164242">
<title>LotR Two Towers Trailer Online</title>
<link>http://slashdot.org/article.pl?sid=02/07/01/164242</link>
<dc:creator>CmdrTaco</dc:creator>
<dc:subject>movies</dc:subject>
<dc:date>2002-07-01T17:08:24+00:00</dc:date>
<slash:department>provided-you-have-sorenson-and-bandwidth</slash:department>
<slash:section>articles</slash:section>
<slash:comments>20</slash:comments>
<slash:hitparade>20,19,11,8,3,0,0</slash:hitparade>
</item>
```

mod_streaming

mod_streaming was designed by me (happily enough) to take care of the additional needs of anyone who wants to create a feed that points to streaming-media presentations. You will notice elements for the live events—start times, end times, and so forth. These can also be used to split a single stream into chunks and provide associated metadata with each section.

Namespace

mod_streaming takes str: as its prefix, and http://hacks.benhammersley.com/rss/streaming/ is its identifying URI. So, its root element looks like this:

```
<rdf:RDF xmlns:rdf="http://www.w3.org/1999/02/22-rdf-syntax-ns#"
        xmlns="http://purl.org/rss/1.0/"
        xmlns:str="http://hacks.benhammersley.com/rss/streaming/"
>
```

Elements

All the elements within mod_streaming are subelements of item except str:type, which can be a subelement of channel as well. All elements are optional.

str:type
> This can take audio, video, or both as its value, and it can be a subelement of either item or channel. video implies a video, regardless of the presence of a soundtrack. both implies a mixture of video and audio items, and hence is for use only within a channel description.

str:associatedApplication
> The name of any special application required to play back the stream.

str:associatedApplication.version
> The version number of the associated application, if applicable.

`str:associatedApplication.downloadUri`
> The URI for downloading the associated application.

`str:codec`
> The name of the codec in which the stream is encoded.

`str:codec.version`
> The version number of the codec, if applicable

`str:codec.downloadUri`
> The URI for downloading the codec.

`str:codec.sampleRate`
> The value of any audio's sample rate, in kHz.

`str:codec.stereo`
> Either stereo or `mono`, depending on the audio being used.

`str:codec.ResolutionX`
> The number of pixels in the X axis (width).

`str:codec.ResolutionY`
> The number of pixels in the Y axis (height).

`str:duration`
> The length of the item, in the W3C format of `HH:MM:SS`.

`str: live`
> Either `live` or recorded, as applicable.

`str:live.scheduledStartTime`
> A W3CDTF-encoded date and time for the start of live broadcasts, or just `HH:MM:SS.ss` for the start time in the timecode of a recording.

`str:live.scheduledEndTime`
> The end time of a live broadcast or recording, in the same format as `str:live.scheduledStartTime`.

`str:live.location`
> This can be a literal string, as per the Dublin Core location guidelines, or it can use RDF with additional location-specific namespaces.

`str:live.contactUri`
> A URI to contact the live show (e.g., `mailto:`, `http:`, `aim:`, or `irc:`). Think "radio phone-in show."

Example

Example 7-18. An RSS 1.0 feed using mod_streaming

```
<?xml version="1.0" encoding="utf-8"?>
<rdf:RDF xmlns:rdf="http://www.w3.org/1999/02/22-rdf-syntax-ns#"
        xmlns="http://purl.org/rss/1.0/"
        xmlns:str="http://hacks.benhammersley.com/rss/streaming/"
>
<channel rdf:about="http://www.streamsRus.com/">
  <title>Streams R Us</title>
```

Example 7-18. An RSS 1.0 feed using mod_streaming (continued)

```
   <link>http://www.streamsRus.com</link>
   <description>Streams R Us: An Entirely Fictional Site</description>
   <str:type>both</str:type>
   <image rdf:resource="http://www.streamsRus.com/icons/stream.jpg" />
<items>
  <rdf:Seq>
    <rdf:li rdf:resource="http://www.streamsRus.com/example.ram" />
    <rdf:li rdf:resource="http://www.streamsRus.com/example2.mp3" />
    <rdf:li rdf:resource="http://www.streamsRus.com/example3.mov" />
  </rdf:Seq>
</items>
</channel>

<item rdf:about="http://www.streamsRus.com/example.ram">
  <title>RSS Rocks Out</title>
  <link>http://www.streamsRus.com/example.ram</link>
  <str:associatedApplication>realplayer</str:associatedApplication>
  <str:associatedApplication.downloadUri>http://www.real.com/
  </str:associatedApplication.downloadUri>
  <str:duration>00:04:30</str:duration>
  <str:live>recorded</str:live>
</item>

<item rdf:about="http://www.streamsRus.com/example2.ram">
  <title>RSS Rocks Out Live</title>
  <link>http://www.streamsRus.com/example2.mp3</link>
  <str:associatedApplication>winamp</str:associatedApplication>
  <str:associatedApplication.downloadUri>http://www.winamp.com/
  </str:associatedApplication.downloadUri>
  <str:duration>00:04:30</str:duration>
  <str:live>live</str:live>
  <str:live.scheduledStartTime>2002:04:03T00:00:00Z</str:scheduledStartTime>
  <str:live.scheduledEndTime>2002:04:03T00:04:30Z</str:scheduledEndTime>
</item>

<item rdf:about="http://www.streamsRus.com/example3.mov">
  <title>RSS Rocks Out Live on Video</title>
  <link>http://www.streamsRus.com/example2.mov</link>
  <str:type>video</str:type>
  <str:codec>sorenson</str:codec>
  <str:associatedApplication>Quicktime</str:associatedApplication>
  <str:associatedApplication.downloadUri>http://www.apple.com/quicktime
  </str:associatedApplication.downloadUri>
  <str:duration>00:02:32</str:duration>
  <str:live>live</str:live>
  <str:live.scheduledStartTime>2002:04:03T00:00:00Z</str:scheduledStartTime>
  <str:live.scheduledEndTime>2002:04:03T00:02:32Z</str:scheduledEndTime>
  <str:codec.ResolutionX>600</str:codec.ResolutionX>
  <str:codec.ResolutionY>400</str:codec.ResolutionY>
  <str:live.ContactUri>mailto:ben@benhammersley.com</str:live.contact.Uri>
</item>

</rdf:RDF>
```

mod_syndication

mod_syndication gives aggregators and feed users an idea of how often the feed changes. By giving this information, you prevent everyone from wasting time and bandwidth by asking for your feed too often or, indeed, too seldom. It is the third module to achieve Standard status.

mod_syndication supersedes the skipHours and skipDays elements of mod_rss091. Clients usually prefer the mod_syndication values over mod_rss091.

Namespace

mod_syndication takes sy: as its prefix and http://purl.org/rss/1.0/modules/ syndication as its identifying URI. Thus:

```
<rdf:RDF xmlns:rdf="http://www.w3.org/1999/02/22-rdf-syntax-ns#"
         xmlns="http://purl.org/rss/1.0/"
         xmlns:sy="http://purl.org/rss/1.0/modules/syndication/"
  >
```

Elements

The mod_syndication elements are all subelements of channel:

sy:updatePeriod
> Takes a value of hourly, daily, weekly, monthly, or yearly.

sy:updateFrequency
> A number representing the number of times the feed should be refreshed during the updatePeriod. For example, an updatePeriod of hourly and an updateFrequency of 2 will make the aggregator refresh the feed twice an hour. If this element is missing, the default is 1.

sy:updateBase
> The date and time, in W3CDTF format, from which all calculations should originate.

Example

Example 7-19. A part of a channel containing the mod_syndication elements

```
<channel rdf:about="http://meerkat.oreillynet.com/?_fl=rss1.0">
<title>Meerkat</title>
<link>http://meerkat.oreillynet.com</link>
<description>Meerkat: An Open Wire Service</description>
<sy:updatePeriod>hourly</sy:updatePeriod>
<sy:updateFrequency>2</sy:updateFrequency>
<sy:updateBase>2000-01-01T12:00+00:00</sy:updateBase>
```

mod_taxonomy

mod_taxonomy allows the classification of objects under a defined taxonomic scheme
—basically, you describe the topics of your objects.

The object can be anything: a channel, an item, or a reference from another module.
Because of this universality, mod_taxonomy can be used heavily throughout an RSS 1.0
feed, which may cause some confusion. As with many modules, a good bit of reformatting may help clarify things.

The taxonomic definitions are always given as URIs. As shown in Chapter 5, URIs
are used, like namespaces, to differentiate between homonyms. Python (the language) and Python (the snake) need to be distinguished, because you may want to
run away from one of them.

One good source of taxonomic URIs is the Open Directory Project, at *http://www.
dmoz.org*. All the examples in this section originate from this source.

Namespace

mod_taxonomy takes the stylish moniker of taxo: and the identifying URI of http://
purl.org/rss/1.0/modules/taxonomy/. Hence, the lovely root element:

```
<rdf:RDF xmlns:rdf="http://www.w3.org/1999/02/22-rdf-syntax-ns#"
  xmlns="http://purl.org/rss/1.0/"
  xmlns:taxo="http://purl.org/rss/1.0/modules/taxonomy/"
  >
```

Elements

mod_taxonomy can be used in two ways: the simple and the more defined. The simple
method uses one element, and it can be used as a subelement of item or channel:

```
<taxo:topics>
<rdf:Bag>
<rdf:li resource="URI TO TAXONOMIC REFERENCE" /
<rdf:li resource="URI TO TAXONOMIC REFERENCE" />
</rdf:Bag>
</taxo:topics>
```

This nesting of elements gives a list of topics that are associated with the channel or
the item that contains it. This structure remains the same, with additional <rdf:li
resource=""/> elements for every new topic.

This provides a straightforward method for giving a list of defining URIs for an RSS
object. Sometimes, however, we'd like to define more details of each of the topic
URIs themselves. For this, we use the taxo:topic element. This element is a subelement of rdf:RDF—i.e., on the same level as channel, item, and so on.

Within the grammar of RDF, taxo:topic allows us to assign metadata to the URI that we use elsewhere in the feed in taxo:topics. It takes one subelement of its own module, taxo:link, and then any other module's element that can be a subelement of channel. The most popular elements come from mod_dublincore:

```
<taxo:topic rdf:about="URI OF TAXONOMIC RESOURCE">
<taxo:link>URL TO TAXONOMIC RESOURCE HERE<taxo:link>
<dc:subject>EXAMPLE</dc:subject>
OTHER ELEMENTS HERE
</taxo:topic>
```

The taxo:topic element itself can contain taxo:topics, as shown in Example 7-19.

Example

Example 7-20. A partial RSS 1.0 feed demonstrating mod_taxonomy

```
<item rdf:about="http://c.moreover.com/click/here.pl?r123" position="1">
  <title>XML: A Disruptive Technology</title>
  <link>http://c.moreover.com/click/here.pl?r123</link>
  <description>
  XML is placing increasingly heavy loads on the existing technical
  infrastructure of the Internet.
  </description>
  <taxo:topics>
    <rdf:Bag>
      <rdf:li resource="http://meerkat.oreillynet.com/?c=cat23">
      <rdf:li resource="http://meerkat.oreillynet.com/?c=47">
      <rdf:li resource="http://dmoz.org/Computers/Data_Formats/Markup_Languages/XML/">
    </rdf:Bag>
  </taxo:topics>
</item>

<taxo:topic rdf:about="http://meerkat.oreillynet.com/?c=cat23">
  <taxo:link>http://meerkat.oreillynet.com/?c=cat23</taxo:link>
  <dc:title>Data: XML</taxo:title>
  <dc:description>A Meerkat channel</dc:description>
</taxo:topic>

<taxo:topic rdf:about="http://dmoz.org/Computers/Data_Formats/Markup_Languages/XML/">
  <taxo:link>http://dmoz.org/Computers/Data_Formats/Markup_Languages/XML/</taxo:link>
  <dc:title>XML</taxo:title>
  <dc:subject>XML</dc:subject>
  <dc:description>DMOZ category</dc:description>
  <taxo:topics>
    <rdf:Bag>
      <rdf:li resource="http://meerkat.oreillynet.com/?c=cat23">
      <rdf:li resource="http://dmoz.org/Computers/Data_Formats/Markup_Languages/SGML/">
      <rdf:li resource="http://dmoz.org/Computers/Programming/Internet/">
    </rdf:Bag>
  </taxo:topics>
</taxo:topic>
```

Example 7-19 shows an item using taxo:topics to describe itself, and a taxo:topic defining two of the taxonomic definitions used. The last taxo:topic uses taxo:topics itself to define its own subject with more finesse.

Note that the taxo:topic elements—which define the URIs we use within the <item> <taxo:topics></taxo:topics></item> section—are on the same level as the item within the document. RSS 1.0's structure, unlike RSS 0.9x, gives them both equal weight.

mod_threading

mod_threading provides a system to describe the children of an item (for example, replies to a weblog entry). This module is still in a state of flux—a great deal of work is being done to finalize a system for the description of message threads within RSS and RDF. This is one of the goals of the ThreadML developmental effort (*http://www.quicktopic.com/7/H/rhSrjkWgjnvRq*).

With this in mind, mod_threading can get complicated quickly. Unfortunately, as complex as you might logically make it, the lack of standardization means that anything but the simplest usage will likely be misunderstood by most parsers. Therefore, in this chapter we restrict ourselves to defining children only within the limited scope of a single document. If true message threading is your goal, check with the mailing lists and weblogs for more details.

Namespace

mod_threading takes the prefix thr: and the identifying URI http://purl.org/rss/1.0/modules/threading/. Hence, the root element:

```
<rdf:RDF xmlns:rdf="http://www.w3.org/1999/02/22-rdf-syntax-ns#"
        xmlns="http://purl.org/rss/1.0/"
        xmlns:thr="http://purl.org/rss/1.0/modules/threading/"
>
```

Element

There's only one element within mod_threading; it's a subelement of item and it contains an rdf:Seq of rdf:li of URIs representing items that are children of the item:

```
<thr:children>
  <rdf:Seq>
    <rdf:li rdf:resource="URI OF CHILD ITEM" />
  </rdf:Seq>
</thr:children>
```

For simplicity's sake, the child item, and hence the URI, must be also contained within the same RSS 1.0 document.

Example

Example 7-21. mod_threading within an item element

```
<item rdf:about="http://c.moreover.com/click/here.pl?r123">
    <title>XML: A Disruptive Technology</title>
    <link>http://c.moreover.com/click/here.pl?r123</link>
    <thr:children>
     <rdf:Seq>
       <rdf:li rdf:resource="http://www.example.com/child1"/>
       <rdf:li rdf:resource="http://www.example.com/child2"/>
       <rdf:li rdf:resource="http://www.example.com/child2"/>
     </rdf:Seq>
    </thr:children>
</item>
```

mod_wiki

Wikis—web pages that grant editing rights to everyone—are increasingly popular, but they give RSS feed creators plenty of special problems. Because wikis contain extensive information about how the page has been edited, and by whom, they require their own module to supply all the necessary elements.

Namespace

mod_wiki's prefix is wiki:, and the identifying URI is http://purl.org/rss/1.0/ modules/wiki/. mod_wiki also uses mod_dublincore for some of its elements. Hence, the lovely root element:

```
<rdf:RDF xmlns:rdf="http://www.w3.org/1999/02/22-rdf-syntax-ns#"
         xmlns="http://purl.org/rss/1.0/"
         xmlns:dc="http://purl.org/dc/elements/1.1/"
         xmlns:wiki="http://purl.org/rss/1.0/modules/wiki/"
   >
```

Elements

wiki:interwiki

An optional subelement of channel, wiki:interwiki refers to the moniker of the wiki in question if it is part of an interwiki setup. It can take two forms, between which you may choose—the simpler:

```
<wiki:interwifi>INTERWIKI MONIKER<wiki:interwiki>
```

or the more complex, which may be unparsable for simple parsers:

```
<wiki:interwiki>
  <rdf:Description link="URL TO WIKI">
    <rdf:value>WIKI NAME</rdf:value>
  </rdf:Description>
</wiki:interwiki>
```

wiki:version

An optional subelement of item, containing the version number of the page.

`wiki:status`

An optional subelement of `item`, denoting it as new, updated, or deleted.

`wiki:importance`

An optional subelement of `item`, describing the importance of the change to the page (either major or minor).

`wiki:diff`

An optional subelement of `item` that provides a URL to the previous version of the page.

`wiki:history`

An optional subelement of `item` that provides a URL to a list of changes to the page.

`wiki:host`

A special optional subelement of the `dc:contributor` element from `mod_dublincore`. It contains the IP address of the person who made the change to the wiki page. It should be in the following format:

```
<dc:contributor>
  <rdf:Description wiki:host="192.168.1.10">
    <rdf:value>A.N.Person</rdf:value>
  </rdf:Description>
</dc:contributor>
```

Example

Example 7-22. mod_wiki within an item element

```
<item rdf:about="http://www.usemod.com/cgi-bin/mb2.
pl?action=browse&amp;id=JohnKellden&amp;revision=30">
  <title>JohnKellden</title>
  <link>http://www.usemod.com/cgi-bin/mb2.pl?JohnKellden</link>
  <description></description>
  <dc:date>2002-07-03T06:47:19+00:00</dc:date>
  <dc:contributor>
  <rdf:Description wiki:host="pc88-86.norrkoping.se" >
  <rdf:value>pc88-86.norrkoping.se</rdf:value>
  </rdf:Description>
  </dc:contributor>
  <wiki:status>updated</wiki:status>
  <wiki:importance>major</wiki:importance>
<wiki:diff>http://www.usemod.com/cgi-bin/mb2.
pl?action=browse&amp;diff=4&amp;id=JohnKellden</wiki:diff>
<wiki:version>30</wiki:version>
  <wiki:history>http://www.usemod.com/cgi-bin/mb2.pl?action=history&amp;id=JohnKellden</
wiki:history>
</item>
```

## CHAPTER 8

RSS 2.0 (Simply Extensible)

Honest disagreement is often a good sign of progress.
—Mahatma Gandhi

Readers who are taking each chapter in order may be puzzled as to why I have gone from RSS 1.0, with its complex RDF capabilities and syntax, back to a much simpler standard. I have done this for two reasons. First, by now you should be fully aware of the concept of XML namespaces and the idea of modules. Second, because RSS 2.0 is the latest RSS standard to be released, and it is the newest thing in this book, it makes sense to go in some sort of chronological order.

Finalized on 19 August 2002, RSS 2.0 was the result of a great deal of argument and distress within the RSS development community. Perhaps inspired by the announcement of this book, the community had spent the summer of 2002 looking for ways to improve the RSS specification and—if possible—recombine the two strands.

The major stumbling blocks were, of course, RDF and modules.

As you will see, the resultant specification managed to incorporate one of these wishes—modules—but again rejected any use of RDF. Further arguments over the name (many people wanted to call it RSS 0.94—0.93 was abandoned previously) and the way in which the specification was decided led, sadly, to a similarly antagonistic position as before, though it did make the simpler strand of RSS a great deal more useful.

The Specification in Detail

RSS 2.0 is basically RSS 0.92 with modules allowed and a handful of additional elements. There are also a small number of rule changes, but we will deal with the new elements first:

comments
> An optional subelement of item that should contain the URL of the comments page for the item. This is primarily used with blogging.

generator

An optional subelement of channel that should contain a string indicating which program has been used to create the RSS file.

author

An optional subelement of item that should contain the email address of the author of the resource referred to within the item.

ttl

An optional subelement of channel that contains a number, which is the number of minutes the reader should wait before refreshing the feed from its source.

pubDate

An optional subelement of item that should contain the date the object referred to by the item was originally published. This date should be in the standard mandated by RFC 822—for example: Sat, 01 Jan 2002 0:00:01 GMT.

guid

An optional subelement of item that should contain a string that uniquely identifies the item. This element has the optional attribute isPermalink, which, if true, denotes that the value of the element can be taken as a URL to the object referred to by the item.

All of these new elements are quite straightforward, with the exception of guid. This requires some more examination.

When a guid Is Not a GUID

The introduction of the guid element caused many people to comment on its ability to cause confusion among users. There is already a concept known as GUID, whose letters stand for the same thing—Globally Unique Identifier.

The idea behind both guid and GUID is that by giving an object a unique string to identify it, we allow RSS-reading applications to record which item it has already seen. A guid is used—instead of relying on the link URL, for example—because we can both ensure that the guid (and hence the item) is uniquely identified (URLs can be reused), and because programmatically it is easier and quicker to distinguish between two simple strings than it is to use any other method.

guid differs from standard GUIDs in that within RSS 2.0 the guid can take any form. It is up to the feed publisher to ensure that the guid is globally unique, whereas the more standard GUID—as defined by the Open Software Foundation—is always a 16-byte integer generated by the OSF GUID algorithm, which takes into account the space and time you are in at the time of its generation. There is nothing to stop you from using that algorithm within your generation of RSS 2.0 feeds, but despite the name you must not assume the guid of another's feed is globally unique. We will discuss implementation of the guid in the next few pages.

Changes from RSS 0.92

Other than the new elements and the introduction of namespaced modules within 2.0, there are only five other changes from the 0.92 specification:

- The root element's version attribute changes to 2.0 and can now contain namespace declarations for new modules, as detailed in the next section.
- image is optional.
- category can be a subelement of channel.
- link can point to any URL, as long as it is part of a registered URI scheme. Hence, https://, javascript://, and aim:// are all allowed.
- The language element can contain any language code defined by the W3C.

Example 8-1 illustrates these changes in a sample RSS 2.0 feed with no modules.

Example 8-1. An RSS 2.0 feed with no modules included

```
<?xml version="1.0"?>
<rss version="2.0">
<channel>
  <title>RSS2.0Example</title>
  <link>http://www.exampleurl.com/example/index.html</link>
  <description>This is an example RSS 2.0 feed</description>
  <language>en-gb</language>
  <copyright>Copyright 2002, Oreilly and Associates.</copyright>
  <managingEditor>example@exampleurl.com</managingEditor>
  <webMaster>webmaster@exampleurl.com</webMaster>
  <rating> </rating>
  <pubDate>03 Apr 02 1500 GMT</pubDate>
  <lastBuildDate>03 Apr 02 1500 GMT</lastBuildDate>
  <docs>http://backend.userland.com/rss</docs>
  <skipDays><day>Monday</day></skipDays>
  <skipHours><hour>20</hour></skipHours>
  <category  domain="http://www.dmoz.org">Business/Industries/Publishing/Publishers/
Nonfiction/Business/O'Reilly_and_Associates/</category>
  <generator>NewsAggregator'o'Matic</generator>
  <ttl>30<ttl>
  <cloud domain="http://www.exampleurl.com" port="80" path="/RPC2"
registerProcedure="pleaseNotify" protocol="XML-RPC" />

  <image>
    <title>RSS2.0 Example</title>
    <url>http://www.exampleurl.com/example/images/logo.gif</url>
    <link>http://www.exampleurl.com/example/index.html</link>
    <width>88</width>
    <height>31</height>
    <description>The World's Leading Technical Publisher</description>
  </image>

  <textInput>
    <title>Search</title>
```

Example 8-1. An RSS 2.0 feed with no modules included (continued)

```
    <description>Search the Archives</description>
    <name>query</name>
    <link>http://www.exampleurl.com/example/search.cgi</link>
  </textInput>

  <item>
    <title>The First Item</title>
    <link>http://www.exampleurl.com/example/001.html</link>
    <description>This is the first item.</description>
    <source url="http://www.anothersite.com/index.xml">Another Site</source>
    <enclosure url="http://www.exampleurl.com/example/001.mp3" length="543210" type"audio/
mpeg"/>
    <category domain="http://www.dmoz.org">Business/Industries/Publishing/Publishers/
Nonfiction/Business/O'Reilly_and_Associates/</category>
    <comments>http://www.exampleurl.com/comments/001.html</comments>
    <author>Ben Hammersley</author>
    <pubDate>Sat, 01 Jan 2002 0:00:01 GMT</pubDate>
    <guid isPermaLink="true">http://www.exampleurl.com/example/001.html</guid>
  </item>

  <item>
    <title>The Second Item</title>
    <link>http://www.exampleurl.com/example/002.html</link>
    <description>This is the second item.</description>
    <source url="http://www.anothersite.com/index.xml">Another Site</source>
    <enclosure url="http://www.exampleurl.com/example/002.mp3" length="543210" type"audio/
mpeg"/>
    <category domain="http://www.dmoz.org">Business/Industries/Publishing/Publishers/
Nonfiction/Business/O'Reilly_and_Associates/</category>
    <comments>http://www.exampleurl.com/comments/002.html</comments>
    <author>Ben Hammersley</author>
    <pubDate>Sun, 02 Jan 2002 0:00:01 GMT</pubDate>
    <guid isPermaLink="true">http://www.exampleurl.com/example/002.html</guid>
  </item>

  <item>
    <title>The Third Item</title>
    <link>http://www.exampleurl.com/example/003.html</link>
    <description>This is the third item.</description>
    <source url="http://www.anothersite.com/index.xml">Another Site</source>
    <enclosure url="http://www.exampleurl.com/example/003.mp3" length="543210" type"audio/
mpeg"/>
    <category domain="http://www.dmoz.org">Business/Industries/Publishing/Publishers/
Nonfiction/Business/O'Reilly_and_Associates/</category>
    <comments>http://www.exampleurl.com/comments/003.html</comments>
    <author>Ben Hammersley</author>
    <pubDate>Mon, 03 Jan 2002 0:00:01 GMT</pubDate>
    <guid isPermaLink="true">http://www.exampleurl.com/example/003.html</guid>
  </item>

</channel>
</rss>
```

Module Support Within RSS 2.0

The key change that RSS 2.0 brings is the ability to use modules. As in RSS 1.0, the use of modules is simply a matter of placing the correct namespace declaration into the root element of the feed and then using the namespace elements with the correct prefix. Unlike 1.0, however, 2.0 modules cannot use RDF for any purpose whatsoever. At least, this is the current thinking of Dave Winer, guardian of the specification.

This is currently a matter of debate, over which much more blood will likely be spilled. When the rules over 1.0 and 2.0 module design have been formalized (I will discuss the latest thinking in Chapter 11) we may be able to use 1.0 modules within 2.0. At the moment, alas, this is not recommended, and for the sake of diplomacy we will deal now solely with specialist 2.0 modules. At this time there is only one: BlogChannel.

BlogChannel Module

Designed by Dave Winer only a week after he formalized RSS 2.0, the BlogChannel module allows the inclusion of data used by weblogging applications and, specifically, the newer generation of aggregating and filtering systems.

It consists of three optional elements, all of which are subelements of channel, and has the following namespace declaration:

```
xmlns:blogChannel="http://backend.userland.com/blogChannelModule"
```

The elements are:

blogChannel:blogRoll

> Contains a literal string that is the URL of an OPML file containing the *blogroll* for the site. A blogroll is the list of blogs that the blog author habitually reads.

blogChannel:blink

> Contains a literal string that is the URL of a site that the blog author recommends the reader visits.

blogChannel:mySubscriptions

> Contains a literal string that is the URL of the OPML file containing the URLs of the RSS feeds to which the blog author is subscribed in her desktop reader.

Example 8-2 shows the beginning of an RSS 2.0 feed using the BlogChannel module.

Example 8-2. An RSS 2.0 feed with the BlogChannel module

```
<?xml version="1.0"?>
<rss version="2.0" xmlns:blogChannel="http://backend.userland.com/blogChannelModule">
<channel>
  <title>RSS2.0Example</title>
  <link>http://www.exampleurl.com/example/index.html</link>
  <description>This is an example RSS 2.0 feed</description>
  <blogChannel:blogRoll>http://www.exampleurl.com/blogroll.opml</blogChannel:blogRoll>
<blogChannel:blink>http://www.benhammersley.com</blogChannel:blink>
```

Example 8-2. An RSS 2.0 feed with the BlogChannel module (continued)

```
<blogChannel:mySubscriptions>http://www.exampleurl.com/mySubscriptions.opml</blogChannel:
mySubscriptions>
```

...

We will discuss OPML, blogrolls, and subscription lists in Chapter 10. In the mean-time, let's look at producing RSS 2.0 feeds.

Producing RSS 2.0 with Blogging Tools

RSS 2.0 is still too young for any dedicated programmatic tools to have appeared, so the vast majority of 2.0 feeds are produced by weblogging tools that use templates. The most popular of these is Movable Type, written by Ben and Mena Trott, which is freely available for for noncommercial use at *http://www.movabletype.org*. In order to discuss a few important implementation points, we will now look at a template for Movable Type, shown in Example 8-3, that produces an RSS 2.0 feed.

Example 8-3. A Movable Type template for producing RSS 2.0

```
<?xml version="1.0"?>
<rss version="2.0">
<channel>
<title><$MTBlogName$></title>
<link><$MTBlogURL$></link>
<description><$MTBlogDescription$></description>
<language>en-gb</language>
<copyright>All content Public Domain</copyright>
<managingEditor>ben@benhammersley.com</managingEditor>
<webMaster>ben@benhammersley.com</webMaster>
<docs>http://backend.userland.com/rss</docs>
<category  domain="http://www.dmoz.org">Reference/Libraries/Library_and_Information_
Science/Technical_Services/Cataloguing/Metadata/RDF/Applications/RSS/</category>
<generator>Movable Type/2.5</generator>
<lastBuildDate><$MTDate format="%a, %d %b %Y %I:%M:00 GMT"$></lastBuildDate>
<ttl>60</ttl>


<MTEntries lastn="15">
<item>
<title><$MTEntryTitle encode_html="1"$></title>
<description><$MTEntryExcerpt encode_html="1"$></description>
<link><$MTEntryLink$></link>
<comments><$MTEntryLink$></comments>
<author><$MTEntryAuthorEmail$></author>
<pubDate><$MTEntryDate format="%a, %d %b %Y %I:%M:00 GMT"$></pubDate>
<guid isPermaLink="false">GUID:<$MTEntryLink$></g<$MTEntryDate format="%a%d%b%Y%I:%M"$></
guid>
</item>
</MTEntries>
```

Example 8-3. A Movable Type template for producing RSS 2.0 (continued)

```
</channel>
</rss>
```

The vast majority of this template is standard Movable Type fare. Taken from one of my own blogs, it uses the `<$MT$>` tags to insert information directly from the Movable Type database into the feed. So far, so simple.

Two things need to be noted. First, the date format:

```
<pubDate><$MTEntryDate format="%a, %d %b %Y %I:%M:00 GMT"$></pubDate>
```

Care must be taken to ensure that the format of the contents of the date fields are correctly formed. RSS 2.0 feeds require their dates to be written to comply with RFC 822—for example: `Mon, 03 Jan 2002 0:00:01 GMT`.

Common errors found in RSS 2.0 feeds include missing commas, seconds values, and time zones. You must ensure that these are all present, as some desktop readers and aggregators are not as forgiving as others.

Implementation of the guid element is equally important. The RSS 2.0 standard does not discuss the form of the guid. It only asks the author to ensure that it is globally unique. There is no scope for the OSF GUID standard to be used within most blogging tools, so we have to formulate our own system.

For the template shown in Example 8-3 I considered various things. First, the guid's purpose is to tell applications if the entry is new or if it has changed. Second, within my own blogs I allow people to add comments to the entries. I consider this a change to the entry, so my guid must reflect this. Because this change is not reflected in the link to the entry, the link alone is not a good guid. So, by combining the link with the last-updated-date value, I am able to make a guid that is globally unique and changes when it needs to. For added measure, I add the string GUID to the front of it to prevent it from looking too much like a retrievable URL—which, of course, it isn't. Hence:

```
<guid isPermaLink="false">GUID:<$MTEntryLink$></g<$MTEntryDate format="%a%d%b%Y%I:
%M"$></guid>
```

Now that we know how to make RSS feeds in all the latest formats, let's move on to Chapter 9, *Using Feeds*.

Blogging?

Weblogging, or "blogging," has been mentioned quite a few times in this chapter—and with good reason: RSS 2.0 is used primarily for weblogging applications, and it was developed mostly over weblogs. O'Reilly publishes a good introduction to blogging—namely, *Essential Blogging* by Cory Doctorow, Rael Dornfest, J. Scott Johnson, Shelley Powers, Benjamin Trott, and Mena G. Trott.

## CHAPTER 9

Using Feeds

*Words ought to be a little wild for they are the
assaults of thought on the unthinking.*
—John Maynard Keynes

Creating your own feed is good fun, but surely the real point of RSS is using feeds created by others. In this chapter, we'll show how to incorporate other RSS 0.9x feeds within your own site, using techniques that you can also build into applications.

To use a feed you must first *parse* it—i.e., convert it from RSS into something more immediately useful to your program. The result may be something that a browser can display, data to be fed into a database, or variables to be used immediately. RSS feeds, because they are in XML, are parsable in many different ways, and the method you use depends on what you want to do with the feed and what sort of access you have to the machine doing the work.

The most common use of RSS feeds is incorporation into web sites, so that's where we'll start.

Using RSS Feeds Inside Another Site

Because RSS feeds change independently of the rest of the content within your page, the most sensible method of displaying the feed is to treat it as an inclusion. There are two ways of doing this: as a *server-side include* (SSI), in which your server inserts the parsed RSS feed into the correct place inside your page, or as a *client-side include*, in which you rely on your user's browser to do the same.

Server-side inclusion depends on settings within your server's configuration. If you have neither control of your own server, nor a friendly system administrator who might be bribed to turn it on for you, you're out of luck here. Client-side inclusion depends on your user's browser allowing the execution of JavaScript. Most do, but some people keep it turned off for security reasons. Anyone using browsers without JavaScript (and this might include PDAs and web-television systems) will not be able to see the feed. You will have to account for this in your design process.

Deciding which method to use is really a matter of how much access you have to the technology that runs your site. At the end of the day, the feed must be parsed into something readable, and this is always done on the server side. So, if you don't have full access to CGI-Bin, you'll be relying on a third-party parsing service. These services give you a line of JavaScript to include in your page's code, which acts as the client-side inclusion. For example, a third party is good for blogs that might be hosted on services that do not allow scripting.

If you have CGI-Bin access, but no server-side inclusion allowed by your host's server settings, you'll need to combine server-side parsing with client-side inclusion. Those of us lucky enough to have full access to our servers can do whatever we like, with all of the toys available and waiting. The most fun, and certainly the most flexible method, is to use server-side parsing and server-side inclusion in combination.

In this section, we'll discuss all the options. But first, let's talk about parsing RSS into something more readable.

Parsing RSS as Simply as Possible

The disadvantage of RSS's split into two separate but similar specifications is that we can never be sure which of the standards our desired feeds will arrive in. If we restrict ourselves to using only RSS 0.9x, it is very likely that the universe will conspire to make the most interesting stuff available solely in RSS 1.0, or vice versa. So, no matter what we want to do with the feed, our approach must be able to handle both standards with equal aplomb. With that in mind, simple parsing of RSS can be done in three different ways:

- XML parsing
- Regular expressions
- XSLT transformations

XML parsers

XML parsers are useful tools to have around when dealing with either RSS 0.9x or 1.0. While RSS 0.9x is a quite simple format, and using a full-fledged XML parser on it does sometimes seem to be like stirring soup with a cement mixer, it does have a distinct advantage over the other methods: *future-proofing*. Depending on how you architect your code, the use of a proper parser may save you a lot of time should the specifications change, or if new elements are introduced. This is especially useful with RSS 1.0 and its ever-growing raft of modules, and it is the method I recommend. For the majority of purposes, the simplest XML parsers are perfectly useful. The Perl module XML::Simple is a good example. Example 9-1 is a simple script that uses XML::Simple to parse both RSS 0.9x and RSS 1.0 feeds into XHTML that is ready for server-side inclusion.

Example 9-1. Using XML::Simple to parse RSS

```perl
#!/usr/local/bin/perl

use strict;
use warnings;

use LWP::Simple;
use XML::Simple;

my $url=$ARGV[0];

# Retrieve the feed, or die gracefully
my $feed_to_parse = get ($url) or die "I can't get the feed you want";

# Parse the XML
my $parser = XML::Simple->new( );
my $rss = $parser->XMLin("$feed_to_parse");

# Decide on name for outputfile
my $outputfile = "$rss->{'channel'}->{'title'}.html";

# Replace any spaces within the title with an underscore
$outputfile =~ s/ /_/g;

# Open the output file
open (OUTPUTFILE, ">$outputfile");

# Print the Channel Title
print OUTPUTFILE '<div class="channelLink">'."\n".'<a href="';
print OUTPUTFILE "$rss->{'channel'}->{'link'}"."'">';
print OUTPUTFILE "$rss->{'channel'}->{'title'}</a>\n</div>\n";

# Print the channel items
print OUTPUTFILE '<div class="linkentries">'."\n"."<ul>";
print OUTPUTFILE "\n";

foreach my $item (@{$rss->{channel}->{'item'}}) {
    next unless defined($item->{'title'}) && defined($item->{'link'});
    print OUTPUTFILE '<li><a href="';
    print OUTPUTFILE "$item->{'link'}";
    print OUTPUTFILE '">';
    print OUTPUTFILE "$item->{'title'}</a></li>\n";
        }

foreach my $item (@{$rss->{'item'}}) {
    next unless defined($item->{'title'}) && defined($item->{'link'});
    print OUTPUTFILE '<li><a href="';
    print OUTPUTFILE "$item->{'link'}";
    print OUTPUTFILE '">';
    print OUTPUTFILE "$item->{'title'}</a></li>\n";
        }

print OUTPUTFILE "</ul>\n</div>\n";
```

Example 9-1. Using XML::Simple to parse RSS (continued)
```
# Close the OUTPUTFILE
close (OUTPUTFILE);
```

This script highlights various issues regarding the parsing of RSS, so it is worth dissecting closely. We start with the opening statements:

```
#!/usr/local/bin/perl

use strict;
use warnings;

use LWP::Simple;
use XML::Simple;

my $url=$ARGV[0];

# Retrieve the feed, or die gracefully
my $feed_to_parse = get ($url) or die "I can't get the feed you want";
```

This is nice and standard Perl—the usual use strict; and use warnings; for good programming karma. Next, we load the two necessary modules: XML::Simple we are aware of already, and LWP::Simple is used to retrieve the RSS feed from the remote server. This is indeed what we do next, taking the command-line argument as the URL for the feed we want to parse. We place the entire feed in the scalar $feed_to_parse, ready for the next section of the script:

```
# Parse the XML
my $parser = XML::Simple->new( );
my $rss = $parser->XMLin("$feed_to_parse");
```

This section fires up a new instance of the XML::Simple module and calls the newly initialized object $parser. It then reads the retrieved RSS feed and parses it into a tree, with the root of the tree called $rss. This tree is actually a set of hashes, with the element names as hash keys. In other words, we can do this:

```
# Decide on name for outputfile
my $outputfile = "$rss->{'channel'}->{'title'}.html";

# Replace any spaces within the title with an underscore
$outputfile =~ s/ /_/g;

# Open the output file
open (OUTPUTFILE, ">$outputfile");
```

Here we take the value of the title element within the channel, add the string .html, and make it the value of $outputfile. This is for a simple reason: I wanted to make the user interface to this script as simple as possible. You can change it to allow the user to input the output filename themselves, but I like the script to work one out automatically from the title element. Of course, many title elements use spaces, which makes a nasty mess of filenames, so we use a regular expression to replace spaces with underscores. We then open up the file handle, creating the file if necessary.

With a file ready for filling, and an RSS feed parsed in memory, let's fill in some of the rest:

```
# Print the Channel Title
print OUTPUTFILE '<div class="channelLink">'."\n".'<a  href="';
print OUTPUTFILE "$rss->{'channel'}->{'link'}".'">';
print OUTPUTFILE "$rss->{'channel'}->{'title'}</a>\n</div>\n";
```

Here we start to make the XHTML version. We take the link and title elements from the channel and create a title that is a hyperlink to the destination of the feed. We assign it a div, so that we can format it later with CSS, and include some new lines to make the XHTML source as pretty as can be:

```
# Print the channel items
print OUTPUTFILE '<div class="linkentries">'."\n"."<ul>";
print OUTPUTFILE "\n";

foreach my $item (@{$rss->{channel}->{'item'}}) {
    next unless defined($item->{'title'}) && defined($item->{'link'});
    print OUTPUTFILE '<li><a href="';
    print OUTPUTFILE "$item->{'link'}";
    print OUTPUTFILE '">';
    print OUTPUTFILE "$item->{'title'}</a></li>\n";
        }

foreach my $item (@{$rss->{'item'}}) {
    next unless defined($item->{'title'}) && defined($item->{'link'});
    print OUTPUTFILE '<li><a href="';
    print OUTPUTFILE "$item->{'link'}";
    print OUTPUTFILE '">';
    print OUTPUTFILE "$item->{'title'}</a></li>\n";
        }

print OUTPUTFILE "</ul>\n</div>\n";

# Close the OUTPUTFILE
close (OUTPUTFILE);
```

The last section of the script deals with the biggest issue for all RSS parsing: the differences between RSS 0.9x and RSS 1.0. With XML::Simple, or any other tree-based parser, this is especially crucial, because the item appears in a different place in each specification. Remember: in RSS 0.9x, item is a subelement of channel, but in RSS 1.0 they have equal weight.

So, in the preceding snippet you can see two foreach loops. The first one takes care of RSS 0.9x feeds, and the second covers RSS 1.0. Either way, they are encased inside another div and made into an ul unordered list. The script finishes by closing the file handle. Our work is done.

Running this from the command line, with the RSS feed from *http://rss. benhammersley.com/index.xml*, produces the result shown in Example 9-2.

Example 9-2. Content_Syndication_with_RSS.html

```
<div class="channelLink">
<a href="http://rss.benhammersley.com/">Content Syndication with XML and RSS</a>
</div>
<div class="linkentries">
<ul>
<li><a href="http://rss.benhammersley.com/archives/001150.html">PHP parsing of RSS</a></
li>
<li><a href="http://rss.benhammersley.com/archives/001146.html">RSS for Pocket PC</a></li>
<li><a href="http://rss.benhammersley.com/archives/001145.html">Syndic8 is One</a></li>
<li><a href="http://rss.benhammersley.com/archives/001141.html">RDF mod_events</a></li>
<li><a href="http://rss.benhammersley.com/archives/001140.html">RSS class for cocoa</a></
li>
<li><a href="http://rss.benhammersley.com/archives/001131.html">Creative Commons RDF</a></
li>
<li><a href="http://rss.benhammersley.com/archives/001129.html">RDF events in Outlook.</a>
</li>
<li><a href="http://rss.benhammersley.com/archives/001128.html">Reading Online News</a></
li>
<li><a href="http://rss.benhammersley.com/archives/001115.html">Hep messaging server</a></
li>
<li><a href="http://rss.benhammersley.com/archives/001109.html">mod_link</a></li>
<li><a href="http://rss.benhammersley.com/archives/001107.html">Individual Entries as RSS
1.0</a></li>
<li><a href="http://rss.benhammersley.com/archives/001105.html">RDFMap</a></li>
<li><a href="http://rss.benhammersley.com/archives/001104.html">They're Heeereeee</a></li>
<li><a href="http://rss.benhammersley.com/archives/001077.html">Burton Modules</a></li>
<li><a href="http://rss.benhammersley.com/archives/001076.html">RSS within XHTML documents
UPDATED</a></li>
</ul>
</div>
```

We can then include this inside another page using server-side inclusion (see later in this chapter.)

After all our detailing of additional elements, I hear you cry, where are they? Well, including extra elements in a script of this sort is rather simple. Here I've taken another look at the second foreach loop from our previous example. Notice the sections in bold type:

```
foreach my $item (@{$rss->{'item'}}) {
    next unless defined($item->{'title'}) && defined($item->{'link'});
    print OUTPUTFILE '<li><a href="';
    print OUTPUTFILE "$item->{'link'}";
    print OUTPUTFILE '">';
    print OUTPUTFILE "$item->{'title'}</a>";
    if ($item->{'dc:creator'}) {
        print OUTPUTFILE '<span class="dccreator">Written  by';
        print OUTPUTFILE "$item->{'dc:creator'}";
        print OUTPUTFILE '</span>';
        }
    print OUTPUTFILE "<ol><blockquote>$item->{'description'}</blockquote></ol>";
    print OUTPUTFILE "\n</li>\n";
        }
```

This section now looks inside the RSS feed for a dc:creator element and displays it if it finds one. It also retrieves the contents of the description element and displays it as a nested item in the list. You might want to change this formatting, obviously.

By repeating the emphasized line, it is easy to add support for different elements as you see fit, and it's also simple to give each new element its own div or span class to control the on-screen formatting. For example:

```
if ($item->{'dc:creator'}) {
    print OUTPUTFILE '<span class="dccreator">Written by';
    print OUTPUTFILE "$item->{'dc:creator'}";
    print OUTPUTFILE '</span>';
}
if ($item->{'dc:date'}) {
    print OUTPUTFILE '<span class="dcdate">Date:';
    print OUTPUTFILE "$item->{'dc:date'}";
    print OUTPUTFILE '</span>';
}
if ($item->{'annotate:reference'}) {
    print OUTPUTFILE '<span class="annotation"><a href="';
    print OUTPUTFILE "$item->{'annotate:reference'}->{'rdf:resource'}";
    print OUTPUTFILE '">Comment on this</a></span>';
}
```

Installing XML Parsers with Expat

Most XML parsers found in scripting languages (Perl, Python, etc.) are really interfaces for Expat, the powerful XML parsing library. They therefore require Expat to be installed. Expat is available from *http://expat.sourceforge.net/* and is released under the MIT License.

As you can see, the final extension prints the contents of the annotate:reference element. This, as we mentioned in Chapter 7, is a single rdf:resource attribute. Note the way we get XML::Simple to read the attribute. It just treats the attribute as another leaf on the tree—you call it in the same way you would a subelement. You can use the same syntax for any attribute-only element.

Regular Expressions

Using regular expressions to parse RSS may seem a little brutish, but it does have two advantages. First, it totally negates the issues regarding the differences between standards. Second, it is a much easier installation: it requires no XML parsing modules, or any dependencies thereof.

Regular expressions, however, are not pretty. Consider Example 9-3, which is a section from Rael Dornfest's lightweight RSS aggregator, Blagg.

Example 9-3. A section of code from Blagg

```
# Feed's title and link
my($f_title, $f_link) = ($rss =~ m#<title>(.*?)</title>.*?<link>(.*?)</link>#ms);

# RSS items' title, link, and description

while ( $rss =~ m{<item(?!s).*?>.*?(?:<title>(.*?)</title>.*?)?(?:<link>(.*?)</link>.
*?)?(?:<description>(.*?)</description>.*?)?</item>}mgis ) {
    my($i_title, $i_link, $i_desc, $i_fn) = ($1||'', $2||'', $3||'', undef);

    # Unescape &amp; &lt; &gt; to produce useful HTML
    my %unescape = ('&lt;'=>'<', '&gt;'=>'>', '&amp;'=>'&', '&quot;'=>'"');
    my $unescape_re = join '|' => keys %unescape;
    $i_title && $i_title =~ s/($unescape_re)/$unescape{$1}/g;
    $i_desc && $i_desc =~ s/($unescape_re)/$unescape{$1}/g;

    # If no title, use the first 50 non-markup characters of the description
    unless ($i_title) {
        $i_title = $i_desc;
        $i_title =~ s/<.*?>//msg;
        $i_title = substr($i_title, 0, 50);
    }
    next unless $i_title;
```

While this looks pretty nasty, it is actually an efficient way of stripping the data out of the RSS file, even if it is potentially much harder to extend. If you are really into regular expressions and do not mind having a very specialized, hard-to-extend system, their simplicity may be for you. They certainly have their place.

Other Outputs and Selective Parsing

In all of our examples so far, we have written the parsed feed to a file handle for use inside another web page. This is just the start. We could use the same basic structure to output to just about anything that handles text. Example 9-4 is a script that sends the top headline of a feed to a mobile phone via the Short Message Service (SMS). It uses the WWW::SMS module, outputting to the first web-based free SMS service it can find that works.

Example 9-4. rsssms.pl sends the first headline title to a mobile phone via SMS

```
#!/usr/local/bin/perl
use strict;
use warnings;
use LWP::Simple;
use XML::Simple;
use WWW::SMS;

# Take the command line arguments, URL first, then complete number of mobile
my $url=$ARGV[0];
my $number=$ARGV[1];
```

Example 9-4. rsssms.pl sends the first headline title to a mobile phone via SMS (continued)

```perl
# Retrieve the feed, or die disgracefully
my $feed_to_parse = get ($url) or die "I can't get the feed you want";

# Parse the XML
my $parser = XML::Simple->new();
my $rss = $parser->XMLin("$feed_to_parse");

# Get the data we want
my $message = "NEWSFLASH:: $rss->{'channel'}->{'item'}->[0]->{'title'}";

# Send the message
my @gateway = WWW::SMS->gateways();
my $sms = WWW::SMS->new($number, $message);
foreach my $gateway(@gateway) {if ($sms->send($gateway)) {
        print 'Message sent!';
          last;
    } else {
        print "Error: $WWW::SMS::Error\n";
    }}
```

You can use the script in Example 9-4 from the command line or crontab like so:

```
perl rsssms.pl http://full.urlof/feed.xml 123456789
```

You can see how one might set this up on crontab to send the latest news at the desired interval. But how about using the system status module, mod_systemstatus, to automatically detect and inform you of system failures? Perhaps you could use something like Example 9-5.

Example 9-5. mod_systemstatusSMS.pl

```perl
#!/usr/local/bin/perl

use strict;
use warnings;
use LWP::Simple;
use XML::Simple;
use WWW::SMS;

# Take the command line arguments, URL first, then complete number
my $url=$ARGV[0];
my $number=$ARGV[1];

# Retrieve the feed, or die gracefully
my $feed_to_parse = get ($url) or die "I can't get the feed you want";

# Parse the XML
my $parser = XML::Simple->new();
my $rss = $parser->XMLin("$feed_to_parse");

# initialise the $message
```

Example 9-5. mod_systemstatusSMS.pl (continued)

```
my $message;

# Look for downed servers
foreach my $item (@{$rss->{'item'}}) {
    next unless ($item->{'ss:responding'}) eq 'false';
    $message .= "Emergency! $item->{'title'} is down.";
        }

# Send the message
if ($message) {
my @gateway = WWW::SMS->gateways();
my $sms = WWW::SMS->new($number, $message);
foreach my $gateway(@gateway) {if ($sms->send($gateway)) {
        print 'Message sent!';
    } else {
        print "Error: $WWW::SMS::Error\n";
    }}
    };
```

Again, run from cron, this little beasty will let you monitor hundreds of machines—as long as they are generating the correct RSS—and inform you of a server outage via your mobile phone.

This combination of selective parsing, interesting output methods, and cron allows us to do many things with RSS feeds that a more comprehensive system may well inhibit. Monitoring a list of feeds for mentions of keywords is simple, as is using RSS feeds of stock prices to alert you of falls in the market. Combining these techniques with Publish and Subscribe systems (discussed in Chapter 12) gives us an even greater ability to monitor the world. Want an IRC channel to be notified of any new weblog postings? No problem. Want an SMS whenever the phrase "Free Beer" appears in your local feeds? Again, no problem.

Transforming RSS with XSLT

The transformation of RSS into another form of XML, using XSLT, is not very common at the moment, but it may soon have its time in the sun. This is because RSS—especially RSS 1.0, with its complicated relationships and masses of metadata—can be reproduced in many useful ways.

While the examples in this book have been text-based and mostly XHTML, there is no reason we cannot render RSS into an SVG graphic, a PDF (via the Apache FOP tool), an MMS-SMIL message for new-generation mobile phones, or any of the hundreds of other XML-based systems. XSLT and the arcane art of writing XSLT style sheets to take care of all of this is a subject too large for this book to cover in detail—for that, check out O'Reilly's *XSLT*, by Doug Tidwell.

Nevertheless, I will show you some nifty stuff. Example 9-6 is an XSLT style sheet that transforms an RSS 1.0 feed into the XHTML we produced in Example 9-2.

Example 9-6. RSS 1.0 Transforming into XHTML fragments

```
<?xml version="1.0"?>

<xsl:stylesheet version = '1.0'
xmlns:xsl="http://www.w3.org/1999/XSL/Transform"
xmlns:rdf="http://www.w3.org/1999/02/22-rdf-syntax-ns#"
xmlns:rss="http://purl.org/rss/1.0/"
exclude-result-prefixes="rss rdf"
>
<xsl:output method="html"/>

<xsl:template match="/">
 <div class="channellink">
  <a href="{rdf:RDF/rss:channel/rss:link}">
   <xsl:value-of select="rdf:RDF/rss:channel/rss:title"/>
  </a>
 </div>
 <div class="linkentries">
  <ul>
   <xsl:apply-templates select="rdf:RDF/*"/>
  </ul>
 </div>
</xsl:template>

<xsl:template match="rss:channel|rss:item">
 <li>
  <a href="{rss:link}">
   <xsl:value-of select="rss:title"/>
  </a>
 </li>
</xsl:template>

</xsl:stylesheet>
```

Again, just like the parsing code in Example 9-1, it is easy to extend this style sheet to take the modules into account. Example 9-7 extends Example 9-6 to look for the description, dc:creator, and dc:date elements. Note the emphasized code—those are the changes.

Example 9-7. Making the XSLT style sheet more useful

```
<?xml version="1.0"?>

<xsl:stylesheet version = '1.0'
xmlns:xsl="http://www.w3.org/1999/XSL/Transform"
xmlns:rdf="http://www.w3.org/1999/02/22-rdf-syntax-ns#"
xmlns:rss="http://purl.org/rss/1.0/"
xmlns:dc="http://purl.org/dc/elements/1.1/"
exclude-result-prefixes="rss   rdf  dc "
>
<xsl:output method="html"/>

<xsl:template match="/">
```

Example 9-7. Making the XSLT style sheet more useful (continued)

```
<div class="channellink">
 <a href="{rdf:RDF/rss:channel/rss:link}">
  <xsl:value-of select="rdf:RDF/rss:channel/rss:title"/>
 </a>
</div>
<div class="linkentries">
 <ul>
  <xsl:apply-templates select="rdf:RDF/*"/>
 </ul>
</div>
</xsl:template>

<xsl:template match="rss:channel|rss:item">
 <li>
  <a href="{rss:link}"><xsl:value-of select="rss:title"/></a>
   <ol>
     <xsl:value-of select="rss:description" />
   </ol>
   <ol>
    <xsl:text>Written  by: </xsl:text>
    <xsl:value-of select="dc:creator"/>
   </ol>
   <ol>
    <xsl:text>Written  on: </xsl:text>
    <xsl:value-of select="dc:date"/>
   </ol>
 </li>
</xsl:template>

</xsl:stylesheet>
```

Client-Side Inclusion

As mentioned in the beginning of this chapter, client-side inclusion is the way to go if you are setting up a third-party parsing service or hosting the majority of the site on a server that forbids server-side scripting. Doing this is very simple. All you need to do is create a script that returns a JavaScript script that displays the necessary XHTML.

To do this, just wrap each line of the XHTML that your ordinary script would produce in a document.writeln( ) function:

```
document.writeln("<h1>This is the heading<h1>");
```

and have the script return this document as the result of a call by the script element from the HTML document. So, the HTML document contains this line:

```
<script src="PATH TO PARSING SCRIPT APPENDED  WITH FEED URL" />
```

The CGI script will return the document.writeln script, which the browser will execute and then parse the resulting XHTML.

The upshot of this technique is that you can start a third-party RSS-parsing service with little effort. All you need to do is distribute the URL of the CGI script you are using and tell people to append the URL of the feed they want to the end of it. Give them the resulting script element to insert into their site code, and everyone is in business:

```
<script src="http://www.bensparsers.com?feed=http://bensfeed.com/index.xml"/>
```

Server-Side Inclusion

The more powerful method is server-side inclusion (SSI). It allows you to parse the feed using any technique and any language you like, and it allows greater flexibility for how the feed is used.

Let's look at an example of how it works. Example 9-8 produces an XHTML page with a server-side include directive.

Example 9-8. An XHTML page with a server-side include

```
<!DOCTYPE html PUBLIC "-//W3C//DTD XHTML 1.1//EN"
    "http://www.w3.org/TR/xhtml11/DTD/xhtml11.dtd">
<html xmlns="http://www.w3.org/1999/xhtml" xml:lang="en">
<head>
<title>An Example of a SSI</title>
</head>
<body>
<h1>This here is a News Feed from a really good site</h1>
<!--#include file="parsedfeed.html" -->
</body>
</html>
```

A server serving the page in Example 9-8 will, if the server is set up correctly, import the contents of *parsedfeed.html* and insert them in place of the SSI directive `<!--#include file="parsedfile.html" -->`.

So, by parsing RSS files into XHTML and saving them to disk, we can use SSI to place them within our existing XHTML page, apply formatting to change the way they look via the site's CSS style sheet, and present them to the end user.

Enabling server-side includes within Apache 1.3.x

Turning on server-side includes within Apache is straightforward, but it involves delving into places where a wrong move can make a nasty mess. Have a coffee, then concentrate. (N.B.: this section discusses Apache Version 1.3.x. Apache's configuration structure may change in later versions. Consult the documentation online at *http://www.apache.org.*)

To permit SSI on your server, you must have the following directive either in your *httpd.conf* file, or in a *.htaccess* file:

```
Options +Includes
```

This tells Apache that you want to permit files to be parsed for SSI directives. Of course, real-world installations are more complicated than that—most Apache installations have multiple `Options` directives set: one for each directory in some cases. You will most likely want to apply the `Options` to the specific directory in which you want SSI enabled—where the document in which you want to include the RSS feeds resides.

Example 9-9 shows the relevant section of the *httpd.conf* file for my own server.

Example 9-9. A section of an Apache http.conf file that allows for CGI and SSI

```
<Directory "/usr/local/apache/htdocs/rss">
Options ExecCGI Includes
DirectoryIndex index.shtml
</Directory>
```

Note that this configuration defines the directory's index page as *index.shtml*, because it is not a good idea to make your browser seek out SSI directives in every page it serves. Rather, you should tell it to look for SSI directives solely in pages that end with a certain file extension, by adding the following lines to your *httpd.conf* file:

```
AddType text/html .shtml
AddHandler server-parsed .shtml
```

This makes Apache search any file ending in *.shtml* (the traditional extension for such things) for SSI directives and replace them with their associated files before serving them to the end user.

This approach has a disadvantage: if you want to add SSI directives to an existing page, you have to change the name of that page. All links to that page will therefore be broken, in order to get the SSI directives to work. So, if you're retrofitting a site with RSS, the other method is to use the XBitHack directive within your *httpd.conf* file:

```
XBitHack on
```

XBitHack tells Apache to parse files for SSI directives if the files have the execute bit set. So, to add SSI directives to an existing page, rather than having to change the filename, you just need to make the file executable using chmod.

Now all that remains is to write the server-side include. Apache's SSI abilities are quite powerful, but we need to concern ourselves only with a limited subset here. If you're curious, take a look at *http://httpd.apache.org/docs/howto/ssi.html*.

Server-side includes with Microsoft IIS

Microsoft's Internet Information Services (IIS) server package comes with server-side includes enabled—by default, it will process any file ending in *.stm*, *.shtm*, or *.shtml*. However, files will be processed only if they're inside directories with Scripts or Execute access permissions.

How Often to Read the Feed

RSS feeds do change, it is true. People update their sites at all times of the day or night, and it would be lovely to have the very latest headlines. Currently, however, it is not a good idea to keep requesting a new RSS feed every few minutes. Etiquette and convention limit our requests for a new file to once every 60 minutes, unless the feed's publisher has specifically said that we can grab it more often, or unless they are using Publish and Subscribe (see Chapter 12).

In many cases, even requesting the feed every hour is too much. Feeds that change only once a day require downloading only once a day. It's a simple courtesy to pay attention to these conventions.

To set these permissions:

1. Open *My Computer*, select the directory in which you want to allow SSI, and right-click to open its property menu.

2. On the Security property menu, select the Windows account for which you want to change permissions.

3. Under Permissions, select the types of access for the selected user or group. Use Allow to specifically allow access and Deny to specifically deny access. For more choices, click Advanced.

## CHAPTER 10

Directories, Web Aggregators, and Desktop Readers

Outside of a dog, a book is man's best friend.
Inside of a dog, it's too dark to read.
—Groucho Marx

There are probably over one million RSS feeds published daily on the Internet, if you include all the webloggers, news sites, Slash sites, and custom channels from crazed content management systems. Add the RSS feeds made by ad hoc searches, collections of live data, and randomly generated MP3 streams, and we're suddenly talking about the sort of information overload that RSS feeds were initially designed to fix. What we need is a catalog, a collection where RSS feeds can be classified and searched, and where users can go to find the feeds on subjects close to their hearts. What we need are *directories* and their slightly more advanced brethren, the *aggregators*.

Directories: Introducing Syndic8

There have always been directories of RSS feeds. From the very beginning, at the My Netscape Network and the HotSauce application before that, people have needed to know where to find the best information. The growth of the standard, however, has not been matched by a growth in directories. Though today's RSS users have many more feed choices, they really are limited to one pure, searchable directory: Jeff Barr's Syndic8 (*http://www.syndic8.com*), shown in Figure 10-1.

Registering Your Feed with Syndic8

The registration process with Syndic8 reflects its community-authored nature and requires the following steps:

1. Submit the URL to feed itself via the Submissions page, *http://www.syndic8.com/suggest.php?Mode=data*.

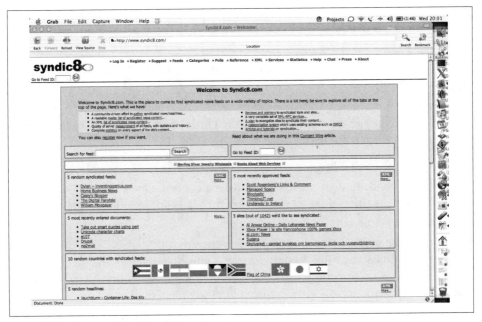

Figure 10-1. A screenshot of Syndic8

2. The new feed is then polled several times to measure reliability and find new items.

3. Once a feed has proven itself to be both reliable and regularly renewed, it is made available for review by a Reviewer.

4. Reviewed and approved feeds are then made available.

Using Syndic8

Before you can access some of the more advanced features the site provides, you must register for a username and password. Technically, you don't need to register to run a search for a site or find RSS feeds, but the other exciting stuff is well worth the effort, and this is your big opportunity to give something back to the RSS community. The content of the Syndic8 databases is enhanced by the volunteer efforts of the Syndic8 community. You should consider joining and giving a few minutes a week to one of the roles offered. You can join by going to *http://www.syndic8.com/ register.php* and filling in the appropriate boxes. You'll find yourself given four options:

Reviewer
I can review syndicated sites for accuracy and approve them.

Evangelist
I can work with nonsyndicated sites to encourage them to syndicate their content.

Scraper

I can do the programming work to scrape a site to syndicate its content.

Fixer

I can work with syndicated sites to help them repair problems with their syndicated information.

Check the ones you feel good about, and get yourself logged on. Now, every time you go back to the site, you can log in and do a little of whatever work needs doing. I encourage you to help out in this way.

Now, back to the searching.

Syndic8 has two methods to search for feeds: via the ordinary text-string search box, which indexes the titles of the feeds, and via the Categories section at the top of the page.

Here we see the whole point of marking up your site with metadata, as described in Chapter 3. Syndic8 classifies feeds with the same hierarchy as the DMOZ Open Directory, but it does so only for feeds that give it the necessary information. So, make sure you mark up your sites before submitting them to Syndic8.

Running a search gives you a list of matching feeds—the small, orange XML buttons link directly to the feed, and the feed title links to the URL given by the `link` subelement of the `channel` section of the feed.

Syndic8 API

Syndic8 really came into its own with the introduction of the XML-RPC API. By allowing the database to be queried programmatically by remote applications, Jeff Barr and the other Syndic8 developers produced a facility perfectly suited for inclusion in more ambitious scripts and applications.

The API works using ordinary XML-RPC, with the requests sent to the listener at *http://www.syndic8.com/xmlrpc.php*.

There are two groups of functions available at Syndic8: the basic set, which anyone can use to query the database in various ways and suggest feeds for inclusion, and the Personal List set, which is available only to users who have the Personal List facility. We will deal with the basic set functions first. These functions are classified according to their various purposes.

The first group finds Syndic8's capabilities:

`syndic8.GetFeedCount`
> *Takes:* nothing
> *Returns:* a number
> This function returns the number of feeds Syndic8 knows about.

`syndic8.GetFeedFields`

Takes: nothing

Returns: an array of strings, each a name of a field

This function returns all the field names that a feed record can have within the Syndic8 database.

`syndic8.GetFeedStates`

Takes: nothing

Returns: an array of structs, each a feed state and its description

This function returns all the possible feed states that Syndic8 supports.

`syndic8.GetLocationSchemes`

Takes: nothing

Returns: an array of strings, each a location scheme

This function returns all the location schemes Syndic8 knows about.

`syndic8.GetToolkits`

Takes: nothing

Returns: an array of strings, each a toolkit name

This function returns all the toolkits Syndic8 knows about.

The second group deals with the categories the feed author assigned to the feed, as discussed in Chapter 3. You can see the categories in action on the Web at *http://www.syndic8.com/feedcat.php*.

`syndic8.GetCategoryChildren`

Takes: nothing

Returns: an array of category names

This function returns the categories that are the immediate children of the given category.

`syndic8.GetCategoryRoots`

Takes: a string, the name of a category

Returns: a string, the name of the first category within the ontology for the given category

This function returns the topmost category for the given category.

`syndic8.GetCategorySchemes`

Takes: nothing

Returns: an array of the supported category schemes

This function returns an array of the supported category schemes.

`syndic8.GetCategoryTree`

Takes: a string, the name of a category scheme

Returns: an array of the categories within the scheme

This function returns an array of all the categories within a scheme.

`syndic8.GetFeedsInCategory`

Takes: a string, either a category name or a category scheme name

Returns: an array of `FeedIDs`

This function returns an array containing the `FeedIDs` of all the feeds within the named category.

The third group allows simple queries of the database:

syndic8.FindFeeds

    Takes: a string pattern to match against all feed fields

    Returns: an array of FeedIDs of matching feeds

This function matches a string against all the text fields of each feed in the feed list and returns the FeedIDs of the matching feeds.

syndic8.FindSites

    Takes: a string

    Returns: an array of FeedIDs of matching feeds

This function matches a string against the SiteURL field of each feed in the feed list (i.e., the content of the link subelement of channel) and returns the FeedIDs of the matching feeds.

syndic8.FindUsers

    Takes: a string

    Returns: an array of UserIDs of matching users

This function matches a string against all text fields of the user list and returns the UserIDs of the matching users.

syndic8.GetUserInfo

    Takes: a string, the UserID of the user

    Returns: a struct containing all the fields in the database pertaining to the user

This returns all known information about a user.

The fourth group allows more complicated database queries:

syndic8.GetChangedFeeds

    Takes: an array of structs, each containing an array of strings that denote the fields to check, a string of the search StartDate (*YYYY-MM-DD*), a string of the search EndDate (*YYYY-MM-DD*), and an array of strings denoting the fields to return

    Returns: an array of structs, each containing the requested fields from feeds with changes in the given date range.

This is a powerful function that returns all the feeds fitting the criteria that are known to have changed within a given date range.

syndic8.GetFeedInfo

    Takes: a single scalar or an array of integer FeedIDs or string FeedURLs, plus, optionally, an array of field names if you want to limit the result

    Returns: an array of all information known about the requested feeds, or just the fields named in the request

The most complicated function in the Syndic8 API, but also the most powerful, this function returns information known about one or more feeds.

syndic8.QueryFeeds

    Takes: three strings; the field to match, an operator on the match (<, >, <=, >=, !=, =, like, or regexp), and the value to match

    Returns: an array of FeedIDs of matching feeds

This function queries the database for feeds matching a single criterion.

By combining these commands, we can ask Syndic8 for all sorts of information regarding a feed, as well as any feed related to it in any way. It is quite simple, therefore, to produce applications that can query Syndic8 for the URL of a site's RSS feed, plus the URLs of any feeds related to it, selecting only those feeds that have been updated within a certain time frame and are written in a certain language.

These functions are universally available—anyone can write a script to call them. The next set of functions are not. They require the user to have an account with Syndic8, and some require the Personal List option to be turned on, which it is now the default for new users.

The first set of Personal List functions we will look at deal with subscription lists. Syndic8 can store subscription lists for its users. The lists are numbered, beginning with 0. The user can add and remove feeds to any subscription list, then query the list or pass it to another application. If you consider it as a remote blogroll, you have precisely the idea.

syndic8.CreateSubscriptionList

> *Takes:* three strings; the UserID, the user's password, either in cleartext or MD5-hashed, and the list name; also, one Boolean value should be listed as Public.
>
> *Returns:* the numerical reference for the new list

This function creates a new subscription list for the user.

syndic8.DeleteSubscriptionList

> *Takes:* two strings; the UserID and the user's password, either in cleartext or MD5-hashed, followed by the integer list reference
>
> *Returns:* 1 on success, 0 on failure

This function deletes the subscription list.

syndic8.GetSubscribed

> This function returns a list of all feeds subscribed to by the user, filtered by the given criteria, including feeds subscribed to by category.

syndic8.GetSubscribedFeeds

> *Takes:* two strings; the UserID and the user's password, either in cleartext or MD5-hashed, followed by the integer list reference and, optionally, an array of string field names
>
> *Returns:* an array of structs; FeedID, DataURL, and Status if field names are not supplied, or requested fields if they are supplied

This function is the same as syndic8.GetSubscribed, except that the returned feeds are only those subscribed to explicitly (i.e., it does not include feeds subscribed to implicity by category).

syndic8.GetSubscribedCategories

> *Takes:* two strings; the UserID and the user's password, either in cleartext or MD5-hashed, followed by the integer list reference
>
> *Returns:* an array of structures, each a scheme and a category

This function returns the categories subscribed to within a certain subscription list.

```
syndic8.GetSubscriptionLists
```
Takes: two strings; the UserID and the user's password, either in cleartext or MD5-hashed

Returns: array of structures, each a list index and a name

This function returns the list of subscription lists for the user.

Subscription lists would be no fun if you couldn't add things to them. The functions return 1, for a successful result, or an error code. Table 10-1 lists Syndic8's error codes.

Table 10-1. Error codes from Syndic8

Value	Name	Meaning
801	errorQUERY_FAILED	A select query failed due to a database problem.
802	errorNO_FEED	The FeedID supplied to the call is not valid.
803	errorNO_USER	The UserID supplied to the call is not valid.
804	errorINVALID_USER	The user name or password is not valid.
805	errorNO_SCHEME	The categorization or location scheme is invalid.
807	errorNO_SET_CATEGORY	The category could not be set.
808	errorMUST_BE_CATEGORIZER	The function requires that the user have the Categorizer role.
809	errorNO_SET_LOCATION	The location could not be set.
810	errorNO_RETRIEVE_BY_CATEGORY	The feeds could not be retrieved for the category.
811	errorNO_SUBSCRIBE_FEED	The subscription request for the feed could not be completed.
812	errorNO_SUBSCRIBE_CATEGORY	The subscription request for the category could not be completed.
813	errorMUST_HAVE_PERSONAL_LIST	The user must have the PersonalList option set to perform the operation.
814	errorSUGGEST_FAILURE	Autosuggesting the DataURL failed.
815	errorNO_DATA_URL	The nonnumeric FeedID/DataURL given to SubscribeFeed did not appear to be a URL.
816	errorNO_UNSUBSCRIBE_FEED	The unsubscription request for the feed could not be completed.
817	errorNO_UNSUBSCRIBE_CATEGORY	The unsubscription request for the category could not be completed.
818	errorNO_DELETE_LIST	The subscription list could not be deleted.
819	errorDUPLICATE_USERID	The given UserID is already in use.
820	errorDUPLICATE_EMAIL	The given Email is already in use.
821	errorINVALID_SPONSOR	The SponsorID or SponsorPassword is not valid.
822	errorMUST_HAVE_CREATE_USER	The sponsor must have the CreateUser option set to perform the operation.
823	errorBAD_QUERY	The query given to QueryFeeds is defective.
824	errorNO_FIELD	An invalid field name was given to GetFeedInfo.
825	errorNO_LIST	An invalid list identifier was given.
826	errorNO_CREATE_LIST	The subscription list could not be created.
827	errorMUST_BE_EDITOR	The caller must have the Editor role.
828	errorBAD_USERID	The supplied UserID is syntactically invalid.

`syndic8.SubscribeFeed`

> *Takes:* two strings; the `UserID` and the user's password, either in cleartext or MD5-hashed, followed by either the
>   integer `FeedID` or a string URL of the RSS feed itself, and then the number of the list you want to subscribe the
>   feed to and a Boolean value of `true` or `false` for "AutoSuggest?"
>
> *Returns:* a success or error code

This function adds the feed to the user's given subscription list. If a `DataURL` is given, the AutoSuggest option is true, and the feed is not known by Syndic8, it will be added to the "suggested" list as if by entered by the `UserID`.

`syndic8.UnSubscribeFeed`

> *Takes:* two strings; the `UserID` and the user's password, either in cleartext or MD5-hashed, followed by the integer
>   `FeedID` and the number of the list you wish to unsubscribe the feed from
>
> *Returns:* a success or error code

This function removes a feed from a subscription list.

`syndic8.SubscribeCategory`

> *Takes:* four strings; the `UserID`, the user's password, either in cleartext or MD5-hashed, the Category scheme, and
>   the category and integer of the subscription list
>
> *Returns:* a success or error code

This function adds all the feeds within the category to a subscription list.

`syndic8.UnSubscribeCategory`

> *Takes:* four strings; the `UserID`, the user's password, either in cleartext or MD5-hashed, the Category scheme, and
>   the category and integer of the subscription list
>
> *Returns:* a success or error code

This function removes all the feeds within a category from a subscription list.

Finally, the Syndic8 API can be used to add feeds to the Syndic8 database. There are two functions to do this, and they return the new `FeedID`, plus a special code, as listed in Table 10-2.

`syndic8.SuggestDataURL`

> *Takes:* a string, the URL of the RSS feed itself
>
> *Returns:* a struct with the `FeedID` (newly created or old) and a suggest-status code

This function suggests a feed from its RSS URL.

`syndic8.SuggestSiteURL`

> *Takes:* a string, the URL of the site itself (i.e., the contents of `channel link`)
>
> *Returns:* a struct with the `FeedID` (newly created or old) and a suggest-status code

This function suggests a feed with its `SiteURL`.

Table 10-2. Response codes from Syndic8 for feed suggestions

Value	Name	Meaning
1	`suggestALREADY_QUEUED`	The `DataURL` is already known, and the site is currently being polled to prepare it for review.
2	`suggestALREADY_EVANGELIZING`	The `SiteURL` is already known, and the site is currently being evangelized.
3	`suggestALREADY_KNOWN`	The `DataURL` or `SiteURL` is already known, and the status is neither queued nor evangelizing.

Value	Name	Meaning
4	suggestACCEPTED	The DataURL or SiteURL was not known. It has been accepted for reviewing or evangelization, as appropriate.
5	suggestERROR	Something went wrong.
6	suggestNO_PREFIX	The URL did not have an *http://* prefix.
7	suggestNO_FETCH	The information referred to by the URL could not be fetched.
8	suggestNOT_FEED	The information referred to by the URL did not appear to be a valid feed.
9	suggestNUMERIC_IP	The URL contained a numeric IP address.
10	suggestBLOCKED	The URL is from a domain or subdomain that is not currently accepted into Syndic8.

We will be using the Syndic8 API again in Chapter 12. In the meantime, let's move on to aggregators.

Web Aggregators: Introducing Meerkat

Meerkat was the first truly open-to-all, searchable, categorized aggregator. Developed by Rael Dornfest, Chair of the RSS 1.0 Working Group and researcher for O'Reilly (the publisher of this book), Meerkat (*http://www.oreillynet.com/meerkat/*) takes the RSS feeds from a whole range of sites, throws all of the items into a big pot, and makes the resulting mix searchable. Aggregating feeds in this way allows for custom feeds to be made—"The latest news on Java," say, or "Everything containing the keyword 'sausages' written in the past 30 minutes."

Meerkat is primarily usable via its web interface, shown in Figure 10-2. This introduces two main concepts for the application: *profiles* and *mobs*. To use either of these features, you must first sign up for a user ID with the O'Reilly Network (*http://www.oreillynet.com*).

Profiles are named sets of query parameters. There are global parameters already loaded into Meerkat, based on subject matter (Apache, Perl, P2P, etc.), and you can save your own from the web interface.

Mobs, on the other hand, are collections of stories. You use a mob like a universally retrievable bookmark list. You can add stories to it via the web interface, send its URL to other people, or even query and display the mob via the Meerkat API.

The what? Well, let me tell you…

The Meerkat API

Like Syndic8, Meerkat offers an API to allow other applications access to its database. Unlike Syndic8, however, Meerkat is not a web service in the XML-RPC/SOAP

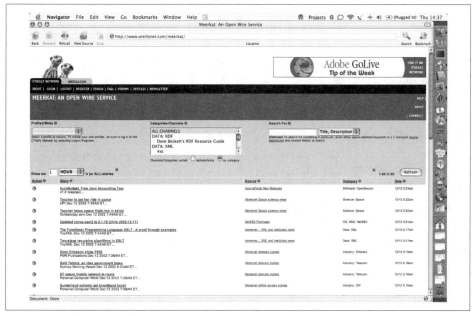

Figure 10-2. A screenshot of Meerkat's front page

mold. Rather, it relies on the REST-architectural system of passing the entire query encoded into a URL. This is very useful in the RSS world, as it allows people to swap URLs of custom feeds from within the existing framework of behavior—not just emailing them or instant messaging to friends, but also by inclusion in blogrolls and mySubscription lists. As such, the REST-based web aggregator provides a different extended service to the directory or the desktop reader.

To query the Meerkat API, you pass it a URL, built up from *http://meerkat.oreillynet. com/?*, and then a query made out of the following parameters (any spaces in URLs are replaced by %20):

s= *(Search For)*
> Instructs Meerkat to search for something in the item's title or description. This can be either a list of keywords separated with a plus sign (+) or a regular expression enclosed in //.
>
> **Example:** *http://meerkat.oreillynet.com/?s=eggs+ham* returns "any stories whose title or description contains either 'eggs' or 'ham'."

sw= *(Search What)*
> Ordinarily, Meerkat's s= parameter will only search through title and description elements. The sw= option instructs Meerkat to search other specified fields. Currently, Meerkat supports only the simpler Dublin Core elements, so sw= can be either blank (hence: title, description) or a combination of dc_ title, dc_creator, dc_subject, dc_description, dc_publisher, dc_contributor,

dc_date, dc_type, dc_format, dc_identifier, dc_source, dc_language, dc_relation, dc_coverage, or dc_rights.

Example: *http://meerkat.oreillynet.com/?s=bod@exampleurl.com&sw=dc_contributor* returns all the item elements for which *bod@exampleurl.com* is listed as contributor.

c= *(Channel)*

This tells Meerkat to display only the requested channel. It takes the numerical channel ID.

Example: *http://meerkat.oreillynet.com/?c=1243* returns only "stories from the 'oreillynet.python' newsgroup."

t= *(Time Period)*

This controls the maximum age of stories that Meerkat displays. It takes a number, followed by: MINUTE, HOUR, DAY, or ALL. The number is optional (and meaningless) when choosing ALL. The default setting is 1HOUR, so you must set this parameter to get anything older.

Example: *http://meerkat.oreillynet.com/?t=7DAY* means "show me stories from the past seven days."

p= *(Profile)*

This displays the stories in the manner chosen by a set profile within Meerkat. You only need to pass it the numerical ID of an existing profile.

Example: *http://meerkat.oreillynet.com/?p=563* shows "all stories caught by profile number 563 (the O'Reilly Network)."

m= *(Mob)*

Very similar to the p= parameter, but displaying stories associated with a particular mob. You pass it the numerical ID of the mob in question.

Example: *http://meerkat.oreillynet.com/?m=123* gets you "stories grouped under mob number 123."

i= *(ID)*

This parameter displays a particular story. Each item in the Meerkat database is assigned a numerical ID. If you know the number, you can point directly at the story. (To find it, go to the web interface, and hold your mouse over the mob icon (ring of dots) to see the story's ID.)

Example: *http://meerkat.oreillynet.com/?i=456* will display only story number 456.

So far, we've seen all the parameters needed to filter exactly which stories to display. If you've been adventurous, you will have found that retrieving the URL query in a browser gives you a fancy HTML result with lots of Meerkat logos and links to the rest of the O'Reilly Network site. These are pretty, and provide much good reading, but they are of little use to someone wanting to grab an RSS feed or another type of output.

Happily, Meerkat introduces the concept of flavors. By setting the parameter _fl to a certain string, you get results back in various ways:

_fl=meerkat
    The default setting, providing the full bells and whistles of the Meerkat page.

_fl=tofeerkat
    A lighter version of the Meerkat page.

_fl=minimal
    A very light version of the Meerkat page.

_fl=rss
    Provides the results as a simple RSS 0.91 feed.

_fl=rss10
    Provides the results as an RSS 1.0 feed.

_fl=xml
    Provides the results in a bespoke XML format.

_fl=js
    Provides the results in a JavaScript file, which, when parsed, displays the results in an XHTML format.

_fl=php
    Provides the results in a PHP-serialized string.

So, now not only can we query the Meerkat database of feeds, but we can also get feedback out again. It gets better. Meerkat offers finer control over exactly what it produces with some Boolean switches (0 = off, 1 = on) that turn various output features on or off:

_de= *(Descriptions)*
    Turns on or off story descriptions or blurbs. You lose some of the story detail but gain a compact display for easy scanning.

    Example: *http://meerkat.oreillynet.com/?_de=0* means "without descriptions."

_ca= *(Categories)*
    Meerkat places each feed into a category hierarchy of its own, and certain flavors display this. If you don't want to use these for anything, you can turn them off.

    Example: *http://meerkat.oreillynet.com/?_ca=0* means "no categorization."

_ch= *(Channels)*
    Turns the channel display on or off for the flavors that care about it.

    Example: *http://meerkat.oreillynet.com/?_ch=0* means "turn off the display of channels."

_da= *(Dates)*
    Turns on or off the display of the date Meerkat first saw the story.

    Example: *http://meerkat.oreillynet.com/?_da=0* means "dates? I don't need no dates."

_dc= *(Dublin Core Metadata)*

> The RSS 1.0 flavor contains mod_dc information. You can remove this information with this parameter.
>
> **Example:** *http://meerkat.oreillynet.com/?_dc=0* means "plain and simple, DC-free is for me."

So, you're asking, how do we stick all these together to make something cool? Well, we separate the parameters with an & character.

For example, a query that produces an RSS 1.0 feed of the keyword search for "Ben" for stories up to a week old looks like this:

> *http://meerkat.oreillynet.com/?s=Ben&_fl=rss10&t=1WEEK*

Whereas a query for anything on Java in the past hour, in RSS 1.0 but without Dublin Core Metadata or Categories, looks like this:

> *http://meerkat.oreillynet.com/?s=Java&_fl=rss10&_dc=0&_ca=0*

Desktop Readers

Incorporation into a web site or online service is one thing, but RSS feeds can be far more useful than that. Desktop readers, a category of software that can display your favorite RSS feeds directly on your desktop, are quickly gaining in popularity. In this section, we look at some examples of good desktop readers and their similarities.

A Little History

The first RSS desktop reader to come to prominence was Carmen's Headline Viewer (CHV). Its origins were shrouded in mystery for a while, but CHV was actually written by Jeff Barr—the man behind Syndic8—and named after his wife. Version 0.1 came out in April 1999, and development continues at the time of this writing. It captured the imagination of many users by giving two advantages over reading RSS feeds over the existing online portals. First, it allowed users to be offline when they read the feeds, which allowed hundreds of sources to be downloaded and perused at a user's leisure in an era when Internet access was expensive in many countries. Second, the author considered a non-browser-based RSS vehicle to be potentially superior.

Since then, desktop readers have flourished. There are currently over 30 different examples listed on the Open Directory Project at *http://www.dmoz.org*. Many are free or cost very little.

Common Features

The evolution of RSS desktop readers is still in its early stages, but already many common features have emerged. Future developers should take note of these, as they are rapidly growing in popularity. Some of them may be refined over the next few years, but it is not expected that any of them will disappear entirely.

Automatic subscribing

Userland Software, whose CEO Dave Winer has been instrumental in the development of RSS 0.9x and 2.0, was one of the first companies to invest commercially in RSS. They produced an RSS-reading feature within their desktop weblogging software, Radio. This introduced a new idea into desktop readers: the subscription icon. Because Radio runs as a web server on port 5335 on the host machine, web sites can display icons that are hyperlinked to an IP address of 121.0.0.1—that of the user's machine. Clicking on the link tells Radio to subscribe to the feed denoted in the URL's attributes. For example, a link to:

> *http://127.0.0.1:5335/system/pages/subscriptions?url=http%3A%2F%2Fwww.*
> *scripting.com%2Frss.xml*

will, when activated, tell Radio to subscribe to the feed at the URL *http://www. scripting.com/rss.xml* (which is actually the feed from Dave Winer's own weblog, Scripting News).

This feature allowed for all Radio-built weblogs to include the requisite coffee-cup icon, shown in Figure 10-3. A circle of virtuous people was attracted to Radio for this feature, using it to produce more icon-decorated sites, which, in turn, attracted more people.

Figure 10-3. The Radio Userland coffee-cup icon

This proved to be such a popular feature that now many of the desktop reader products (and web-based aggregators too, for that matter) allow for the same thing, with similar methods of invoking the subscription function:

Amphetadesk
> *http://127.0.0.1:8888/index.html?add_url=URL_OF_RSS*

Fyuze
> *http://fyuze.com/customize/clickthru.php?url= URL_OF_RSS*

Headline Viewer
> *http://127.0.0.1:8900/add_provider?url= URL_OF_RSS*

Syndic8
> *http://www.syndic8.com/feedinfo.php?FeedDataURL= URL_OF_RSS*

Radio
> *http://127.0.0.1:5335/system/pages/subscriptions?url=URL_OF_RSS*

Web site publishers who want to make it easy for the users of these products to subscribe can provide links in these formats. At the time of this writing a small effort is underway to standardize the port number and path that the desktop readers listen on, so that only one URL need be given by the web site publisher to support, for example, Radio, Amphetadesk, and Headline Viewer together.

Support is also growing for desktop readers to support subscription requests in which the user gives only the URL of the main page of the site. Assuming that this page contains the relevant `<link rel="">` tag, as discussed in Chapter 4, the reader should be able to determine the path to the RSS file it seeks. As we have already seen, desktop readers could use the Syndic8 API to find the URL of the RSS feed, if Syndic8 contains the correct information (but I am unaware of one that does as yet).

Automatic discovery of feed URLs can be very useful, especially when the user is trying to subscribe to a large number of feeds in one go: by importing someone's blogroll, for example.

Blogrolls and subscription lists

As RSS gains popularity among the weblogging community, it has become an interesting fashion to provide a link to a list of all the feeds you subscribe to and the sites you read. The list of sites you read is called a *blogroll* and the list of subscribed-to feeds is called a *subscription list*.

Publishing your blogroll or subscription list is interesting for a few reasons. First, it allows all sorts of digital social network stuff to go on: your readers can see who you read, they can read the same, you form communities, and by reading other people's blogrolls you can get an interesting insight into the mind and interests of the person whose site you visit every day.

Second, and more important for us here, it means that desktop readers can import the subscription list and subscribe you en masse to all the feeds listed. To do this, we need such files to be in a standard format. Luckily, one format has been co-opted to do the job: OPML.

Outline Processor Markup Language (OPML)

OPML is a simple XML format, originally developed for the markup of outlines. The OPML specification defines an outline as "a tree, where each node contains a set of named attributes with string values."

Example 10-1 shows a reduced version of my own blogroll. (I actually have close to 100 sites in my blogroll, but you will get the point here.) Notice that an OPML file consists of a root element of `opml`, followed by a `head` element, which contains a sub-element of `title`. Following that is a `body` element, which may have one or more `outline` elements, each containing various attributes. Each `outline` element contains the details of a site to which I am subscribed.

Example 10-1. An example of a blogroll OPML file

```
<?xml version="1.0"?>
<opml version="1.1">
<head>
<title>mySubscriptions</title>
</head>
<body>

  <outline
text="Aaron Swartz: The Weblog"
description="&quot;the world's most influential teen who is not in a bubble-gum pop
outfit&quot; (Joey deVilla)"
title="Aaron Swartz: The Weblog"
type="rss"
version="RSS"
htmlUrl="http://www.aaronsw.com/weblog/"
xmlUrl="http://www.aaronsw.com/weblog/index.xml"/>

<outline
text="BBC News | Front Page"
description="Updated every minute of every day"
title="BBC News | Front Page"
type="rss"
version="RSS"
htmlUrl="http://news.bbc.co.uk/go/rss/-/1/hi/default.stm" xmlUrl="http://www.bbc.co.uk/
syndication/feeds/news/ukfs_news/front_page/rss091.xml"/>

<outline
text="Ben Hammersley.com"
description="Ben Hammersley.com - Stuff you'll like to read."
title="Ben Hammersley.com"
type="rss"
version="RSS"
htmlUrl="http://www.benhammersley.com/"
xmlUrl="http://www.benhammersley.com/index.rdf"/>

  <outline text="Blackbeltjones Work"
description="a blog about experience design, design matters and occasionally other stuff
like tech, science and comicbooks."
title="Blackbeltjones Work"
type="rss"
version="RSS"
htmlUrl="http://www.blackbeltjones.com/work/" xmlUrl="http://www.blackbeltjones.com/work/
xml_index.xml"/>

  </body>
</opml>
```

As you can see from this example, the outline element has seven attributes:

text=""
> This holds the string that, if displayed as an outline, would appear at that node. Depending on the application, either this or the title attribute is used as the name of the feed. As such, they are usually identical.

description=""
> The contents of the description subelement of channel within the feed. It therefore contains a short description of the feed.

title=""
> As with the text attribute, this holds the title of the feed to which you are subscribed.

type=""
> When OPML is being used for other purposes, type denotes what sort of branch of the outline this section is. For our purposes it is always "rss".

version=""
> This denotes the format of the file to which the branch links. Here it is always "RSS".

htmlURL=""
> The URL of the HTML representation of the feed (i.e., the page itself).

xmlURL=""
> The URL of the feed itself.

Subscription lists and blogrolls can also be listed within link elements inside the head section of an HTML page, in a manner similar to RSS feeds, like so:

```
<link rel="subscriptions" type="text/x-opml" title="Subscriptions" href="URL_TO_
SUBSCRIPTIONS">

  <link rel="blogroll" type="text/x-opml" title="Blogroll" href="URL_TO_BLOGROLL">
```

Now that we have discussed the generalities of desktop readers, let's move on to Chapter 11, where we will design a new RSS module and expand two of the most popular desktop readers to handle it.

Developing New Modules

Inventions reached their limit long ago, and I see no
hope for further development.
—Sextus Julius Frontinus

In this chapter, we will create a new module and extend a desktop reader (Ampheta-Desk) to understand it. We will also discuss the differences between the RSS 1.0 and RSS 2.0 data models and the effect of these differences on module design.

We have already dealt with the RDF data model in detail in Chapter 5, so we must now look at RSS 2.0.

Namespaces and Modules with RSS 2.0

RSS 2.0 introduces namespaced modules to the simple strand of RSS. The specification document states:

> A RSS feed may contain elements not described on this page, only if those elements are defined in a namespace. The elements defined in this document are not themselves members of a namespace, so that RSS 2.0 can remain compatible with previous versions in the following sense—a version 0.91 or 0.92 file is also a valid 2.0 file. If the elements of RSS 2.0 were in a namespace, this constraint would break, a version 0.9x file would not be a valid 2.0 file.

Other than not defining a namespace for the core elements of RSS 2.0, the modules work in the same way as the modules for RSS 1.0: declare the module's namespace in the root element (which in the case of RSS 2.0 is, of course, rss) and then use the module elements as directed by their specification. Parsers that do not recognize the namespace just ignore the new elements.

Differences from RSS 1.0

Whether or not RSS 1.0 modules can be reused within RSS 2.0 is currently a matter of debate. To do so requires the feed author to declare two additional namespaces within the root element: the namespace of the module and the namespace of RDF.

Some people find this additional complexity distasteful, and others find the rejection of the additionally powerful metadata a great shame. Still others, however, are using modules that declare the rdf:resource attribute without flinching.

While this argument rages (I advise you to check out the relevant email lists for the latest blows and parries), we can always bear in mind the simple way to convert between the default module styles, which we will consider now.

RSS 1.0 modules, you will remember, declare everything in terms of RDF resources. This is done with the rdf:resource attribute. For example, a fictional element pet: image, used to denote an image of the feed author's pet, would be written:

```
<pet:image rdf:resource="URI_OF_IMAGE"/>
```

whereas in RSS 2.0, the default lack of RDF means you must just declare the URI of the image as a literal string:

```
<pet:image>URI_OF_IMAGE</pet:image>
```

But the differences go deeper than this, as we will now see as we design a new module: mod_Book.

Case Study: mod_Book

My wife and I are currently planning on moving from London, England, to Sweden. To that effect, much of the contents of our home is already in storage, and most of this is books. We sent 86 tea chests full of books to the warehouse, and we still have plenty more to go.

Many people really like our books, many people like to borrow them, and for many reasons it would be quite cool to be able to put the details of books we have into an RSS feed. When we unpack the books, we will most likely scan their barcodes and order our library (we're geeky like that), so we will have all sorts of data available.

So, the challenge is to design an RSS module for both 1.0 and 2.0 that can deal with books.

What Do We Know?

The first thing to think about is precisely what knowledge we already have about the thing we are trying to describe. With books, we know a great deal:

- The title
- The author
- The publisher
- The ISBN number
- The subject

- The date of publication
- The content itself

There are also, alas, things that we might think we know, but which we in fact do not. In the case of books, unless we are dealing with a specific edition in a specific place at a specific time, we do not know the number of pages, the price, the printer, the paper quality, or how critics received it. We might think we do—after all, I bought most of these books, and I can touch them and pick them up—but for the sake of sharable data these are not universally useful values. They will change with time and are not internationally sharable. Remember that once it has left your machine, the data you create—in this case each item—is lost to you. As the first author, it is your responsibility to create it in such a way that it retains its value for as long as possible with as wide an audience as possible.

So, rule 1 of module design is: *decide what data you know, and what data you do not know*.

Can We Express This Data Already?

Rule 2 of module design is: *if possible, use another module's element to deliver the same information*.

This is another key point. It is much less work to leverage the efforts of others, and when many people have spent time introducing Dublin Core support to desktop readers, for example, we should reward them by using Dublin Core as much as possible. Module elements need to be created only if there is no suitable alternative already in the wild.

So, to reexamine our data:

The title
> Titles can be written within the core `title` element of either 1.0 or 2.0, or within the `dc:title` element of the Dublin Core module. One should always strive to use the core namespace first, so `title` it is.

The author
> Here we have the first core split between 1.0 and 2.0. In 2.0, we can use the core author element. There is no such thing in 1.0, so we are forced to use the `dc:creator` element of Dublin Core. Because one should always strive to use the core namespace first, RSS 2.0 users should use `author`. But because we want to have as simple a module specification as possible, we might like to use the same element in both module versions. One way of doing this would be to import the RSS 2.0 namespace into the 1.0 feed and use `author` in both. However, this cannot be done. RSS 2.0's root namespace is `""`. We can't import that, as we don't have a namespace URI to point to. We could possibly use the URL of the 2.0 specification document as the URI, declare `xmlns:rss2="http://backend.userland.com/rss"`, and then use `rss2:author`, but because the URI is different,

technically this does not refer to the same vocabulary as the one used in RSS 2.0. As we will see, using the same element—even if it is in a slightly different syntax—is very useful indeed for the authors of RSS applications. So, for the sake of simplicity, I'm opting for dc:creator. We also have the option of using dc:contributor to denote a contributor.

The publisher

Publishers are lovely people and happily have their very own Dublin Core element, dc:publisher.

The ISBN number

ISBN numbers are fantastically useful here. Because the ISBN governing body ensures that each ISBN number is unique to its book, this can serve as a globally unique identifier. What's more, we can even turn an ISBN into a URI by using the format *urn:isbn:0123456789*. For RSS 1.0, this will prove remarkably useful, as we will discuss in a moment. Meanwhile, denoting the ISBN is a good idea. Let's invent a new element. Choosing book as the namespace prefix, let's call it book:isbn.

The subject

A book's subject can be a matter of debate—especially with fiction—so it may not be entirely sane to make this element mandatory or to trust it. Nevertheless, we do have ways of writing it. RSS 2.0's core element category may help here, as would dc:subject, especially when used with RSS 1.0 mod_taxonomy.

All of these schemes, however, rely on being able to place the subject within a greater hierarchy. Fortunately, library scientists are hard at work on this, and there are many to choose from. For our purposes, we will use the Open Directory hierarchy—just to provide continuity throughout this book.

The date of publication

Again, here we have a clash between the extended core of RSS 2.0 and RSS 1.0's use of Dublin Core. Within RSS 2.0 we have pubDate available, and within RSS 1.0 we rely on dc:date. Given that Dublin Core is more widely recognized within the RDF world and perfectly valid within the RSS 2.0 world, it saves time and effort to standardize on it. This is a good example of rule 3: *as you cannot tell people what they can't do with your data, you must make it easy for them to do what they want.*

The content itself

We have the content itself. The core description does not work here—we're talking about the content, not a précis of it, and we certainly do not want to include all of the content, so content:encoded is out too. We really need an element to contain an excerpt of the book, the opening paragraph, for example.

Hurrah! We can invent a new element! Let's call it book:openingPara.

So, out of all the information we want to include, we need to invent only two new elements: book:isbn and book:openingPara. This is not a bad thing: modules do not just consist of masses of new elements slung out into the public. They should also include guidance as to the proper usage of existing modules in the new context. Reuse and recycle as much as possible.

To summarize, we now have:

```
<title/>
<dc:author/>
<dc:publisher/>
<book:isbn/>
<dc:subject/>
<dc:date/>
<book:openingPara/>
```

Putting the New Elements to Work with RSS 2.0

Before creating the feed item, we need to decide on what the link will point to. Given that my book collection is not web-addressable in that way, I'm going to point people to the relevant page on *http://isbn.nu*—Glenn Fleishman's book-price comparison site.

For an RSS 2.0 item, we can therefore use Example 11-1.

Example 11-1. mod_Book for RSS 2.0

```
<item>
  <title>Down and Out in the Magic Kingdom</title>
  <link>http://isbn.nu/0765304368/</link>
  <dc:author>Cory Doctorow</dc:author>
  <dc:publisher>Tor Books</dc:publisher>
  <book:isbn>0765304368</book:isbn>
  <dc:subject>Fiction</dc:subject>
  <dc:date>2003-02-01T00:01+00:00</dc:date>
  <book:openingPara> I lived long enough to see the cure for death; to see the rise of the
Bitchun Society, to learn ten languages; to compose three symphonies; to realize my
boyhood dream of taking up residence in Disney World; to see the death of the workplace
and of work.</book:openingPara>
</item>
```

As you can see in this simple strand of RSS 2.0, the inclusion of book metadata is easy. We know all about the book, and a mod_Book-compatible reader can allow us to read the first paragraph and, if it appeals, to click on the link and buy it. All is good.

Putting the New Elements to Work with RSS 1.0

With RSS 1.0, we must make a few changes. First, we need to assign the book a URI for the rdf:about attribute of item. This is not as straightforward as you might think. We need to think about precisely what we are describing. In this case, the choice is between a specific book—the one that is sitting on my desk right now—and the concept of that book, of which my specific book is one example.

The URI determines this. If I make the URI *http://www.benhammersley.com/ myLibrary/catalogue/0765304368*, then the item refers to my own copy: one discreet object.

If, however, I make the URI *urn:isbn:0765304368*, then the item refers to the general concept of Cory Doctorow's book. For our purposes here, this is the one to go for. If I were producing an RSS feed for a lending library, it might be different. Example 11-2 makes these changes to mod_Book in RSS 1.0.

Example 11-2. mod_Book in RSS 1.0

```
<item rdf:about="urn:isbn:0765304368">
  <title>Down and Out in the Magic Kingdom</title>
  <link>http://isbn.nu/0765304368/</link>
  <dc:author>Cory Doctorow</dc:author>
  <dc:publisher>Tor Books</dc:publisher>
  <book:isbn>0765304368</book:isbn>
  <dc:subject>Fiction</dc:subject>
  <dc:date>2003-02-01T00:01+00:00</dc:date>
  <book:openingPara> I lived long enough to see the cure for death; to see the rise of the
Bitchun Society, to learn ten languages; to compose three symphonies; to realize my
boyhood dream of taking up residence in Disney World; to see the death of the workplace
and of work.</book:openingPara>
</item>
```

The second thing to think about is the preference for all the element values within RSS 1.0 to be rdf:resources and not literal strings. To this end, we need to assign URIs to each of the values we can. It is possible within RSS 1.0 to keep extending all the information you have to greater and greater detail. At this point, you must think about your audience. If you foresee people using the feed for only the simplest of tasks—such as displaying the list in a reader or on a site—then you can stop now. If you foresee people using the data in deeper, more interesting applications, then you need to give guidance as to how far each element should be extended.

For the purposes of this chapter, we need to go no further, but for an example we will anyway. Example 11-3 expands the dc:author element via RDF and the use of a new RDF vocabulary—FOAF, or Friend of a Friend (see *http://www.rdfweb.org*).

Example 11-3. Expanding the module even further

```
<?xml version="1.0"?>
<rdf:RDF
xmlns:rdf="http://www.w3.org/1999/02/22-rdf-syntax-ns#"
xmlns:dc="http://purl.org/dc/elements/1.1/"
xmlns:foaf="http://xmlns.com/foaf/0.1/"
xmlns:book="http://www.exampleurl.com/namespaces"
xmlns="http://purl.org/rss/1.0/"
>

<item rdf:about="urn:isbn:0765304368">
  <title>Down and Out in the Magic Kingdom</title>
```

Example 11-3. Expanding the module even further (continued)

```
<link>http://isbn.nu/0765304368/</link>
<dc:author rdf:resource="mailto:doctorow@craphound.com" />
<dc:publisher>Tor Books</dc:publisher>
<book:isbn>0765304368</book:isbn>
<dc:subject>Fiction</dc:subject>
<dc:date>2003-02-01T00:01+00:00</dc:date>
  <book:openingPara> I lived long enough to see the cure for death; to see the rise of the
Bitchun Society, to learn ten languages; to compose three symphonies; to realize my
boyhood dream of taking up residence in Disney World; to see the death of the workplace
and of work.</book:openingPara>
</item>

<dc:author rdf:about="mailto:doctorow@craphound.com">
 <foaf:Person>
   <foaf:name>Cory Doctorow</foaf:name>
   <foaf:title>Mr</foaf:title>
   <foaf:firstName>Cory</foaf:firstName>
   <foaf:surname>Doctorow</foaf:surname>
   <foaf:homepage rdf:resource="http://www.craphound.com"/>
   <foaf:workPlaceHomepage rdf:resource="http://www.eff.org/" />
 </foaf:Person>
</dc:author>

</rdf:RDF>
```

Because only you, as the module designer, know the scope of the data you want to put across, you must document your module accordingly. Speaking of which…

Documentation

You *must* document your module. It is obligatory. The place to do this is at the address you are using as the namespace URI. Without documentation, no one will know precisely what you mean, and no one will be able to support your module. Without support, the module is worthless on the wider stage.

Extending Your Desktop Reader

Of the 30 or so desktop viewers to appear, most are closed source and either share-ware or try-then-buy packages. For our pedagogic purposes, therefore, they are not much good. (As products in their own right, of course, things may be a different. I am not making any comment as to the value of commercial packages, apart from the fact that I can't show you their code and explain how it works. For commercial success, this is irrelevant, but for this book it is quite key.)

For our purposes, therefore, one relative newcomer gives us plenty of scope. So, for the rest of this chapter, we will look at the brainchild of Morbus Iff (or Kevin Hemenway to the uncool): AmphetaDesk.

Introducing AmphetaDesk

AmphetaDesk was started by Morbus Iff in January 2001 and continues in development. In this book, we will be working with Version 0.93. Apart from being a very popular tool for reading RSS feeds, AmphetaDesk's internal architecture makes it eminently hackable and a great way to learn how to use RSS feeds in your own programs. It also runs on Windows, Linux, and Mac OS, so most readers will be able to try it out.

The system works like this: the workings are written in Perl and HTML templates and come accompanied by an operating system–specific program that acts as the Perl interpreter. Because of this, you can access and change the source code even while the program is running, and you will see the changes happen immediately. Plus, you can add any feature you like by just dropping the correct Perl module into the right directory and writing a template file to call it.

In this section, we will download AmphetaDesk, install it, and examine how it works, and then move on to customizing it.

Installing AmphetaDesk

Installing AmphetaDesk is simplicity itself—download the latest version from *http://www.disobey.com/amphetadesk/*, unpack the archive, and save the resulting directory structure and files to wherever you want to keep it. You are then presented with the following files and directories:

/AmphetaDesk.exe
> The AmphetaDesk runtime file. This is the file you run to use the program. It contains all the necessary aspects of Perl needed by your machine to go about its RSS-reading business.

/AmphetaDesk.pl
> The Perl version of the AmphetaDesk runtime file.

/data/myChannels.opml
> An OPML file containing the details of the feeds to which you are subscribed.

/data/mySettings.xml
> An XML file containing the user's settings.

/data/channels/
> A directory to contain local copies of the subscribed-to feeds.

/data/internal/
> This directory contains files created and used as the program is running, namely:

> */data/internal/version.txt*
>> This file contains the version number of the AmphetaDesk installation you are using. It is compared at startup with a version on the AmphetaDesk server, and appropriate messages are displayed.

/data/internal/AmphetaDesk.log

This file, recreated every time you run AmphetaDesk, contains the logged messages from the program—very useful for debugging.

/data/lists/

The directory that stores lists of RSS feeds (called *channels* in this context) that you can add to your AmphetaDesk display. It consists of:

/data/lists/services-channels-complete.xml

This lists all the channel services that are still publishing something. The feed is not checked for anything at all, bar actually being there to read.

/data/lists/services-channels-failure.xml

This lists all the feeds that have failed to be retrieved correctly three times in a row.

/data/lists/services-channels-recent.xml

This is a cut-down version of the complete list, removing only those feeds known definitively to have not updated within the month.

/docs

The directory that contains the system documentation and one subdirectory:

/docs/images

The directory that contains images for use within the documentation.

/lib

The directory that contains the Perl modules used by the program. It contains:

AmphetaDesk.pm

This controls the data traffic between the different modules and the templates.

/lib/AmphetaDesk/

This directory contains all the original modules used within the workings of AmphetaDesk. These include:

/lib/AmphetaDesk/Channels.pm

AmphetaDesk::Channels handles the parsing of the feed. It takes the feed and returns it in a common data structure, regardless of which version of RSS you are using.

/lib/AmphetaDesk/ChannelsList.pm

AmphetaDesk::ChannelsList handles the channel listing in the "Add a Channel" section of the program. It takes an OPML file and converts it into something more useful for displaying on the screen.

/lib/AmphetaDesk/MyChannels.pm

AmphetaDesk::MyChannels handles all the functions that deal with the user's subscription list.

/lib/AmphetaDesk/Settings.pm

AmphetaDesk::Settings controls the program settings: loading, saving, and providing an API for changing every tweakable configuration.

/lib/AmphetaDesk/Utilities.pm

AmphetaDesk::Utilities provides all the little functions needed to make RSS readers run nicely—strip_newlines_and_tabs, for example.

/lib/AmphetaDesk/Versioning.pm

AmphetaDesk::Versioning handles the versioning of the package—it checks to see if the installation you are using is the latest, by comparing */data/internal/version.txt* with the AmphetaDesk server's mirror.

/lib/AmphetaDesk/WebServer.pm

AmphetaDesk::WebServer provides a subclass of the HTTP::Daemon module used to serve the pages the system creates. As the author says in the comments, "This package is here merely to provide a subclass for HTTP::Daemon so that we can override the product_tokens routine and set our own Server name."

/lib/AmphetaDesk/WWW.pm

AmphetaDesk::WWW provides functions that work to retrieve data from the Net.

/lib/Text/Template.pm

The classic Text::Template module, written by Mark-Jason Dominus, deals with replacing text in templates. As the user interface to AmphetaDesk is written in templates, this module is required to make it work.

/lib/XML/Simple.pm

Our old friend from Chapter 8, XML::Simple is a simple XML parser. AmphetaDesk uses it to make sense of the feeds it retrieves.

/templates/default

The *templates* directory and its subdirectories hold the template files that AmphetaDesk parses through Text::Template. It is here that we find *index.html*—the page that displays the feeds' content—which we will now customize.

index.html

AmphetaDesk works by first downloading the feed and then using *Channels.pm* to convert it to a common data structure. This lessens the load on the next section, the templates, as they need to give the address of the data they want within only one structure, and not two different versions for 1.0 and 2.0.

If you open *index.html* in a text editor, you will find, about halfway down, the following code:

```
foreach my $item (@{$data->{item}}) {

# check to see if mod_content is used, which is a module to RSS 1.0
# allowing more data in a feed as well as embedded HTML. this is NOT
# a full implementation, as it'll only support CDATA's. if it does
# exist, then we stick the data into our $item->{description}.
```

```
my $rdf_value = $item->{"content:items"}{"rdf:Bag"}{"rdf:li"}{"content:item"}{"rdf:
value"}
if defined($item->{"content:items"}{"rdf:Bag"}{"rdf:li"}{"content:item"}{"rdf:
value"});
        $item->{description} = $rdf_value if defined($rdf_value);

# display the actual item.
$OUT .= qq{          };

$OUT .= qq{<tr><td width="15" bgcolor="#ffffff"> </td><td bgcolor="#ffffff"
align="left">};

$OUT .= qq{<a href="$item->{link}" target="$link_target">} if $item->{link};
$OUT .= qq{$item->{title}} if $item->{title};
$OUT .= qq{</a>} if $item->{link};

$OUT .= qq{ $item->{description} } if $item->{description};

$OUT .= qq{</td></tr>\n};

        }
```

As you can see, this will step through each `item` in the feed, take the contents of the `link`, `title`, and `description` elements, and output some HTML with the form:

```
<a href="LINK" target="_blank">TITLE</a> DESCRIPTION
```

Those links are surrounded by some table markup to make them look pretty, as shown in Figure 11-1.

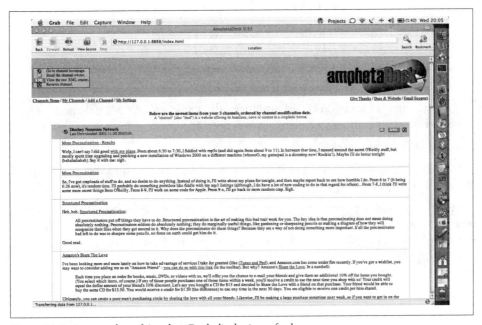

Figure 11-1. A screenshot of AmphetaDesk displaying a feed

Adding code to this template to allow it to display your module is therefore quite straightforward. Note the section of the code that does the work:

```
$OUT .= qq{<a href="$item->{link}" target="$link_target">} if $item->{link};
$OUT .= qq{$item->{title}} if $item->{title};
$OUT .= qq{</a>} if $item->{link};

$OUT .= qq{$item->{description} } if $item->{description};

$OUT .= qq{</td></tr>\n};
```

By slipping in our own code, we can take the value we want from our module. In this case, I'd like to allow people to buy one of the books in my feed from the popular online store Amazon.com.

By experimentation, I know that the URL *http://www.amazon.com/exec/obidos/ASIN/* followed by the ISBN number will lead to the correct page. This seems to be a good use for the book:isbn element.

I also know that people using my module might not have included a description element. So, I will want to get book:openingPara in there somewhere.

No problem:

```
$OUT .= qq{<a href="$item->{link}" target="$link_target">} if $item->{link};
$OUT .= qq{$item->{title}} if $item->{title};
$OUT .= qq{</a>} if $item->{link};

$OUT .= qq{<a href="http://www.amazon.com/exec.obidos/ASIN/$item->{"book:isdn"}">Buy
At Amazon</a>} if $item->{"book:isdn"};

$OUT .= qq{$item->{description} } if $item->{description};
$OUT .= qq{<blockquote>$item->{"book:openingPara"}</blockquote> } if $item->{"book:
openingPara"};

$OUT .= qq{</td></tr>\n};
```

Note that whereas $item->{title} produces the value of the title element, if you want to bring in a namespaced element, you need to wrap it in quotes:

```
$item->{"book:openingPara"}
```

If you save *index.html* and refresh it in your browser, you will find that the template will now display mod_Book information. Cool, huh?

You can now add support for your own modules in the same way. Be sure to pass any changes you make back to Morbus Iff at *http://www.disobey.com/amphetadesk*. He will likely include it in the next release, and you will have made the RSS world a better place for it.

## CHAPTER 12

Publish and Subscribe

*The trouble with being punctual is that
there's nobody there to appreciate it.*
—Franklin P. Jones

The traditional guidelines for the use of RSS feeds present a small problem. There is always going to be a balance between the need to be up-to-date and the need to refrain from abusing the feed publisher's server by requesting the feed every few seconds. While the norm is to request the feed a maximum of once an hour, many feeds deserve following much more closely. Conversely, many feeds update only once a day, or less often. Requesting those once an hour is a waste of time and resources and potentially expensive for the publisher. In this chapter, we look at the two systems currently prescribed for RSS feeds to solve these problems.

Introducing Publish and Subscribe

The problems of efficient delivery of information have existed for far longer than RSS has, as have techniques for addressing them. Indeed, both the systems described in this chapter follow the classic Gang of Four "Observer" design pattern. It is perhaps from the other title of this pattern that the name of the technique arises: Publish and Subscribe.

Let's think of the situation from above. We have a feed, and this feed has its users. The users take the feed and do what they will—we've already seen some examples of potential uses in the previous chapters—but each of the users depends on his copy of the feed (whether in memory, or converted to another format and saved) being up-to-date. In order for this to happen, the users *subscribe* to a system that watches the feed continuously. This system then *publishes* notifications to all of the users when the feed changes. The users are then responsible for updating their copies of the feed, ordinarily by requesting it from the server.

There are two ways of implementing such a system within RSS: one with the relevant elements included in RSS 0.92 and 2.0, and the other suggested by an RSS 1.0 module. We will deal with these in turn.

Publish and Subscribe Within RSS 0.92 and 2.0

RSS 0.92's Publish and Subscribe system is the result of work by Userland Software, and its CEO Dave Winer. It was introduced with, and perhaps inspired, the release of RSS 0.92, and features heavily in Userland products. Furthermore, its workings are based on XML-RPC and SOAP, two protocols that Winer was instrumental in starting. But that is not to say that RSS 0.92's Publish and Subscribe is in any way proprietary—it is not.

We have three characters to watch in this drama: the user, the feed, and the Publish and Subscribe system, better known as the cloud. Here is the process:

1. The user's system sends a message, via either XML-RPC, SOAP, or HTTP-POST, to the cloud to subscribe. This message contains five parameters:
   - The name of the procedure that the cloud should call to notify the user of changes.
   - The TCP port on which the user's system is listening.
   - The path to the user's system. This is all that is needed, as the user's system will be running either XML-RPC or SOAP, both of which use HTTP as their transport layer, and the cloud can determine the IP address of the caller from the initial request. This has a nice security benefit: one user cannot make a registration call on behalf of another.
   - A string indicating which protocol to use, either XML-RPC or SOAP, when the cloud messages the user.
   - A list of URLs of RSS files to be watched.

2. If the registration is successful, the cloud returns true; if not, it returns an error.

3. Somewhat later on, the cloud either detects or is informed of a change in the feed.

4. The cloud messages the user using the protocol requested, giving the URL of the changed feed.

5. The user requests the fresh feed from its server and does what she likes with it.

Note that by design, the RSS 0.92 Publish and Subscribe system expires subscriptions after 25 hours, forcing them to be renewed every day.

As we have already seen in Chapter 4, the RSS 0.92 Publish and Subscribe system is denoted in the RSS feed with the cloud element:

```
<cloud domain="DOMAIN NAME or IP ADDRESS of the cloud"
       port="TCP port on which the cloud is listening"
       path="The path to the cloud's listener"
       registerProcedure="The procedure name to register with the cloud"
       protocol="either xml-rpc or soap, case-sensitive" />
```

You see that we talk of passing messages via XML-RPC or SOAP? These may require some explanation. The two protocols are the basis of the fashionable technology known collectively as *web services*. We have already used some web services in previous chapters: getting information from Google using SOAP, for example. With those examples, we were passing a query, encoded in XML, and getting a set of results back, also encoded in XML. In the case of RSS 0.92 Publish and Subscribe, we are doing something similar: passing XML-encoded messages between systems. What makes the RSS 0.92 Publish and Subscribe system different from the other uses of web services we have already seen is that the user's system has to not only pass a message and wait for a reply, but also continually listen for other systems trying to talk to it. For this reason, it cannot be used with machines that reside behind Network Address Translation (NAT) systems. The user's machine must be directly addressable from the rest of the Internet, and it must be listening for people trying to do so.

To see how this works in practice, we will now build our own basic RSS 0.92 Publish and Subscribe system.

Learning XML-RPC and SOAP

O'Reilly publishes some very good books on the implementation of XML-RPC and SOAP. You may be interested in reading the following:

- *Programming Web Services with XML-RPC*, by Simon St. Laurent, Joe Johnston, and Edd Dumbill
- *Web Services Essentials*, by Ethan Cerami
- *Programming Web Services with SOAP*, by Doug Tidwell, James Snell, and Pavel Kulchenko

---

RSS 0.92 Publish and Subscribe has, at the time of this writing, been publicly implemented twice. Userland Software incorporates it directly into their own products, and NewsIsFree (*http://www.newsisfree.com*), the RSS aggregator site run by Mike Krus, uses it as well. Both services produce feeds with a `cloud` element, and both run servers that will notify you of changes to the feeds.

These are both nice services, but what if you want to use your own Publish and Subscribe system to update, say, a web site's rendering of a feed? No problem—we just roll our own Publish and Subscribe system, as we will in a moment.

Publish and Subscribe with RSS 1.0

As it stands, the RSS 0.92 version of Publish and Subscribe is currently unavailable to standard RSS 1.0 users; it exists neither in the core specification nor in any published modules known to me. But that is not to say that you cannot create a module to import the `cloud` element. You are, of course, at liberty to do so.

Meanwhile, the rest of us may be looking at the mod_changedpage module. This Publish and Subscribe module, written by Aaron Swartz, is fundamentally different from the system used with RSS 0.92. Where the latter uses web services protocols to communicate between systems, mod_changedpage uses simple HTTP POST procedures to handle the same job.

It works like this: the RSS 1.0 feed's channel contains the single element cp:server, which contains simply the URL of the Publish and Subscribe service for the feed. A user who wants to subscribe to notifications for this feed sends an HTTP POST request to that URL, taking two parameters:

responder
>   The URL of the user's mod_changedpage system

target
>   The URL of the feed we want to monitor:

>>   *responder=http%3A%2F%2FURL.OF*
>>   *USERSSYSTEM&target=httP%3A%2F%2FURL OF FEED*

(Notice that the :// of the URLs within the parameters are entity encoded as %3A%2F%2F.)

The original proposal document for this specification states:

> Additional attributes should be allowed before or after the URL. Implementations should ignore attributes they don't understand. The order of the attributes is not significant. Content-Type should be specified as "application/x-www-form-urlencoded".

> If this sounds familiar, it should be. This is how HTML forms are encoded, as described in the HTML spec.

Either way, the URL is received at the Publish and Subscribe service, which returns a HTTP status code of 200 if the subscription is successful and an HTTP status code of 400 if the subscription failed (it is also recommended that a 400 code should be accompanied by a plain-text file explaining the error as far as possible).

When the feed updates, the Publish and Subscribe system sends a similar HTTP POST request, with one parameter—the URL of the changed feed:

>   *url=http %3A%2F%2FURL.OF.CHANGEDFEED*

The user's system can then do what it likes with that feed.

Rolling Your Own: LinkPimp PubSub

Having said all that, and given that there are currently no implementations of mod_changedpage to receive pages from, we will concentrate on working with cloud. What's more, every cloud implementation in the wild uses XML-RPC, so, for simplicity, this is all we will support here. Extending the script to support SOAP and HTTP-POST would not be hard, if necessary, but it probably won't be necessary.

The following Publish and Subscribe (PubSub) system is for web sites displaying various feeds, rendered into XHTML and inserted onto the page using a server-side include. It is currently working live on the test site: *http://www.linkpimp.com*.

This system also incorporates two other things we have already discussed. First, it renders the feed into XHTML—we can leave the on-screen formatting to a style sheet—but the subroutine that does this is quite obvious in the code and can be turned to do something else—send IM notifications, for example.

Second, it uses Syndic8's API and subscription list service to tell it which feeds to examine. This allows us not only to play with the Syndic8 system, but also to add or remove feeds from the site without touching its code. I can merely log on to Syndic8 and subscribe to a feed there, and it should be incorporated into the site within the hour. It is rough and ready, but you will undoubtedly get ideas of your own from it.

The system comes in two parts:

LinkpimpClient.pl
> This script retrieves a subscription list from Syndic8, using that site's XML-RPC interface, checks to see if any of the feeds contain a cloud element, and subscribes, if necessary. It then renders the feeds into XHTML, if necessary, and saves them to disk. It then creates a new file called *feeds.shtml*, which contains the server-side include instructions to include the feeds. This script is run hourly. Example 12-1, later in this chapter, contains the complete listing.

LinkpimpListener.pl
> This script listens out for Publish and Subscribe notifications and refreshes the rendered feed when necessary. This script is run as a daemon. Example 12-2, later in this chapter, contains the complete listing.

Running the system creates three files internal to its working:

logfile.txt
> The system creates a verbose log, for purposes of explaining what is happening. You can disable this, if you wish.

pubsub.txt
> This file holds the URL and last-subscription-time of all the feeds to which you have Publish and Subscribe subscriptions. It must not be deleted. *LinkpimpStrimmer.pl* keeps it healthy, by stripping it of URLs older than 24 hours.

Feeds.shtml
> This file contains the server-side include instructions for displaying the feeds on your page. In turn, it should be called in with its own SSI directive from your customer-facing page, using the command:
>
> ```
> <!--#include file="feeds.shtml" -->
> ```

LinkpimpClient.pl

LinkpimpClient.pl deals with the majority of the tasks needed for this system. Although feeds can be PubSub-enabled via XML-RPC, SOAP, HTTP POST, or not at all, and while for completeness we should be able to deal with all of these situations to make a Publish and Subscribe system fully spec-compliant, XML-RPC is the only system being used at the moment and the only one we will discuss here.

So, onward! Example 12-1 shows the entire program listing, but first let's step through the interesting bits to illustrate a few points.

After setting up the necessary variables and loading the modules, we get to the section of the program that deals with the current subscriptions. When the program is run for the first time, this section is irrelevant, but since we'll probably run this script every hour from cron, it soon becomes necessary. Subscriptions last for 25 hours, so we need to make sure they are renewed in time.

```
logger ("\n Program started. Let's go!\n");

# First we need to strim the PubSub records and remove all the old entries.

# Work out the time 25 hours ago (1 hour = 3600 seconds, so 25 hours = 90000 seconds)
my $oldestpossibletime = time() - 90000;

logger ("The oldest allowable  subscription  cannot have been made earlier than
$oldestpossibletime");

# Open the subscriber list created by pubSubListener and stick it in an array.
open (PUBSUBLIST, "<$pubsublog");
my @lines = <PUBSUBLIST>;
close (PUBSUBLIST);

# Clear the subscriber list.
unlink ($pubsublog) or die "Can't delete the data file\n";
logger ("Old Subscription list deleted");

# We need to prevent the file being empty, even if there are no subscriptions, so:
open (NEWPUBSUBLIST, ">$pubsublog");
print NEWPUBSUBLIST "This holds the details of all your subscriptions , 0000001\n";

# Go through each line, splitting it back into the right variables.
foreach $line (@lines) {
            my ($rssUrl , $time) = split (/,/, "$line");

    # If the time the notification request was made ($time) is later than 25 hours
ago
    # ($oldestpossibletime) then stick that line back into the data file.

                if ($time > $oldestpossibletime)
            {
            print NEWPUBSUBLIST "$line\n";
                    };
            };
```

```
    logger ("New PubSublist written");

    close (NEWPUBSUBLIST);
```

We're storing the current subscriptions in a file called *pubsub.txt*. This section opens the file, loads it into an array, and then deletes it. We then rewrite the file line-by-line if, and only if, the line is younger than the oldest possible time allowed (i.e., 24-hours old).

We then open the new file and read the lines into another array, which we will work with later:

```
# Now, we reopen the pubsublog, and load it as a string for use later
open (PUBSUB, "$pubsublog");
$/ = '';
my $content_of_pubsublog = <PUBSUB>;
```

Notice the $/=''; line. This changes the delimiter for the line-input operator used in the next line. By default, saying my$content_of_pubsublog=<PUBSUB>; only loads the file until the first new line. By setting the delimiter to null, we have the operator just scoop the whole file up in one swallow.

The next section then loads the subscription list from Syndic8 in the manner described in Chapter 10. We then enter a loop, loading the RSS files one-by-one, and examine them for PubSub-related elements:

```
# Take the next line from the array of DataURLs
foreach $url (@edited_subscribed_feeds_list) {
            logger ("Now working with $url");
            # Check the feed is not on the list of subscribed-to feeds
            if ($content_of_pubsublog =~ m/$url/i ) {
            logger ("Subscription already present, it seems. Excellent. I will get
on with the next one.");
            #We leave the main loop and move onto the next URL
            } else {
            # Retrieve the RSS feed
              $retrieved_feed = get ($url);
              logger ("Retrieved Feed from $url");
            # Examine for <cloud>
              if ($retrieved_feed =~ m/<cloud/) {
              &there_is_a_cloud
              } else {
              logger("There is no cloud element");
              # Stick it through print_html, with an error trap here
              eval {&print_html};
              logger ("The parsing choked on $url with this error\n $@ \n") if
$@;

            }
            };
```

This section runs a series of tests. First it checks to see if we are already subscribed to the feed. If so, we move straight on to the next one. Why? Because one of the reasons for Publish and Subscribe is to lessen the load on the publisher's server. If we were to retrieve the feed every hour anyway, we would ruin this aspect of the idea.

If we are not subscribed, we retrieve the feed and run the other tests, using regular expressions to check for cloud elements. I realize the mention of regexps will have sent many of you into a swoon. They are here because they fulfill a very simple purpose (in other words: tough). Because these elements appear only when Publish and Subscribe is allowed for, if they are found, we can spin the program off into the relevant subroutine. If no cloud element is found, we just go straight-ahead and parse the feed using the subroutine &print_html, which works as we described in Chapter 8. If we find a cloud element, we spin the program off to the there_is_a_cloud subroutine

RSS 0.92's Publish and Subscribe standard requires dealing with either XML-RPC or SOAP, depending on the whim of the publisher. Our system must be able to deal with both. Here it is:

```
sub there_is_a_cloud {

    logger ("We're not subscribed, so I will attempt to subscribe to the $url");

    # First we must parse the <cloud> element with $retrieved_feed. This is in a set
format:
    # e.g <cloud domain="www.newsisfree.com" port="80" path="/RPC"
registerProcedure="hpe.rssPleaseNotify" protocol="xml-rpc" />
    # We'll do this with XML::Simple.

    my $parsed_xml = XMLin($retrieved_feed);

    my $cloud_domain = $parsed_xml->{channel}->{cloud}->{domain};
    my $cloud_port = $parsed_xml->{channel}->{cloud}->{port};
    my $cloud_path = $parsed_xml->{channel}->{cloud}->{path};
    my $cloud_registerProcedure = $parsed_xml->{channel}->{cloud}->{registerProcedure};
    my $cloud_protocol = $parsed_xml->{channel}->{cloud}->{protocol};

    logger ("We have retrieved the PubSub data from the RSS 0.92 feed.");
    logger ("The cloud domain is $cloud_domain");
    logger ("The port is $cloud_port");
    logger ("The path is $cloud_path");
    logger ("The port is $cloud_registerProcedure");
    logger ("The protocol is $cloud_protocol");

    # The protocol is all important. We need to differentiate between SOAP users, those
who like XML-RPC, and the big men of HTTP-POST.

    if ($cloud_protocol eq "xml-rpc") {
        # Marvellous. That done, we spawn a new xml:rpc client.
        my $pubsub_call = Frontier::Client -> new ( url => "http://$cloud_domain:
$cloud_port$cloud_path",
                    debug => 0,
                    use_objects => 1);
        # Then call the remote procedure with the rss url, as per the spec.

        $pubsub_call->call($cloud_registerProcedure,$pubsub_listening_procedure,$pubsub_
port,$pubsub_path,$cloud_protocol,$url);
```

```
        logger ("I've asked for the subscription");
            } else {
                logger ("The protocol requested is not yet supported");
                return 1;
                }

    # Now add the url and the time it was made to the pubsublog
    open (PUBSUBLOG, ">>$pubsublog");
    my $time = time( );
    print PUBSUBLOG "$url , $time\n";
    close PUBSUBLOG;

    # That's it: return to the next one in the list.
    };
```

In this script, we have checked for the protocol attribute of the cloud element and reacted accordingly. We then parse the feed for the first time in the usual way and move onto the next URL.

The complete listing is shown in Example 12-1.

Example 12-1. LinkpimpClient.pl

```perl
#!/usr/bin/perl -w

use diagnostics;
use warnings;

use XML::RSS;
use XML::Simple;
use LWP::Simple;
use Frontier::Client;
use Frontier::RPC2;
use File::Copy;
use SOAP::Lite;
use LWP::UserAgent;

# User changable variables

my $logging          = "1";
my $logfile          = "logfile.txt";
my $pubsublog        = "pubsub.txt";
my $includefile      = "feeds.shtml";
my $tempincludefile  = "feeds.shtml.tmp";

my $syndic8_userid    = "bhammersley";
my $syndic8_password  = "joe90";
my $syndic8_list_id   = "0";
my $syndic8_XMLRPC_path = "http://www.syndic8.com:80/xmlrpc.php";

my $pubsub_listening_procedure = "updatedFeed";
my $pubsub_port                = "8889";
my $pubsub_path                = "/RPC2";
my $pubsub_protocol            = "xml-rpc";
```

Example 12-1. LinkpimpClient.pl (continued)

```perl
my $content;
my $file;
my $line;

our $url;
our $retrieved_feed;
our $feed_spec;


####################################################

logger ("\n Program started. Let's go!\n");

# First we need to strim the pubsub records and remove all the old entries.

# Work out the time 25 hours ago (1 hour = 3600 seconds, so 25 hours = 90000 seconds).
my $oldestpossibletime = time() - 90000;

logger ("The oldest allowable subscription cannot have been made earlier than
$oldestpossibletime");

# Open the subscriber list created by pubSubListener and stick it in an array.
open (PUBSUBLIST, "<$pubsublog");
my @lines = <PUBSUBLIST>;
close (PUBSUBLIST);

# Clear the subscriber list.
unlink ($pubsublog) or die "Can't delete the data file\n";
logger ("Old Subscription list deleted");

# We need to prevent the file being empty, even if there are no subscriptions, so:
open (NEWPUBSUBLIST, ">$pubsublog");
print NEWPUBSUBLIST "This holds the details of all your subscriptions , 0000001\n";

# Go through each line, splitting it back into the right variables.
foreach $line (@lines) {
            my ($rssUrl , $time) = split (/,/, "$line");

            # If the time the notification request was made ($time) is later than 25
hours ago
            # ($oldestpossibletime) then stick that line back into the data file.

                    if ($time > $oldestpossibletime)
                {
                print NEWPUBSUBLIST "$line\n";
                        };
                };
logger ("New PubSublist written");

close (NEWPUBSUBLIST);

# Now, we reopen the pubsublog, and load it as a string for use later
```

Example 12-1. LinkpimpClient.pl (continued)

```perl
open (PUBSUB, "$pubsublog");
$/ = '';
my $content_of_pubsublog = <PUBSUB>;

# and we finally close the filehandle.
close (PUBSUB);

##########

# Use xmlrpc to ask for list of feeds from syndic8, and create object from result.
my $syndic8_xmlrpc_call = Frontier::Client -> new ( url => $syndic8_XMLRPC_path,
                debug => 0,
                use_objects => 1
              );

my $syndic8_xmlrpc_returned_subscriber_list = $syndic8_xmlrpc_call ->
call('syndic8.GetSubscribed',$syndic8_userid,$syndic8_password,$syndic8_list_id) or die
"Cannot retrieve Syndic8 list";
logger ("Retrieved Syndic8 subscription list");

# Place the dataurls from the subscriber list into an array.
my @edited_subscribed_feeds_list = map { $_->{dataurl} } @$syndic8_xmlrpc_returned_
subscriber_list;

# Take the next line from the array of DataURLs.
foreach $url (@edited_subscribed_feeds_list) {
                logger ("Now working with $url");
                # Check the feed is not on the list of subscribed-to feeds
                if ($content_of_pubsublog =~ m/$url/i ) {
                logger ("Subscription already present, it seems. Excellent. I will get on
with the next one.");
                #We leave the main loop and move onto the next URL
                } else {
                # Retrieve the RSS feed
                  $retrieved_feed = get ($url);
                  logger ("Retrieved Feed from $url");
                # Examine for <cloud>
                  if ($retrieved_feed =~ m/<cloud/) {
                  &there_is_a_cloud
                  } else {
                  logger("There is no cloud element");
                  # Stick it through print_html, with an error trap here
                  eval {&print_html};
                  logger ("The parsing choked on $url with this error\n $@ \n") if $@;
                  }
                };

### Replace the include file with the temporary one, and do it fast!
move ("$tempincludefile", "$includefile");

### Clean up and exit the program.
logger ("We're all done here for now. Exiting Program.\n\n");
```

Example 12-1. LinkpimpClient.pl (continued)

```perl
END;

######
## THE SUBROUTINES
######

sub there_is_a_cloud {

  logger ("We're not subscribed, so I will attempt to subscribe to the $url");

  # First we must parse the <cloud> element with $retrieved_feed. This is in a set format:
  # e.g <cloud domain="www.newsisfree.com" port="80" path="/RPC" registerProcedure="hpe.
rssPleaseNotify" protocol="xml-rpc" />
  # We'll do this with XML::Simple.

  my $parsed_xml = XMLin($retrieved_feed);

  my $cloud_domain = $parsed_xml->{channel}->{cloud}->{domain};
  my $cloud_port = $parsed_xml->{channel}->{cloud}->{port};
  my $cloud_path = $parsed_xml->{channel}->{cloud}->{path};
  my $cloud_registerProcedure = $parsed_xml->{channel}->{cloud}->{registerProcedure};
  my $cloud_protocol = $parsed_xml->{channel}->{cloud}->{protocol};

  logger ("We have retrieved the PubSub data from the RSS 0.92 feed.");
  logger ("The cloud domain is $cloud_domain");
  logger ("The port is $cloud_port");
  logger ("The path is $cloud_path");
  logger ("The port is $cloud_registerProcedure");
  logger ("The protocol is $cloud_protocol");

  # The protocol is all important. We need to differentiate between  SOAP users, those who
like XML-RPC, and the big men of HTTP-POST

  if ($cloud_protocol eq "xml-rpc") {
     # Marvellous. That done, we spawn a new xml:rpc client.
       my $pubsub_call = Frontier::Client -> new (  url => "http://$cloud_domain:$cloud_
port$cloud_path",
                 debug => 0,
                 use_objects => 1);
     # Then call the remote procedure with the rss url, as per the spec.

     $pubsub_call->call($cloud_registerProcedure,$pubsub_listening_procedure,$pubsub_
port,$pubsub_path,$cloud_protocol,$url);

     logger ("I've asked for the subscription");
         } else {
             logger ("The protocol requested is not yet supported");
             return 1;
              }

  # Now add the url, and the time it was made to the pubsublog.
  open (PUBSUBLOG, ">>$pubsublog");
```

Example 12-1. LinkpimpClient.pl (continued)

```perl
  my $time = time();
  print PUBSUBLOG "$url , $time\n";
  close PUBSUBLOG;

  # That's it: return to the next one in the list.
  };

######
######

sub logger {
    if ($logging eq "1") {
    open( LOG, ">>$logfile" );
    print LOG @_, "\n";
    close LOG;
    return 1;
    } else {
    return 1;}

    }

######
######

sub includefile {
     ## In order to prevent a race condition, or duplicate feeds, we can't just append
directly to the include file itself
     ## so we create a temporary include file, and then replace the real one with the
temporary one right at the end of the program.
     open (INCLUDEFILE, ">>$tempincludefile");
    print INCLUDEFILE '<!--#include file="'.$outputfile.'" -->'."\n"."<br/>"."\n";
     close INCLUDEFILE;
     return 1;
     }

#######
#######

sub print_html {

  # Create new instance of XML::RSS.
  my $rss = new XML::RSS;

  # Parse the $url and stick it in $rss.
  logger ("Now trying to parse $url");
  my $feed_to_parse = get ($url);
  $rss->parse($feed_to_parse);

  # Decide on name for outputfile.
  our $outputfile = "$rss->{'channel'}->{'title'}.html";
  $outputfile =~ s/ /_/g;
```

Example 12-1. LinkpimpClient.pl (continued)

```
# Open the output file.
logger ("I'm going to call the output file $outputfile");
open (OUTPUTFILE, ">$outputfile");

# Print the channel title.
print OUTPUTFILE '<div class="channel_link">'."\n".'<a href="';
print OUTPUTFILE "$rss->{'channel'}->{'link'}";
print OUTPUTFILE '">';
print OUTPUTFILE "$rss->{'channel'}->{'title'}</a>\n</div>\n";

# Print channel image, checking first if it exists.
if ($rss->{'image'}->{'link'}) {
  print OUTPUTFILE '<div class="channel_image">'."\n".'<a href="';
  print OUTPUTFILE "$rss->{'image'}->{'link'}";
  print OUTPUTFILE '">'."\n";
  print OUTPUTFILE '<img src="';
  print OUTPUTFILE "$rss->{'image'}->{'url'}";
  print OUTPUTFILE '" alt="';
  print OUTPUTFILE "$rss->{'image'}->{'title'}";
  print OUTPUTFILE '"/>'."\n</a>\n</div>";
  print OUTPUTFILE "\n";
        }

# Print the channel items.
print OUTPUTFILE '<div class="linkentries">'."\n"."<ul>";
print OUTPUTFILE "\n";

foreach my $item (@{$rss->{'items'}}) {
  next unless defined($item->{'title'}) && defined($item->{'link'});
  print OUTPUTFILE '<li><a href="';
  print OUTPUTFILE "$item->{'link'}";
  print OUTPUTFILE '">';
  print OUTPUTFILE "$item->{'title'}</a></li>\n";
        }
  print OUTPUTFILE "</ul>\n</div>\n";

# Close the OUTPUTFILE

close (OUTPUTFILE);
logger ("and lo $outputfile has been written.");

# Add to the include-file
includefile ($outputfile);
}
```

LinkpimpListener.pl

The other half of a Publish and Subscribe system is the listener. All the listener does is sit on a port—in this case, it is defaulting to port 8888, but you can change that—and wait for an update notification. It takes that notification and retrieves the refreshed feed, parsing it and saving it to disk, where the web server can retrieve it the next time someone requests the page. The complete listing is shown in Example 12-2.

Example 12-2. LinkpimpListener.pl

```perl
#!usr/bin/perl -w
use strict;
use HTTP::Daemon;
use Frontier::RPC2;
use HTTP::Date;
use XML::RSS;
use LWP::Simple;

# ------USER CHANGABLE VARIABLES HERE -------

my $listeningport = "8888";

# -------------------------------------------

my $methods     = {'updateFeed'              => \&updateFeed};
our $host = "";


# --------------- Start the server up -----------------------

my $listen_socket = HTTP::Daemon->new(
                    LocalPort => $listeningport,
                        Listen    => 20,
                        Proto     => 'tcp',
                        Reuse     => 1
                        );

die "Can't create a listening socket: $@" unless $listen_socket;

while (my $connection = $listen_socket->accept) {
    $host = $connection->peerhost;
    interact($connection);
    $connection->close;
      }

# ------------- The Interact subroutine, as called when a peer connects

sub interact {
    my $sock = shift;
    my $req;
    eval {
        $req = $sock->get_request;
        };

    # Check to see if the contact is both xml and to the right path.
    if( $req->header('Content-Type') eq 'text/xml'&& $req->url->path eq '/RPC2')
        {
        my $message_content      = ($req->content);
```

Example 12-2. LinkpimpListener.pl (continued)

```perl
            if( $main::Fork ){
                    my $pid = fork();
                    unless( defined $pid ){
                                                # check this response
                                                my $res = HTTP::Response->new(500,'Internal
Server Error');

                                                $sock->send_status_line();
                                                $sock->send_response($res);
                                                }
                    if( $pid == 0 ){
                                    $sock->close;
                                    $main::Fork->();
                                    exit;
                                    }

                    $main::Fork = undef;
                    }

        my $conn_host = gethostbyaddr($sock->peeraddr,AF_INET) || $sock->peerhost;

        my $res = HTTP::Response->new(200,'OK');
        $res->header(
                date            => time2str(),
                Server          => 'PubSubServer',
                Content_Type    => 'text/xml',
                );

        $res->content($res_xml);
        $sock->send_response($res);

# -----------------------------------------------------------------------

# ---- updateFeed -----

sub updateFeed      {

my ($url) = @_;

# Create new instance of XML::RSS

my $rss = new XML::RSS;

# Parse the $url and stick it in $rss

my $feed_to_parse = get ($url);
$rss->parse($feed_to_parse);

# Decide on name for outputfile

my $outputfile = "$rss->{'channel'}->{'title'}.html";
$outputfile =~ s/ /_/g;
# Open the output file
```

Example 12-2. LinkpimpListener.pl (continued)

```perl
open (OUTPUTFILE, ">$outputfile");

# Print the channel title.

print OUTPUTFILE '<div id="channel_link"><a href="';
print OUTPUTFILE "$rss->{'channel'}->{'link'}";
print OUTPUTFILE '">';
print OUTPUTFILE "$rss->{'channel'}->{'title'}</a></div>\n";

# Print channel image, checking first if it exists.

if ($rss->{'image'}->{'link'}) {
    print OUTPUTFILE '<div id="channel_image"><a href="';
    print OUTPUTFILE "$rss->{'image'}->{'link'}";
    print OUTPUTFILE '">';
    print OUTPUTFILE '<img src="';
    print OUTPUTFILE "$rss->{'image'}->{'url'}";
    print OUTPUTFILE '" alt="';
    print OUTPUTFILE "$rss->{'image'}->{'title'}";
    print OUTPUTFILE '"/></a>';
    print OUTPUTFILE "\n";
                    }
# Print the channel items.

    print OUTPUTFILE '<div id="linkentries">';
    print OUTPUTFILE "\n";

foreach my $item (@{$rss->{'items'}}) {
    next unless defined($item->{'title'}) && defined($item->{'link'});
    print OUTPUTFILE '<li><a href="';
    print OUTPUTFILE "$item->{'link'}";
    print OUTPUTFILE '">';
    print OUTPUTFILE "$item->{'title'}</a><BR>\n";
                    }
    print OUTPUTFILE "</div>\n";

# If there's a textinput element...

if ($rss->{'textinput'}->{'title'}) {
    print OUTPUTFILE '<div id="textinput">';
    print OUTPUTFILE '<form method="get" action="';
    print OUTPUTFILE "$rss->{'textinput'}->{'link'}";
    print OUTPUTFILE '">';
    print OUTPUTFILE "$rss->{'textinput'}->{'description'}<br/>/n";
    print OUTPUTFILE '<input type="text" name="';
    print OUTPUTFILE "$rss->{'textinput'}->{'name'}";
    print OUTPUTFILE '"><br/>/n';
    print OUTPUTFILE '<input type="submit" value="';
    print OUTPUTFILE "$rss->{'textinput'}->{'title'}";
    print OUTPUTFILE '"></form>';
    print OUTPUTFILE '</div>';
                    }
```

Example 12-2. LinkpimpListener.pl (continued)

```
# If there's a copyright element...

if ($rss->{'channel'}->{'copyright'}) {
    print OUTPUTFILE '<div id="copyright">';
    print OUTPUTFILE "$rss->{'channel'}->{'copyright'}</div>";

                        }
# Close the OUTPUTFILE.

close (OUTPUTFILE);
}

# ----------------

};
};
```

The XML You Need for RSS

The purpose of this appendix is to introduce you to XML. A knowledge of XML is essential if you want to write RSS documents directly, rather than having them generated by some utility. If you're already acquainted with XML, you don't need to read this appendix. If not, read on.

The general overview of XML given in this appendix should be more than sufficient to enable you to work with the RSS documents that you will be using. For further information about XML, the O'Reilly books *Learning XML* by Erik T. Ray, and *XML in a Nutshell* by Elliotte Rusty Harold and W. Scott Means, are invaluable guides, as is the weekly online magazine *XML.com*.

Note that this appendix makes frequent reference to the formal XML 1.0 specification, which can be used for further investigation of topics that fall outside the scope of RSS. Readers are also directed to the "Annotated XML Specification," written by Tim Bray and published online at *http://XML.com*, which provides an illuminating explanation of the XML 1.0 specification, and "What is XML?," by Norm Walsh, also published on *XML.com*.

What Is XML?

XML (Extensible Markup Language) is an Internet-friendly format for data and documents, invented by the World Wide Web Consortium (W3C). "Markup" denotes a way of expressing the structure of a document within the document itself. XML has its roots in a markup language called SGML (Standard Generalized Markup Language), which is used in publishing and shares this heritage with HTML. XML was created to do for machine-readable documents on the Web what HTML did for human-readable documents—that is, provide a commonly agreed-upon syntax, so that processing the underlying format becomes a commodity and documents are made accessible to all users.

Unlike HTML, though, XML comes with very little predefined. HTML developers are accustomed to both the notion of using angle brackets (< >) for denoting elements (that is, syntax), and also the set of element names themselves (such as head, body, etc.). XML shares only the former feature (i.e., the notion of using angle brackets for denoting elements). Unlike HTML, XML has no predefined elements, but is merely a set of rules that lets you write other languages like HTML. (To clarify XML's relationship with SGML: XML is an SGML subset. In contrast, HTML is an SGML application. RSS uses XML to express its operations and thus is an XML application.)

Because XML defines so little, it is easy for everyone to agree to use the XML syntax and then build applications on top of it. It's like agreeing to use a particular alphabet and set of punctuation symbols, but not saying which language to use. However, if you're coming to XML from an HTML background (and have an interest in extending RSS), then you may need to prepare yourself for the shock of having to choose what to call your tags!

Knowing that XML's roots lie with SGML should help you understand some of XML's features and design decisions. Note that although SGML is essentially a document-centric technology, XML's functionality also extends to data-centric applications, including RSS. Commonly, data-centric applications do not need all the flexibility and expressiveness that XML provides and limit themselves to employing only a subset of XML's functionality.

Anatomy of an XML Document

The best way to explain how an XML document is composed is to present one. The following example shows an XML document you might use to describe two authors:

```
<?xml version="1.0" encoding="us-ascii"?>
<authors>
    <person id="lear">
        <name>Edward Lear</name>
        <nationality>British</nationality>
    </person>
    <person id="asimov">
        <name>Isaac Asimov</name>
        <nationality>American</nationality>
    </person>
    <person id="mysteryperson"/>
</authors>
```

The first line of the document is known as the *XML declaration*. This tells a processing application which version of XML you are using (the version indicator is mandatory) and which character encoding you have used for the document. In this example, the document is encoded in ASCII. (The significance of character encoding is covered later in this chapter.)

If the XML declaration is omitted, a processor will make certain assumptions about your document. In particular, it will expect it to be encoded in UTF-8, an encoding of the Unicode character set. However, it is best to use the XML declaration wherever possible, both to avoid confusion over the character encoding and to indicate to processors which version of XML you're using.

Elements and Attributes

The second line of the example begins an element, which has been named authors. The contents of that element include everything between the right angle bracket (>) in <authors> and the left angle bracket (<) in </authors>. The actual syntactic constructs <authors> and </authors> are often referred to as the element *start tag* and *end tag*, respectively. Do not confuse tags with elements! Note that elements may include other elements, as well as text. An XML document must contain exactly one root element, which contains all other content within the document. The name of the root element defines the type of the XML document.

Elements that contain both text and other elements simultaneously are classified as *mixed content*. RSS doesn't generally use mixed content.

The sample authors document uses elements named person to describe the authors themselves. Each person element has an attribute named id. Unlike elements, attributes can contain only textual content. Their values must be surrounded by quotes. Either single quotes (') or double quotes (") may be used, as long as you use the same kind of closing quote as the opening one.

Within XML documents, attributes are frequently used for metadata (i.e., "data about data"), describing properties of the element's contents. This is the case in our example, where id contains a unique identifier for the person being described.

As far as XML is concerned, the order in which attributes are presented in the element start tag does not matter. For example, these two elements contain the same information, as far as an XML 1.0–conformant processing application is concerned:

```
<animal name="dog" legs="4"/>
<animal legs="4" name="dog"/>
```

On the other hand, the information presented to an application by an XML processor upon reading the following two lines will be different for each animal element, because the ordering of elements is significant:

```
<animal><name>dog</name><legs>4</legs></animal>
<animal><legs>4</legs><name>dog</name></animal>
```

XML treats a set of attributes like a bunch of stuff in a bag—there is no implicit ordering—while elements are treated like items on a list, where ordering matters.

New XML developers frequently ask when it is best to use attributes to represent information and when it is best to use elements. As you can see from the authors example, if order is important to you, then elements are a good choice. In general, there is no hard-and-fast "best practice" for choosing whether to use attributes or elements.

The final author described in our document has no information available. All we know about this person is his or her id, mysteryperson. The document uses the XML shortcut syntax for an empty element. The following is a reasonable alternative:

```
<person id="mysteryperson"></person>
```

Name Syntax

XML 1.0 has certain rules about element and attribute names. In particular:

- Names are case-sensitive: e.g., `<person/>` is not the same as `<Person/>`.
- Names beginning with "xml" (in any permutation of uppercase or lowercase) are reserved for use by XML 1.0 and its companion specifications.
- A name must start with a letter or an underscore, not a digit, and may continue with any letter, digit, underscore, or period. (Actually, a name may also contain a colon, but the colon is used to delimit a namespace prefix and is not available for arbitrary use as of the Second Edition of XML 1.0. Knowledge of namespaces is not required for understanding RSS, but for more information see Tim Bray's "XML Namespaces by Example," published at *http://www.xml.com/pub/a/1999/01/namespaces.html.*)

A precise description of names can be found in Section 2.3 of the XML 1.0 specification, at *http://www.w3.org/TR/REC-xml#sec-common-syn.*

Well-Formedness

An XML document that conforms to the rules of XML syntax is known as *well-formed*. At its most basic level, well-formedness means that elements should be properly matched, and all opened elements should be closed. A formal definition of well-formedness can be found in Section 2.1 of the XML 1.0 specification, at *http://www.w3.org/TR/REC-xml#sec-well-formed.* Table A-1 shows some XML documents that are not well-formed.

Table A-1. Examples of poorly formed XML documents

Document	Reason it's not well-formed

`<foo>`
    `<bar>`
    `</foo>`
`</bar>`
	The elements are not properly nested, because `foo` is closed while inside its child element `bar`.

`<foo>`
    `<bar>`
`</foo>`
	The `bar` element was not closed before its parent, `foo`, was closed.

`<foo baz>` `</foo>`	The `baz` attribute has no value. While this is permissible in HTML (e.g., `<table border>`), it is forbidden in XML.
`<foo baz=23>` `</foo>`	The `baz` attribute value, `23`, has no surrounding quotes. Unlike HTML, all attribute values must be quoted in XML.

Comments

As in HTML, it is possible to include comments within XML documents. XML comments are intended to be read only by people. With HTML, developers have occasionally employed comments to add application-specific functionality. For example, the server-side include functionality of most web servers uses instructions embedded in HTML comments. XML provides other means of indicating application processing instructions. A discussion of processing instructions (PIs) is outside the scope of this book. For more information on PIs, see Section 2.6 of the XML 1.0 specification, at *http://www.w3.org/TR/REC-xml#sec-pi*. Comments should not be used for any purpose other than those for which they were intended.

The start of a comment is indicated with <!--, and the end of the comment is indi­cated with -->. Any sequence of characters, aside from the string --, may appear within a comment. Comments tend to be used more in XML documents intended for human consumption than those intended for machine consumption. Comments aren't widely used in RSS.

Entity References

Another feature of XML that is occasionally useful when writing RSS documents is the mechanism for escaping characters.

Because some characters have special significance in XML, there needs to be a way to represent them. For example, in some cases the < symbol might really be intended to mean "less than," rather than to signal the start of an element name. Clearly, just inserting the character without any escaping mechanism would result in a poorly formed document, because a processing application would assume you were starting another element. Another instance of this problem is needing to include both double quotes and single quotes simultaneously in an attribute's value. Here's an example that illustrates both these difficulties:

```
<badDoc>
  <para>
    I'd really like to use the < character
  </para>
  <note title="On the proper 'use' of the " character"/>
</badDoc>
```

XML avoids this problem by the use of the predefined entity reference. The word *entity* in the context of XML simply means a unit of content. The term *entity reference* means just that, a symbolic way of referring to a certain unit of content. XML predefines entities for the following symbols: left angle bracket (<), right angle bracket (>), apostrophe ('), double quote ("), and ampersand (&).

An entity reference is introduced with an ampersand (&), which is followed by a name (using the word "name" in its formal sense, as defined by the XML 1.0 specification), and terminated with a semicolon (;). Table A-2 shows how the five predefined entities can be used within an XML document.

Table A-2. Predefined entity references in XML 1.0

Literal character	Entity reference
<	&lt;
<	&gt;

Table A-2. Predefined entity references in XML 1.0 (continued)

Literal character	Entity reference
'	&apos;
"	&quot;
&	&amp;

Here's our problematic document, revised to use entity references:

```
<badDoc>
  <para>
    I'd really like to use the &lt; character
  </para>
  <note title="On the proper &apos; use &apos;  of the &quot;character"/>
</badDoc>
```

Being able to use the predefined entities is often all you need for RSS; in general, entities are provided as a convenience for human-created XML. XML 1.0 allows you to define your own entities and use entity references as shortcuts in your document. Section 4 of the XML 1.0 specification, available at *http://www.w3.org/TR/REC-xml#sec-physical-struct*, describes the use of entities.

Character References

You may find *character references* in the context of RSS documents. Character references allow you to denote a character by its numeric position in Unicode character set (this position is known as its *code point*). Table A-3 contains a few examples that illustrate the syntax.

Table A-3. Example character references

Actual character	Character reference
1	&#48;
A	&#65;
~	&#xD1;
®	&#xAE;

Note that the code point can be expressed in decimal or, with the use of x as a prefix, in hexadecimal.

Character Encodings

The subject of *character encodings* is frequently a mysterious one for developers. Most code tends to be written for one computing platform and, normally, to run within one organization. Although the Internet is changing things quickly, most of us have never had cause to think too deeply about internationalization.

XML, designed to be an Internet-friendly syntax for information exchange, has internationalization at its very core. One of the basic requirements for XML processors is that they support the Unicode standard character encoding. Unicode attempts to include the requirements of all the world's languages within one character set. Consequently, it is very large!

Unicode encoding schemes

Unicode 3.0 has more than 57,700 code points, each of which corresponds to a character. (You can obtain charts of all these characters online by visiting *http://www.unicode.org/charts/*.) If you were to express a Unicode string by using the position of each character in the character set as its encoding (in the same way as ASCII does), expressing the whole range of characters would require four *octets* for each character. (An octet is a string of eight binary digits, or bits. A byte is commonly, but not always, considered the same thing as an octet.) Clearly, if a document is written in 100 percent American English, it will be 4 times larger than required—all the characters in ASCII fitting into a 7-bit representation. This places a strain on both storage space and on memory requirements for processing applications.

Fortunately, two encoding schemes for Unicode alleviate this problem: UTF-8 and UTF-16. As you might guess from their names, applications can process documents in these encodings in 8- or 16-bit segments at a time. When code points are required in a document that cannot be represented by one chunk, a bit-pattern is used to indicate that the following chunk is required to calculate the desired code point. In UTF-8, this is denoted by the most significant bit of the first octet being set to 1.

This scheme means that UTF-8 is a highly efficient encoding for representing languages using Latin alphabets, such as English. All of the ASCII character set is represented natively in UTF-8—an ASCII-only document and its equivalent in UTF-8 are identical byte-for-byte.

This knowledge will also help you debug encoding errors. One frequent error arises because of the fact that ASCII is a proper subset of UTF-8—programmers get used to this fact and produce UTF-8 documents, but use them as if they were ASCII. Things start to go awry when the XML parser processes a document containing, for example, characters such as Á. Because this character cannot be represented using only one octet in UTF-8, this produces a two-octet sequence in the output document; in a non-Unicode viewer or text editor, it looks like a couple of characters of garbage.

Other character encodings

Unicode, in the context of computing history, is a relatively new invention. Native operating system support for Unicode is by no means widespread. For instance, although Windows NT offers Unicode support, Windows 95 and 98 do not.

XML 1.0 allows a document to be encoded in any character set registered with the Internet Assigned Numbers Authority (IANA). European documents are commonly encoded in one of the ISO Latin character sets, such as ISO-8859-1. Japanese documents commonly use Shift-JIS, and Chinese documents use GB2312 and Big 5.

A full list of registered character sets can be found at *http://www.iana.org/assignments/character-sets*.

XML processors are not required by the XML 1.0 specification to support any more than UTF-8 and UTF-16, but most commonly support other encodings, such as US-ASCII and ISO-8859-1. Although most RSS transactions are currently conducted in ASCII (or the ASCII subset of UTF-8), there is nothing to stop RSS documents from containing, say, Korean text. However, you will probably have to dig into the encoding support of your computing platform to find out if it is possible for you to use alternate encodings.

Validity

In addition to well-formedness, XML 1.0 offers another level of verification, called *validity*. To explain why validity is important, let's take a simple example. Imagine you invented a simple XML format for your friends' telephone numbers:

```
<phonebook>
  <person>
    <name>Albert Smith</name>
    <number>123-456-7890</number>
  </person>
  <person>
    <name>Bertrand Jones</name>
    <number>456-123-9876</number>
  </person>
</phonebook>
```

Based on your format, you also construct a program to display and search your phone numbers. This program turns out to be so useful, you share it with your friends. However, your friends aren't so hot on detail as you are, and they try to feed your program this phone book file:

```
<phonebook>
  <person>
    <name>Melanie Green</name>
    <phone>123-456-7893</phone>
  </person>
</phonebook>
```

Note that, although this file is perfectly well-formed, it doesn't fit the format you prescribed for the phone book, and you find you need to change your program to cope with this situation. If your friends had used number as you did to denote the phone number, and not phone, there wouldn't have been a problem. However, as it is, this second file is not a valid phonebook document.

Document Type Definitions (DTDs)

For validity to be a useful general concept, we need a machine-readable way of saying what a valid document is—that is, which elements and attributes must be present and in what order. XML 1.0 achieves this by introducing *document type definitions* (DTDs). For the purposes of RSS, you don't need to know much about DTDs. Rest assured that RSS does have a DTD, and it spells out in detail exactly which combinations of elements and attributes make up a valid document.

The purpose of a DTD is to express the allowed elements and attributes in a certain document type and to constrain the order in which they must appear within that document type. A DTD is generally composed of one file, which contains declarations defining the element types and attribute lists. (In theory, a DTD may span more than one file; however, the mechanism for including one file inside another—*parameter entities*—is outside the scope of this book.) It is common to mistakenly conflate element and element types. The distinction is that an element is the actual instance of the structure as found in an XML document, whereas the element type is the kind of element that the instance is.

Putting It Together

If you want to validate RSS against a DTD, you may need to know how to link a document to its defining DTD. This is done with a document type declaration, `<!DOCTYPE ...>`, inserted at the beginning of the XML document, after the XML declaration in our fictitious example:

```
<?xml version="1.0" encoding="us-ascii"?>
<!DOCTYPE authors SYSTEM "http://example.com/authors.dtd">
<authors>
    <person id="lear">
        <name>Edward Lear</name>
        <nationality>British</nationality>
    </person>
    <person id="asimov">
        <name>Isaac Asimov</name>
        <nationality>American</nationality>
    </person>
    <person id="mysteryperson"/>
</authors>
```

This example assumes the DTD file has been placed on a web server at *example.com*. Note that the document type declaration specifies the root element of the document, not the DTD itself. You could use the same DTD to define person, name, or nationality as the root element of a valid document. Certain DTDs, such as the DocBook DTD for technical documentation (see *http://www.docbook.org*), use this feature to good effect, allowing you to provide the same DTD for multiple document types.

A validating XML processor is obligated to check the input document against its DTD. If it does not validate, the document is rejected. To return to the phone book example, if your application validated its input files against a phone book DTD, you would have been spared the problems of debugging your program and correcting your friend's XML, because your application would have rejected the document as being invalid. While some of the programs that read RSS files do worry about validation, most do not.

XML Namespaces

XML 1.0 lets developers create their own elements and attributes, but it leaves open the potential for overlapping names. "Title" in one context may mean something entirely different than "Title" in a different context. The "Namespaces in XML" specification (which can be found at *http://www.w3.org/TR/REC-xml-names*) provides a mechanism developers can use to identify particular vocabularies using Uniform Resource Identifiers (URIs).

RSS 1.0 uses the URI *http://purl.org/rss/1.0/* for its base namespace. The URI is just an identifier—opening that page in a web browser reveals some links to the RSS, XML 1.0, and Namespaces in XML specifications. Programs processing documents with multiple vocabularies can use the namespaces to figure out which vocabulary they are handling at any given point in a document.

Namespaces are very simple on the surface but are a well-known field of combat in XML arcana. For more information on namespaces, see *XML In a Nutshell* or *Learning XML*. The use of namespaces in RSS is discussed in much greater detail in Chapters 6 and 7.

Tools for Processing XML

While RSS can be parsed directly using text-processing tools, XML parsers are often more convenient. Many parsers exist for using XML with many different programming languages. Most are freely available, and the majority are open source.

Selecting a Parser

An XML parser typically takes the form of a library of code that you interface with your own program. The RSS program hands the XML over to the parser, and the parser hands back information about the contents of the XML document. Typically, parsers do this either via events or via a document object model.

With event-based parsing, the parser calls a function in your program whenever a *parse event* is encountered. Parse events include things like finding the start of an element, the end of an element, or a comment. Most Java event-based parsers follow a standard API called SAX, which is also implemented for other languages such as Python and Perl. You can find more about SAX at *http://www.saxproject.org*.

Document object model (DOM)–based parsers work in a markedly different way. They consume the entire XML input document and hand back a tree-like data structure that the RSS software can interrogate and alter. The DOM is a W3C standard; documentation is available at *http://www.w3.org/DOM*.

Choosing whether to use an event- or DOM-based model depends on the application. If you have a large or unpredictable document size, it is better to use event-based parsing for reasons of speed and memory consumption (DOM trees can get very large). If you have small, simple XML documents, using the DOM leaves you less programming work to do. Many programming languages have both event-based and DOM support.

As XML matures, hybrid techniques that give the best of both worlds are emerging. If you're interested in finding out what's available and what's new for your favorite programming language, keep an eye on the following online sources:

XML.com Resource Guide
   http://xml.com/pub/resourceguide

XMLhack XML Developer News
   http://xmlhack.com

Free XML Tools Guide
   http://www.garshol.priv.no/download/xmltools

XSLT Processors

Many XML applications involve transforming one XML document into another or into HTML. The W3C has defined a special language, called XSLT, for doing transformations. XSLT processors are becoming available for all major programming platforms.

XSLT works by using a style sheet, which contains templates that describe how to transform elements from an XML document. These templates typically specify what XML to output in response to a particular element or attribute. Using a W3C technology called *XPath* gives you the flexibility not only to say "do this for every person element," but also to give instructions as complex as "do this for the third person element, whose name attribute is Fred."

Because of this flexibility, some applications have sprung up for XSLT that aren't really transformation applications at all, but take advantage of the ability to trigger actions on certain element patterns and sequencers. Combined with XSLT's ability to execute custom code via extension functions, the XPath language has enabled applications such as document indexing to be driven by an XSLT processor.

The W3C specifications for XSLT and XPath can be found at *http://w3.org/TR/xslt* and *http://w3.org/TR/xpath*, respectively. For more information on XSLT, see Doug Tidwell's *XSLT* (O'Reilly). For more on XPath, see John Simpson's *XPath and XPointer* (O'Reilly).

Useful Sites and Software

Since RSS is a technology born of the Web, it is not a surprise that a great deal of good information can be gleaned within your browser. This appendix will give you links to some excellent resources, including client software.

Specification Documents

http://web.resource.org/rss/1.0
> The RSS 1.0 Specification

http://backend.userland.com/rss
> The RSS 2.0 Specification

http://backend.userland.com/rss09
> The RSS 0.92 Specification

http://backend.userland.com/rss091
> The RSS 0.91 Specification

http://purl.org/rss/1.0/modules
> The RSS 1.0 modules known to the working group

Mailing Lists

http://groups.yahoo.com/group/rss-dev
> rss-dev—the RSS 1.0 Interest Group list

http://groups.yahoo.com/group/syndication
> Syndication—a general list for RSS matters

http://groups.yahoo.com/group/syndic8
> Syndic8—a list for Syndic8 support matters

http://groups.yahoo.com/group/RSS2-Support
> RSS2 Support—support for RSS 2.0 matters

http://groups.yahoo.com/group/aggregators/
> Aggregators—a list for discussion of aggregator software

Validators

Online validators can check to ensure your feeds are correctly formed:

http://feeds.archive.org/validator
  The most up-to-date validator, optimized for RSS 2.0

http://www.ldodds.com/rss_validator/1.0/validator.html
  Leigh Dodd's experimental RSS 1.0 validator

http://aggregator.userland.com/validator
  Userland Software's RSS validator

http://www.w3.org/RDF/Validator
  The W3C's RDF validator

Desktop Readers

http://bitworking.org/Aggie.html
  Aggie—a .NET-based application for reading RSS files. Open source, for Windows and Linux-with-Mono.

http://www.disobey.com/amphetadesk
  AmphetaDesk—a Perl-based desktop reader that runs in the browser. Windows, Linux, and Mac OS versions available.

http://www.oreillynet.com/~rael/lang/perl/blagg
  Blagg—a news aggregator for the Bloxsom weblogging system.

http://www.cincomsmalltalk.com/BottomFeeder
  BottomFeeder—a Smalltalk desktop RSS Reader. Open source, runs on Windows, Mac, and various Unix flavors.

http://www.headlineviewer.com
  Carmen's Headline Viewer—a shareware news reader client for Windows.

http://www.feedreader.com
  FeedReader—a freeware application for Windows.

http://www.fetchserver.com
  Fetch—an "Enterprise RSS" client and server system, for internal corporate messaging and information flow.

http://members.bellatlantic.net/~vze3szvh/friday
  Friday—a Java front-end for viewing news aggregation sites and site syndication feeds on mobile devices.

http://www.furrygoat.com
  The Furrygoat Experience—a PocketFeed for Pocket PC RSS aggregator.

http://fyuze.com
  fyuze—acts as a personal news portal for searching, sorting, and sifting daily news from RSS feeds.

http://www.johnmunsch.com/projects/HotSheet

Hotsheet—a Java-based desktop news reader. Works on Windows, Mac, Linux, and anything else with a Java Virtual Machine.

http://www.blueelephantsoftware.com

InfoSnorkel News Aggregator—a Windows application that aggregates RSS feeds, plus content from sites without feeds.

http://www.jayeckles.com/news

JERSS—allows seamless integration of RSS news feeds into web sites. It is a Java servlet generating JavaScript objects the web author can manipulate.

http://www.serence.com/site.php?page=prod_klipfolio

Klipfolio—a Windows-based desktop news reader. Reads simple XML files that point to RSS feeds.

http://www.mulle-kybernetik.com/software/MulleNewz

MulleNewz—a Mac OS X docking RSS reader.

http://www.jmagar.com

MyHeadlines—a content syndication search engine and news reader that can be integrated into a web site running PHP and MySQL.

http://radio.weblogs.com/0100875/outlines/myRadio

myRadio—an extension to Radio Userland aggregation from RSS to any data source, including XML, HTML, and SOAP.

http://ranchero.com/software/netnewswire

NetNewsWire Lite—an OS X desktop RSS reader, written in Cocoa.

http://www.newsisfree.com

NewsIsFree—a directory of feeds that also allows for personalized news pages.

http://www.proggle.com/novobot

Novobot—a heavily featured desktop news reader that can also scrape non-RSS'd sites.

http://www.postal-code.com/phpnuke/html/sections.php?op=listarticles&secid=9

Pineapple—a web site news aggregator for Mac OS X.

http://www.furrygoat.com/Software/PocketFeed/index.html

PocketFeed—an RSS/RDF news aggregator that runs on Pocket PC 2002 PDAs.

http://radio.userland.com

Radio Userland—a news aggregator included with a weblog software application for Mac and Windows platforms.

http://40hz.org/Raissa

Raissa—a headline and news reader for Newton MessagePad.

http://reptile.openprivacy.org

Reptile—a P2P project, with RSS reading.

http://sourceforge.net/projects/rssview

> RSS Viewer—a Java-based, open source RSS reader.

http://homepage.mac.com/stas/slashdock.html

> Slashdock—a simple Mac OS X application that fetches and updates headlines for the latest postings on Slashdot-compatible sites and RSS-compatible sites.

http://www.nongnu.org/straw

> Straw—a desktop news aggregator for the GNOME environment, with project information, news, and downloads.

http://www.eastgate.com/Tinderbox

> Tinderbox—a Mac OS feed reader.

Index

Symbols

< > (angle brackets)
    <!-- and --> in XML comments, 183
    < (left angle bracket), XML entity
        for, 183
    > (right angle bracket), XML entity
        for, 183
& (ampersand)
    separating Meerkat query
        parameters, 144
    XML entity for, 183
' and " (single and double quotes) in XML
    attributes, 181
' (apostrophe), XML entity for, 183
" (double quotes), XML entity for, 183

A

admin elements, 73
Administration module, 73
ag elements, 74
age of stories displayed on Meerkat, 142
Aggregation module, 74
aggregators, 7
    Meerkat, 140–144
        querying the API, 141–144
        REST architecture, 141
    NewsisFree.com, 163
    registering with, 40
alternative resources (RDF), list of, 53
alternative title for related item, 91
Amazon.com web services, 67

AmphetaDesk, 156–160
    index.html file, 158
    installing, 156
AmphetaDesk::Channels module, 157
AmphetaDesk::ChannelsList module, 157
annotate element, 76
Annotation module, 75
Apache servers, enabling server-side
        includes, 129–130
Apple, HotSauce application, 2
application/rss+xml MIME type, 39
applications
    program used to generate RSS file, 111
    required to play back streamed
        media, 101
arcs, RDF, 47
ASCII, 186
attributes
    outline element, 148
    rdf:about, 50
    rdf:parseType, 83
    rdf:Parsetype and xmlns, 84
    XML
        choosing between attributes and
            elements, 181
        rules for names (Version 1.0), 182
audio
    mod_audio module, 77
    mod_streaming elements for, 101
authors
    author element, 111
        RSS 1.0, 151
    blog, information about, 114
    XML document describing, 180

We'd like to hear your suggestions for improving our indexes. Send email to *index@oreilly.com*.

codec for streamed media, 102
comments
    comment element, 110
    displayable at each karma threshold, 100
    number attached to an article, 100
    in XML documents, 182
company elements, 80
Company module, 80
contacts (for live shows), 102
containers, RDF
    rdf:Alt element, 53
    rdf:Bag element, 52, 84
        rdf:li subelements, 84
    rdf:Seq element, 53
content
    Content module, 72
    description for books (book:openingPara
        element), 152
    different formats for same content, 92
    mod_content module, 81–86
Content Management Systems (CMS)
    feed creation in, 33
    producing HTML and RSS feed, 11
    structure of, 10
content: namespace, 81
content syndication
    defined, 1
    history of, 1
    reasons for, 8
content:encoding element, 83
    rdf:about attribute, 84
    subelement of content:item, 84
content:format element, 82
    rdf:about attribute, 84
    subelement of content:item, 84
content:item element
    containing other RSS feeds, 85
    content:encoding subelement, 83
    rdf:about attribute, 84
    subelement of rdf:li, 84
    subelements, 84
content:items element, 84
Content-Type header, HTTP, 92
contributors (dc:contributor element), 87
    wiki:host subelement, 109
copyrights
    copyright element in RSS 0.91
        document, 28
    dc:rights element, 89
    implications for RSS feeds, 8
    rss091:copyright element, 96
corporate intranets, use of RSS, 7

coverage (dc:coverage element), 88
cp element, 79
cp:server element, 164
CreateSubscriptionList function
    (Syndic8), 137
creators (dc:creator element), 87, 123, 151
crontab, sending feeds from, 125

D

data model, RDF, 47
databases of RDF-based documents, 49
data-centric applications in XML, 180
dataset, 87
dates and times
    date fields for RSS 2.0, 116
    date Meerkat first saw story, turning
        on/off, 143
    date or date range (dc:coverage), 88
    dc:date element, 152
    dcterms:created element, 91
    dcterms:issued element, 91
    end date of an event (ev:enddate
        element), 94
    last build date of a feed
        (rss091:lastBuildDate), 96
    last modification of related item content
        (dcterms:modified), 91
    publishing date, 152
        dc:date element, 87
        pubDate element, 111
    response time (average) of the server, 99
    server statistics, 99
    start and end dates, searches by feed
        changes, 136
    start date of an event (ev:startdate), 94
    time period for stories on Meerkat, 142
    times for start, end, and duration of
        streamed media, 102
    time-to-live (ttl element), 111
days (rss091:day element), 96
dc elements, 86
dc:relation element, 91
DCSV (Dublin Core Structured Values), 93
dcterms: namespace, 91
dcterms:extent element, 91
dcterms:medium element, 92
declarations, XML, 180
DeleteSubscriptionList function
    (Syndic8), 137
department an article appears in, 100
description elements, 123
    dc:description element, 87

About the Author

Ben Hammersley is an English emigré, living in Sweden with his wife, three greyhounds, a few hundred deer, and a two-way satellite connection. For a day job, he writes for the British national press, appearing in *The Times*, *The Guardian*, and *The Observer*, but in his free time he blogs excessively at *www.benhammersley.com* and runs the *Lazyweb.org* ideas site. As a member of the RSS 1.0 Working Group, he survived the Great Fork Summer, and as a journalist, he was accosted by the secret police of two countries. To this day, he doesn't know which was worse.

Colophon

Our look is the result of reader comments, our own experimentation, and feedback from distribution channels. Distinctive covers complement our distinctive approach to technical topics, breathing personality and life into potentially dry subjects.

The animal on the cover of *Content Syndication with RSS* is an American kestrel (*Falco sparverius*). Though it is also commonly known as a "sparrow hawk," because it occasionally eats sparrows and other small birds, this name does not accurately reflect the American kestrel's much more diverse diet. American kestrels also eat small mammals, insects, reptiles, and amphibians. In the summer, or in warmer climates, their diet consists primarily of insects.

American kestrels are the smallest, most colorful, and most common falcons in North America. On average, they are 8.5 to 11 inches long, with a wingspan of 19 to 22 inches, and they weigh between 3.5 and 6 ounces. Though males and females are similar in size, they differ in their markings and coloration. Both sexes have reddish-brown backs and tails and two black stripes on their faces. Adult males have slate-blue wings and are redder than females. Females are browner, with reddish wings and black bands on their tails.

Kestrels nest throughout North America in small cavities, such as tree holes, building eaves, or human-provided nesting boxes. The female lays between three and seven eggs, about half of which usually develop into healthy young. The off-white or pinkish eggs hatch after incubating for 28 to 30 days, and the young fledglings leave the nest 28 to 30 days later. While the female and young hatchlings nest, the male hunts and brings them food. Kestrels are quite noisy; their high-pitched call of excitement or alarm is a sharp "klee, klee, klee."

Brian Sawyer was the production editor and copyeditor for *Content Syndication with RSS*. Colleen Gorman was the proofreader. Tatiana Apandi Diaz and Claire Cloutier provided quality control. Genevieve D'Entremont provided production support. Ellen Troutman Zaig wrote the index.

Ellie Volckhausen designed the cover of this book, based on a series design by Edie Freedman. The cover image is a 19th-century engraving from the Dover Pictorial

Archive. Emma Colby produced the cover layout with QuarkXPress 4.1 using Adobe's ITC Garamond font.

David Futato designed the interior layout. This book was converted by Joe Wizda to FrameMaker 5.5.6 with a format conversion tool created by Erik Ray, Jason McIntosh, Neil Walls, and Mike Sierra that uses Perl and XML technologies. The text font is Linotype Birka; the heading font is Adobe Myriad Condensed; and the code font is LucasFont's TheSans Mono Condensed. The illustrations that appear in the book were produced by Robert Romano and Jessamyn Read using Macromedia FreeHand 9 and Adobe Photoshop 6. This colophon was written by Brian Sawyer.

Other Titles Available from O'Reilly

XML

XML in a Nutshell, 2nd Edition

By Elliotte Rusty Harold &
W. Scott Means
1st Edition December 2000
400 pages, ISBN 0-596-00058-8

This powerful new edition provides
developers with a comprehensive
guide to the rapidly evolving XML
space. Serious users of XML will find
topics on just about everything they need, from funda-
mental syntax rules, to details of DTD and XML Schema
creation, to XSLT transformations, to APIs used for processing XML documents. Simply put, this is the only reference of its kind among XML books.

XSLT Cookbook

By Sal Mangano
1st Edition December 2002
450 pages, ISBN 0-596-00372-2

This book offers the definitive collection of solutions and examples that
developers at any level can use immediately to solve a wide variety of XML
processing issues. As with our other Cookbook titles,
XSLT Cookbook contains code recipes for specific programming problems. But more than just a book of cut-
and-paste code, *XSLT Cookbook* enables developers to
build their programming skills and their understanding
of XSLT through the detailed explanations provided with
each recipe.

Learning XML

By Erik T. Ray with
Christopher R. Maden
1st Edition January 2001
368 pages, ISBN 0-596-00046-4

XML (Extensible Markup Language) is
a flexible way to create "self-describing
data"—and to share both the format
and the data on the World Wide Web, intranets, and elsewhere. In *Learning XML*, the authors explain XML and
its capabilities succinctly and professionally, with references to real-life projects and other cogent examples.
Learning XML shows the purpose of XML markup itself,
the CSS and XSL styling languages, and the XLink and
XPointer specifications for creating rich link structures.

XML Schema

By Eric van der Vlist
1st Edition June 2002
400 pages, 0-596-00252-1

The W3C's XML Schema offers a powerful set of tools for defining accept-
able XML document structures and
content. While schemas are powerful,
that power comes with substantial complexity. This book
explains XML Schema foundations, a variety of different
styles for writing schemas, simple and complex types,
datatypes and facets, keys, extensibility, documentation,
design choices, best practices, and limitations. Complete
with references, a glossary, and examples throughout.

XSLT

By Doug Tidwell
1st Edition August 2001
473 pages, ISBN 0-596-00053-7

XSLT (Extensible Stylesheet Language
Transformations) is a critical bridge
between XML processing and more
familiar HTML, and dominates the
market for conversions between XML vocabularies. Useful as XSLT is, its complexities can be daunting. Doug
Tidwell, a developer with years of XSLT experience, eases
the pain by building from the basics to the more complex and powerful possibilities of XSLT, so you can jump
in at your own level of expertise.

Java & XML, 2nd Edition

By Brett McLaughlin
2nd Edition September 2001
528 pages, ISBN 0-596-00197-5

New chapters on Advanced SAX,
Advanced DOM, SOAP, and data bind-
ing, as well as new examples throughout, bring the second edition of *Java
& XML* thoroughly up to date. Except for a concise introduction to XML basics, the book focuses entirely on using
XML from Java applications. It's a worthy companion for
Java developers working with XML or involved in messaging, web services, or the new peer-to-peer movement.

O'REILLY®

To order: 800-998-9938 • *order@oreilly.com* • *www.oreilly.com*
Online editions of most O'Reilly titles are available by subscription at *safari.oreilly.com*
Also available at most retail and online bookstores.

How to stay in touch with O'Reilly

1. Visit our award-winning web site

http://www.oreilly.com/

★ "Top 100 Sites on the Web"—PC Magazine
★ CIO Magazine's Web Business 50 Awards

Our web site contains a library of comprehensive product information (including book excerpts and tables of contents), downloadable software, background articles, interviews with technology leaders, links to relevant sites, book cover art, and more. File us in your bookmarks or favorites!

2. Join our email mailing lists

Sign up to get email announcements of new books and conferences, special offers, and O'Reilly Network technology newsletters at:

http://elists.oreilly.com

It's easy to customize your free elists subscription so you'll get exactly the O'Reilly news you want.

3. Get examples from our books

To find example files for a book, go to:

http://www.oreilly.com/catalog

select the book, and follow the "Examples" link.

4. Work with us

Check out our web site for current employment opportunities:

http://jobs.oreilly.com/

5. Register your book

Register your book at:

http://register.oreilly.com

6. Contact us

O'Reilly & Associates, Inc.
1005 Gravenstein Hwy North
Sebastopol, CA 95472 USA
TEL: 707-827-7000 or 800-998-9938
(6am to 5pm PST)
FAX: 707-829-0104

order@oreilly.com
For answers to problems regarding your order or our products. To place a book order online visit:

http://www.oreilly.com/order_new/

catalog@oreilly.com
To request a copy of our latest catalog.

booktech@oreilly.com
For book content technical questions or corrections.

corporate@oreilly.com
For educational, library, government, and corporate sales.

proposals@oreilly.com
To submit new book proposals to our editors and product managers.

international@oreilly.com
For information about our international distributors or translation queries. For a list of our distributors outside of North America check out:

http://international.oreilly.com/distributors.html

adoption@oreilly.com
For information about academic use of O'Reilly books, visit:

http://academic.oreilly.com

O'REILLY®

To order: *800-998-9938* • *order@oreilly.com* • *www.oreilly.com*
Online editions of most O'Reilly titles are available by subscription at *safari.oreilly.com*
Also available at most retail and online bookstores.